HEART at WORK

HEART at WORK

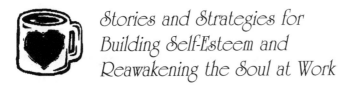

Stories and Strategies for Building Self-Esteem and Reawakening the Soul at Work

Jack Canfield
and
Jacqueline Miller

McGraw-Hill

New York   San Francisco   Washington, D.C.   Auckland   Bogatá
Caracas   Lisbon   London   Madrid   Mexico City   Milan
Montreal   New Delhi   San Juan   Singapore
Sydney   Tokyo   Toronto

McGraw-Hill

A Division of The **McGraw·Hill** Companies

1 2 3 4 5 6 7 8 9 0   DOC/DOC   9 0 1 0 9 8 7 6

ISBN 0-07-011643-1

Printed and bound by Donnelley/Crawfordsville

 This book is printed on recycled, acid-free paper containing a minimum of 50% recycled, de-inked fiber.

Some people come into our lives and quietly go; others stay for a while and leave footprints on our hearts and we are never the same.

Anonymous

We would like to dedicate this book to all people everywhere who have made a commitment to making their workplaces more joyful, humane, affirming, validating, caring, respectful, esteeming, healthy, empowering and spirit-filled places to be. We admire your courage and your willingness to take a stand on your values and your vision. We hope this book will make your efforts easier.

CONTENTS

Foreword / *Willis Harman*   xi

Acknowledgments   xv

Introduction   1

1 SELF-ESTEEM and YOU   7

Developing Your Personal Signature / *Barbara Glanz*   8

The Acorn Principle / *Jim Cathcart*   11

Our Deepest Fear / *Nelson Mandela*   14

Who Will Play Your Music? / *Michael Jones*   15

Integrity and Self-Esteem / *Nathaniel Branden*   19

On Living a Lie / *Richard Brodie*   20

Maintain Your Integrity / *Source Unknown*   25

What Is Integrity? / *Jack Hawley*   26

Impeccability / *Jack Hawley*   28

Entrepreneurs and Self-Esteem / *Wilson L. Harrell*   29

Victory Formula / *Lou Holtz*   32

A Million Dollar Lesson / *Petey Parker*   34

Do What You Love—The Money Will Follow /   35

Work Is Love Made Visible / *Kahlil Gibran*   36

Reverence in the Workplace / *Jack Hawley*   37

Mine Are the Small Initials / *Mildred Brown Duncan*   39

Learning a Lesson / *Susan Cunningham Euker*   41

The Question / *Bob Moore*   43

Look Where You Want to Go / *Jim Donovan*   44

Fired / *Mary A. Long*   45

The Women of Ahmedabad / *Gloria Steinem*   49

The Kingdom of Heaven / *Thich Nhat Hahn*   52

2   The Basic Principles of Managing for High Self-Esteem   53

Positive Self-Esteem at Work: The Eight Behavioral Keys / *Kathy L. Indermill*   54

Self-Esteem and the Managing of Others / *Ken Blanchard*   62

The Worth Ethic / *Kate Ludeman*   66

Self-Esteem and Work / *Will Schutz*   73

All You Have to Do Is Ask! / *Steven Boehler*   83

Radical Reliance on Self-Esteem / *Bud Seith with Jacklyn Wilferd*   85

Treated with Respect / *Robert Levering and Milton Moskowitz*   90

The Value of Respect / *Chérie Carter-Scott*   92

Respect, Caring and Big Loving / *Jack Hawley*   100

The Screamer / *Joe Black*   103

A Master of Human Relations / *Source Unknown*   105

The Fun Minute Manager: An Interview with Ken Blanchard / *Joel Goodman and Ken Blanchard*   106

From Who to Why / *James O'Toole*   111

Taking Responsibility / *Michael J. Wyman*   112

Let Complainers Solve the Problems / *Excerpted from the Pryor Report*   114

The Bridge Between Self-Esteem and a Changing Work Environment / *Bob Moawad*   115

3   The Importance of Caring   120

Threads / *James Autry*   121

What's in a Name? / *Robert Levering and Milton Moskowitz*   122

A Most Important Question / *JoAnn C. Jones*   124

Consistency and Equity / *Dr. Tim Johnson*   125

The Invisible Sign / *Mary Kay Ash*   126

Jessie's Glove / *Rick Phillips*   131

Caring and the Bottom Line / *Christina Campbell*   132

The Power of Four Letter Words! / *Anita Roddick*   133

A Pair of Socks / *Trevor B. Kwok*   139

All in a Day's Work / *Naomi Rhode*   140

Touching / *Sid Friedman*   142

It Can't Happen Here? / *Jack Canfield*   143

4   The IMPORTANCE and POWER of ACKNOWLEDGMENT   **144**

How to Really Motivate an Employee / *Source Unknown*   145

All in the Family: Building Self-Esteem at Home and
   at Work / *Harvey Mackay*   146

Applying the Principles of Family Counseling to Corporate
   Meetings / *Susan E. Davis*   149

The Amazing Power of Acknowledgment^{SM} /
   Michael J. Wyman   151

Love and the Cabbie / *Art Buchwald*   154

The Last Supper / *Excerpted from Bits & Pieces*   156

The Power of Unkind Words / *E. J. Michael*   157

All You Need to Know / *Steve Wilson*   158

The Wranglers vs. the Stranglers / *Ted Engstrom*   160

Praising Your Way to Team Success / *Ronald E. Guzik*   161

The Power of a Blue Ribbon / *Helice Bridges*   165

The Power of a Note / *Fred Bauer*   168

Three Simple Points / *Source Unknown*   172

Rub Somebody the Right Way / *Bob Nelson*   174

Feel Like the Job's Too Big? / *Mother Theresa*   182

5   CEOs on SELF-ESTEEM   **183**

The King's Great Gift / *Anonymous*   186

Lillian Vernon on Self-Esteem / *Lillian Vernon*   187

Self-Esteem in the Nonprofit World / *L. Hunter Lovins*   189

A New Paradigm / *Michael Ray and Alan Rinzler*   *193*

Rewards Beyond the Bottom Line / *Gil Amelio*   *194*

Cultivating Self-Esteem / *Horst M. Rechelbacher*   *196*

Managing to Laugh / *John Imlay, Jr.*   *200*

Meditation in the Workplace / *Robert Roth*   *202*

Managing from Within / *John Goodman*   *204*

Pride of Ownership / *Jack Stack*   *210*

Self-Esteem at Rhino Records / *Richard Foos*   *213*

On Self-Esteem / *L.S. Barksdale*   *216*

A Capitalist Looks at Self-Esteem in the Workplace /
  George E. McCown   *221*

6 FURTHER INSIGHTS   **228**

Self-Esteem in the Workplace / *Emmett E. Miller*   *229*

You Can't Cut Your Way to Prosperity / *Joel Brockner*   *233*

Self-Esteem: A Formula for 21st Century Living
  and Working / *John Vasconcellos*   *236*

Spirituality in the Workplace / *Martin Rutte*   *242*

Self-Esteem and the Impact of Change / *Ichak Adizes*   *249*

Self-Esteem and Women / *Mary Kay Ash*   *251*

Spirituality—The Heart and Soul of Every Successful
  Business / *Terry Cole-Whittaker*   *252*

Afterthoughts / *Jack Canfield and Jacqueline Miller*   **258**

More Heart at Work   **263**

Resources   **264**

About the Authors and Contributors   **274**

Endnotes and Permissions   **281**

FOREWORD

 The work environment in modern organizations leads to a parching of the human spirit. In reaction against this, people are speaking out for "heart at work," for "spirit in the workplace." We find a growing insistence that every part of society—especially the workplace where so many spend so large a portion of their lives—be conducive to the fullest development of the human being.

One sometimes hears a defense of "heart at work" with arguments that boil down to "Spirit in the workplace leads to even more profits." While this may be true in some cases, it misses the real point.

There was a time when it was not too hard to equate being "hard at work" with "heart at work." The farmer who loved his land and his animals; the seamstress who took pride in the results of her handiwork; the craftsman obtaining deep satisfaction from his creation—all exemplified this. People ask why work in the modern corporation cannot be fulfilling as it once was for many in a simpler economy. To answer that, we must explore some aspects of the modern, publicly owned corporation.

The Rouse Corporation a quarter of a century ago (when it was much smaller than it eventually became) achieved a high degree of buy-in to the announced three principles of the corporation. The first principle was that the company is, first and foremost, a place where a certain group of people (employees and managers) gather to create fulfilling lives for themselves. Second, the company seeks to make a contribution to society—in the case of this particular company, through land development (such as the "new town" (then) of Columbia, Maryland). Third, it is the goal of all involved to do those first two things well enough to make a profit and stay in business.

As some companies become larger and publicly owned, the fiduciary responsibility to the shareholders squeezes out other values. Part of the problem, then, is this belief that the company exists for the stockholders. This leads us to ask: What is a corporation for? What is the economy for? The economy was supposed to serve the society; it appears that the modern idea is that most of the rest of society serves the economy. Something has gone wrong fundamentally, and it is this belief system that each of us buys into.

The role of the company in society is presently being questioned. Despite big gains in productivity and products, most employees are not sharing in the rewards while shareholders and option-laden corporate officials most definitely are. Average worker compensation has been going down for a decade; more than one in five work in part-time or temporary jobs; fewer workers have health insurance or pensions. Capitalism has come to be about paying workers less so shareholders can be paid more. The rising economic tide that once lifted everyone in America is now lifting a few yachts and causing a lot of little rowboats to flounder. What's clear is that both conservatives and liberals want corporations to do more for society than boost their stock prices. The story we hear so often is that due to the competitive environment, even though on the one hand people are insisting increasingly on participation and an environment where quality of relationships counts, "downsizing" leads to more work being piled on the shoulders of fewer workers, and "heart" gets squeezed out.

Spirit or heart in the workplace is only one of a number of minor temblors pointing to a tectonic shift taking place in modern culture. It behooves us to understand that broader cultural movement. Basic questions are being asked about matters thought to have been settled generations ago. What is society about? Economic production? The things that were supposed to serve society (economic production) have come to drive society (economic growth). We have acquiesced in the belief that the primary function of the corporation is financial return to the shareholders.

There are probably two chief contributing forces to this movement. One of these is people's growing awareness that an important spiritual, ethical, and ecological dimension has been neglected in modern society. This force is coupled with growing dissatisfaction with the impacts of the present economic and political order on their lives and those of their children and grandchildren, and on their desire for a better world.

Around the world, society is presently in a period of transition. The shape of the new is not yet discernible, although we seem to see elements of it in an assortment of new kinds of entrepreneurial enterprises, new forms of community, alternative economies, and other social innovations which embody values and principles congenial to a new, more heartfelt paradigm.

Tens of millions of persons in North America and similar numbers in Europe, with many more around the world, are voicing this discontent with the dis-spirited workplace. It is something happening throughout the modernized world.

"Heart at work" is in actuality a code phrase for a revolutionary reconception of what the corporation, the economy, and society are really for.

Jack Canfield and Jacqueline Miller have taken the power of storytelling to new heights by using stories and strategies to open our hearts and breathe some life back into the workplace.

A broad cross section of issues and stories and strategies and individuals, from Mary Kay to Jack Stack and from political leaders to cab drivers, has been assembled here to provocatively and profoundly make a bold and loud statement. It is time to soften the workplace and look at what we are doing in relation to each other and work.

WILLIS HARMAN
INSTITUTE OF NOETIC SCIENCES

Acknowledgments

I use not only all the brains I have, but all I can borrow.

Woodrow Wilson

We gratefully acknowledge the following people who contributed to making this book happen:

Georgia Noble, Jack's wife, for living through one more book project and being a space of centeredness, sanity and support in the midst of what often felt like total chaos.

Andrew Michael, Jackie's husband, for surviving Jackie's first book project and all of her time spent away from home at Jack's house in Santa Barbara, and for all the project management he provided for the book and for being the genuine conduit for this entire project. Andy, thank you for your guidance.

Patty Aubery, who tirelessly supervised the writing, typing and editing of this book. Patty, you are amazing under pressure. There are not enough words to express our gratitude.

Nancy Mitchell, who was the first to finish the manuscript and offer valuable feedback, who spent countless weekends at the office to finish this project and who spent hundreds of hours tracking down permissions for many of the stories and articles used in this book—all in record time!

Heather McNamara, who has become indispensable for the production, editing and compiling of our books. She was always willing to go the extra mile day after day to get it done. Thanks, Heather!

Kim Wiele, who did everything from marketing and sales to accounting and customer service in the office so that we could totally focus on this book for the last three months of 1995.

Veronica Valenzuela, the latest edition to our staff, who jumped right in and handled whatever needed to be done.

Trudy Klefsted at Office Works and Wanda Pate, who typed many of the original entries for the book.

Anne Wilson Schaef for her wonderful book *Native Wisdom for White Minds: Daily Reflection Inspired by the Native People of the World* from which we used a few poignant quotes.

John Grimes for generously donating his marvelous cartoons to Partnerships for Change. What talent! And thanks for believing in all the projects underway at Partnerships for Change.

Doug Kruschke, Walter Scott and Judy Haldeman who read the manuscript and shared incredibly valuable feedback and insights with us.

The following people who read parts of the manuscript and offered valuable feedback all along the way: Jan Ballard, Steve Cashdollar, Dominic Cirincione, Kate Driesen, Pam Finger, Sean Griffin, Betty Mazetti Hatch, Jennifer Hawthorne, Dee Hock, Rachel Hott, Ruth Johnston, Robin Kotock, Elisa Lodge, Penelope Ludwig, Roxanne McDougall, Jill Miller, Rebecca Robertson, Martin Rutte, Michael Owen Schwager, Marci Shimoff, John Tate, James Wanless, Richard and Maureen Wilcinski, Brad Winch and Michael Wyman.

The following people at McGraw-Hill: Philip Ruppel, who believed in the project from the beginning; Betsy Brown, our editor, who fully understood the scope and impact of our project and supported us throughout the process; Allyson Arias, who read and commented on the manuscript, and Danielle Munley, who offered enthusiastic support at every stage of the project.

Martin Rutte, Maida Rogerson and Tim Clauss, who gave us several key stories at the very end of the project. Thanks for your selfless generosity.

John Vasconcellos for creating the California Task Force to Promote Self-Esteem and Personal and Social Responsibility, which led to the Self-Esteem in the Workplace Conference where the idea for this book was hatched.

Dr. Emmett Miller for inviting Jackie into the Self-Esteem Task Force arena and for always being the real thing.

Michael Owen Schwager who came up with the title and various key marketing strategies. Michael, thanks for your creative wisdom and loyal support and for being a sounding board. Thanks also for all the wonderful people you introduced us to.

Susan Skye, who provided some much needed facilitation when we got bogged down.

Finally we'd like to acknowledge all the people who helped in ways we can't detail here, but without whom we never would have completed this book: Sam Albert, Mary Apic, Joe Bailey, Sondra Barrett, Warren Bennis, Richard Brodie, Christen Brown, Juanita Brown, Holly Buttner, Peter Cameo, Christina Campbell, Dr. Ben Carson, Leslie Carson, Richard

Carlson, Diane Carter, Bonnie Colleen, Nancy Conrad, Pete Conrad, Lisa Conte, Charles Coonradt, Marguerite Craig, Sandy Davis, David Delker, Constance Demby, Gun Denhart, Paul Dolan, Ann Duquette, Nancy Dutcher, Brooke Medicine Eagle, Dick Elkus, Liz Fetter, Eileen Fisher, Sid Friedman, Donald Gardner, Leeza Gibbons, Jane Goodall, Nick Graham, Leah Griesmann for early editing, Dr. Patrick Griffin, Norah Hart, Andy Hasse, Bart Harvey and the Enterprise Foundation, Jack Hawley, Kate Healy, Hazel Henderson, Gary Herbertson, Elizabeth Hin, Ellison Horne, Marlow Hotchkiss, Caroline Rose Hunt, Dr. Tim Johnson, Prasad Kaipa, Jack Kemp, Charles Kernaghan, Nancy Larsen, Walter Lembi, Learn-It Inc, Elisa Lodge, Clem Long, Ronald Long, Dora Love, Diana Marto, Hanoch McCarty, Roxanne McDougall, Allen McReynolds, Andy Mecca, Ken Michael, Shelah Michael, Emmett Miller, the late John F. Miller, Libby Miller (Jackie's mother), Maurice Miller, Tom Miller, Josie Natori, Valerie Oberle, Audrey Rice Oliver, Jon L. Pierce, Parkinson Pino, John Quigley, Rashani, Robert Reasoner, David Rivard, Rebecca Robertson, Majel Rodenberry, Buck Rodgers, Barbara Rodstein, Rose Russo, Gae Schulman, Walter Scott, Diane Sherwood, David Sibbet, Denise Slattery, Jack Stack, Bill Stark, Mark Stubis, John Tate, Joshua Taylor, Leslie Temple Thurston, Eric Utne, Alis Valencia, Lillian Vernon, Jim Wanless, Matt Weinstein, Ruth Forbes Young, the late Arthur Young, Wendy Zhorne and Shoya Zichy.

Because of the overwhelming size of this project, we are sure that we have left out some names of people who helped us. We apologize to you for our oversight, and yet we are eternally grateful to you for your valuable support and understanding.

My intention always has been to arrive at human contact without enforcing authority. A musician, after all, is not a military officer. What matters most is human contact. The great mystery of music making requires real friendship among those who work together. Every member of the orchestra knows I am with him or her in my heart.

Carlo Maria Giulini
Former Conductor
Los Angeles Philharmonic

SOURCE: Reprinted by permission of John Grimes. © John Grimes.

Introduction

This is not
the age of information.

This is not
the age of information.

Forget the news,
and the radio,
and the blurred screen.

This is the time
of loaves
and fishes.

People are hungry,
and one good word is bread
for a thousand.

David Whyte

The heart of the workplace has been broken. It is no wonder that people are dropping out of jobs at alarming rates—from long-held senate seats and secure positions on Wall Street to jobs at all levels in the corporate world. For those of us who choose to see, we find insecurity, fear, despair, resignation and cynicism are at an all-time high. Profound catastrophic social changes are upon us and all of our systems seem to be on self-destruct. Employees have been told they are "unessential" by government shutdowns, computerization and the effects of greed-motivated downsizing. The message is "profits come before people," and as a result, the dreams of a better life have become the nightmares of disappointment for far too many people. Stress-related illnesses are occurring at epidemic rates and murder has become the number one cause of death in the workplace.

Wretchedly soulless work is rampant, and, thanks to an increase in spiritual awareness and personal development, people no longer want to be part of an organization that is not responsible socially and environmentally. Many more people want to make a difference, not just a living.

As we interviewed Fortune 100 CEOs, fledgling entrepreneurs, corporate consultants, university professors, managers, assistants, employees, the self-employed, government officials, members of the military, psychologists and career counselors, we were continuously struck by how many people discussed not only their human needs but also their "spiritual" values. Many CEOs told us they felt they were being divinely guided and "embraced by the arms of God." Managers discussed the challenges of integrating their spiritual beliefs into their management practices, and over and over again, we heard people express how divine intervention had led them to their current job, "calling" or line of work.

Whether it was a farmer choosing what chemical fertilizer to use or an air quality control engineer monitoring air pollution emissions, people felt better knowing they were contributing to the greater good of their community, the nation and the world.

It may be someone at Patagonia knowing that 10% of their company's profits were going to support charities and causes they had helped choose, a Mary Kay distributor who was proud that her company had won the United Nations Environmental Program Award for using recycled packaging and avoiding animal experimentation, or a press operator at QuadGraphics who is proud that his company produces less waste product than any other printer in America. People like to know their company, government agency or store is making a positive difference rather than creating problems in the world.

People want to feel that who they are and what they do matter. We now spend over 60% of our life at work and we want that work to be connected with what we believe is important in the world. We don't want to work at a company that pollutes our air and water. Our children and our neighbors breathe that air and drink that water. We don't want to go to bed at night knowing we have lied to make a sale or keep a client. We want to feel good about ourselves and our actions.

People want to be able to come to a place of work where they feel loved, appreciated and cared about rather than demeaned, ignored or taken for granted.

Deep down everybody wants to engage in work that is productive, fun, meaningful and masterful. Everybody wants to belong, to contribute, to matter and to make a difference. And, finally, everyone wants to hear the words, "Thank you. You make a difference!"

How This Book Came to Be

The idea for this book emerged at the end of a conference on Self-Esteem in the Workplace that was sponsored by the State of California as part of the dissemination process for its historic Task Force to Promote Self-Esteem and Personal and Social Responsibility. The two of us were discussing what a wonderful day it had been and how useful it would be to share the ideas and strategies that had been presented there with a much wider audience. We agreed to compile a book of articles by the world's leading experts in the field of self-esteem in the workplace, CEOs who were actively and intentionally building self-esteem in their corporations and corporate consultants engaged in conducting seminars, workshops and training on self-esteem and spirit in the workplace.

As we began the process, it seemed like it would be a simple project. In fact it turned out to be one of the most challenging and ultimately most enlightening projects either of us has ever taken on. We had both been working in the field of self-esteem for over 20 years, and we thought we knew a lot about the topic—which we did. However, the more we got into this project, the more we began to realize how much we didn't know.

It seems that our level of self-esteem affects everything in our lives, including our work, and everything at work has the potential to affect our self-esteem. The more we explored self-esteem in the workplace, the more we realized that people were doing hundreds of things that we had not been aware of previously and that were indeed effective in building self-esteem in the workplace. Before we knew it, we had over 200 potential chapters from some of the brightest and most caring people in the world. We came to realize that we had enough material for three books: one of powerfully moving personal stories that would touch the hearts and souls of all people who worked; another for managers composed of well thought-out articles on the best concepts, principles and steps for building self-esteem at work; and a third for CEOs and other leaders, which would contain stories and statements by fellow CEOs about what they were doing or had done to create high self-esteem and release human potential in their organizations.

Our publisher wanted one universal book that could easily be read and appreciated by people from every spectrum of the workplace—CEOs, entrepreneurs, managers, supervisors, employees and consultants. That made the project much more difficult because, at the level of form, our interests are somewhat different. However, we discovered that, at the level of principles, values and what matters to the heart, we are all the same.

What has finally emerged is a book that we believe has successfully combined the best of all three books into one.

This book contains the personal stories of workers, managers, corporate leaders, trainers and consultants sharing their heartfelt experiences and insights about what makes work more humane, more fulfilling and more heartfelt. The stories are bursting with the importance of self-esteem, self-acceptance, love, caring, recognition, purpose, respect, integrity, commitment and courage—what might be called qualities of the spirit—in the workplace.

This book also contains pieces by CEOs, managers, consultants and organizational psychologists who are actively engaged in the day-to-day practice of creating a new kind of organization that respects people, that encourages the full expression of its employees, that embraces truth, that empowers its workers, that respects and cares about the environment and that produces products and services that make a difference.

The stories and insights of these enlightened leaders offer positive visions of hope and practical road maps for creating organizations that build rather than destroy self-esteem and acknowledge and honor the human spirit.

The purpose of this book is to breathe some life back into the workplace. We want people to breathe a sigh of relief knowing that there are people who work from the heart, put people first and still make a healthy profit. We hope their stories, insights and visions will inspire you to do the same.

Anecdotes are sometimes the best vehicles of truth, and if striking and appropriate are often more impressive and powerful than argument.

Tyrone Edwards

How to Read This Book

We have collected and sequenced close to 100 pieces—some short, some long—that present, elucidate and provide practical solutions to key issues in the arenas of self-esteem and spirit in the workplace. You will have to exercise determination and discernment as you read. The short personal stories are the easiest to read and digest. They will touch you on many levels and do their work almost on a subconscious level.

The contributions that are more theoretical and analytical will demand a little more commitment to extract their full value. They will require you to think, decide and plan a course of action. While we believe it is important to touch you at the emotional level, which is where motivation and a commitment to change come from, we also believe that it is important to exercise your mind and challenge your belief systems. This creates a holistic approach, one that we believe will have the deepest impact on your behavior. Ultimately, each contribution to this book is simply one person's experience of what is important. It is never the total truth. Each story and essay is only one facet on a many-faceted diamond. It takes all the facets to make a complete diamond. We invite you to explore every facet as completely as you can and then trust your own perceptions and conclusions as to what is important for you and for your organization.

How to Get the Most Value from This Book

To get the most value out of this book, we recommend that you reread it at least three times within the next year. The reason for this is twofold. First, there is so much gold in this book that you cannot possibly retain, understand and integrate it all in one reading. There is simply too much to digest all at once. The second reason is that some of the articles seem to reveal more and more with each reading—especially those written by CEOs and management consultants. These articles tend to be a bit more theoretical and therefore take a little more concentration to read. They are also packed with so much information and so many practical things that you can do to transform yourself and your workplace that it would take months to implement all the suggestions. We encourage you to keep revisiting these articles both to see how you are doing and to gain new insights as to what to do next.

Again, we recommend that you don't try to read this book all in one sitting. Read until you feel moved to do something else. Perhaps you'll be moved to duplicate a story and share it with your co-workers. Perhaps you'll be moved to attack your job with more vigor, commitment and passion. Perhaps you'll be moved to call up co-workers and tell them how much you appreciate them and their influence in your life. Perhaps you'll be moved to try some specific technique to recognize and reward an employee. Or, perhaps you may be moved to simply do something nice for yourself, like take a walk or do some relaxation exercises. We invite you to trust your impulses and honor them.

Next Steps

Finally, at the end of the book is a list of resources that you can utilize to build and maintain your own self-esteem, build the self-esteem of your employees, enhance your management skills and transform your organizations. We have included books, audio tapes, video tapes, training programs and consultants that will extend and deepen the themes addressed in this book. We have also provided you with information on how to contact the contributors to this book.

Your Letters, Stories, Techniques and Approaches

We are eager to hear from you. We want to hear your reactions to this book, what you have done to build and maintain self-esteem and spirit in *your* workplace and anything else you would like to share with us.

We also invite you to share stories, poems, articles and other pieces—written either by you or by someone else—that you think we ought to include in future books about *Heart at Work*. Our addresses, fax numbers, e-mail addresses and web site information all appear at the back of this book.

Let the Journey Begin!

As you begin this journey into the heart at work—the realm of self-esteem and spirit in the workplace—let us thank you for having the willingness, commitment and courage to open yourself to being touched by those we have gathered together here so that you may turn and touch those who have chosen to gather together around you. Whether you are an employee, a middle manager, an executive or a company president, you have the opportunity to create more joyful, fulfilling and self-actualizing workplaces.

As you begin this journey, we wish you many hours of enjoyable and enlightening reading. Bon voyage!

1 SELF-ESTEEM and YOU

How I feel about and behave toward myself is the basic determinant of most of my behavior. If I improve my self-regard, I will find that dozens of behaviors change automatically. If, for example, I increase my feelings of self-competence, I will probably be less defensive, less angered by criticism, less devastated if I do not get a raise, less anxious when I come to work, better able to make decisions, less afraid of making decisions, and more able to appreciate and praise other people.

Will Schutz

Developing Your
Personal Signature

Barbara Glanz

Professional Speaker
Author, *The Creative Communicator—399 Tools to Communicate Commitment Without Boring People to Death!* and *CARE Packages for the Workplace— Dozens of Little Things You Can Do to Regenerate Spirit at Work*

There is nothing better for a man than to rejoice in his work.

The Bible, Ecclesiastes 3:22

If you are called to be a street sweeper, sweep streets even as Michelangelo painted, or Beethoven composed music, or Shakespeare wrote poetry. Sweep streets so well that all the hosts of heaven and earth will pause to say, "Here lived a great street sweeper who did his job well."

Martin Luther King, Jr.

Last fall I was asked to speak to 3000 employees of a large supermarket chain in the Midwest on "Building Customer Loyalty and Regenerating the Spirit in Your Workplace."

One of the ideas I stressed was the importance of "adding a personal signature to your work." With all the downsizing, re-engineering, overwhelming technological changes and stress in the workplace, I think it is essential for each of us to find a way we can really feel good about ourselves and our jobs. One of the most powerful ways to do this is to do something that differentiates you from all the other people who do the same thing you do.

Some of the examples I shared were a United Airlines pilot, who, after everything is under control in the cockpit, goes to the computer and at random selects several people on board the flight and hand writes them a thank you note for their business. A graphic artist I work with always encloses a piece of sugarless gum in everything he sends his customers so you never throw anything from him away!

A Northwest Airlines baggage attendant decided that his personal signature would be to collect all the luggage tags that fall off customer's suitcases, which in the past have been simply tossed in the garbage, and in his free time he sends them back with a note thanking them for flying Northwest. A senior manager with whom I worked decided that his personal signature would be that whenever he sends his employees a memo

8   Heart at Work

that he knows they won't like very much, he staples a piece of Kleenex to the corner of the memo!

After sharing several other examples of how people add their unique spirit to their jobs, I challenged the audience to get their creative juices going and to come up with their own creative personal signature.

About three weeks after I had spoken to the supermarket employees, my phone rang late one afternoon. The person on the line told me that his name was Johnny and that he was a bagger in one of the stores. He also told me that he was a person with Down's Syndrome. He said, "Barbara, I liked what you said!" Then he went on to tell me that when he'd gone home the night of my presentation, he had asked his dad to teach him to use the computer.

He said they set it up in three columns, and each night now when he goes home, he finds a "thought for the day." He said when he can't find one he likes, he "thinks one up!" Then he types it into the computer, prints out multiple copies, cuts them out, and signs his name on the back of each one. The next day as he bags customer's groceries, "with flourish" *he puts a thought for the day in each person's groceries*, adding his own personal signature in a heartwarming, fun and creative way.

One month later the manager of the store called me. He said, "Barbara, you won't believe what happened today … When I went out on the floor this morning, the line at Johnny's checkout was *three times longer* than any other line! I went ballistic yelling, 'Get more lanes open! Get more people out here!' but the customers said, 'No no! We *want* to be in Johnny's lane—we want the thought for the day!'"

He said one woman even came up and told him, "I only used to shop once a week, and now I come here every time I go by because I want the thought for the day!" (Imagine what that does to the bottom line!) He ended by saying, "Who do you think is the *most important person* in our whole store?" Johnny, of course!

Three months later he called me again, "You and Johnny have transformed our store! Now in the floral department when they have a broken flower or an unused corsage, they go out on the floor and find an elderly woman or a little girl and pin it on them. One of our meat packers loves Snoopy, so he bought 50,000 Snoopy stickers, and each time he packages a piece of meat, he puts a Snoopy sticker on it. We are having so much fun, and our customers are having so much fun!" THAT is spirit in the workplace!

A man lamented to his rabbi: "I'm frustrated that my work leaves me no time for study or prayer." The rabbi replied: "Perhaps your work is more pleasing to God than study or prayer."

Hasidic Tale

The Acorn Principle

Jim Cathcart

President, Jim Cathcart Company
Professional Speaker
Past President, National Speakers Association
Author, *Relationship Selling*

To be nobody but yourself in a world which is doing its best to make you everybody else—means to fight the hardest battle which any human being can fight and never stop fighting.

e.e. cummings

The acorn principle states that your greatest, fastest and easiest growth always comes from your natural abilities. The source of the acorn metaphor is that most people tend to look at other people as if they can change them into whatever they want. What they ought to be doing is looking within those people to see what kind of seed is on the inside. Just like a tree, every person has a seed.

For years there has been a debate among psychologists, psychiatrists and philosophers over what makes persons what they are. Is it nature (their genetics) or is it nurture (the experiences they have had throughout their lives) that cause them to be what they are? The answer is both. The way I suggest you approach developing yourself and others—especially if you want those others to be fulfilled in their work, to be happy in their relationships and to be proud of themselves—is to nurture their nature.

A lot of managers get it backwards. They look at that little acorn that they see inside somebody, and they say, "Acorn, I think you have potential. I think with a little training, and a little hard work, you could be a giant redwood." In fact, the only thing an acorn is going to be is an oak, but it could be a wonderful one if you developed it right.

Then this misled manager comes back and says, "Acorn, here's what I'm going to do for you. I'm going to work with you to help develop your redwood skills. Here's a tape I want you to listen to called *The Power of Positive Redwood Thinking* by Dr. Norman Vincent Tree. Here's a book on the history of some of the great redwoods of all time. Learn from their example. I'd also like you to start networking with redwoods. Just take a redwood to lunch, find out what they're like, and ask them their secrets. I also want you to say a daily affirmation I've written for you. It says, 'I am a redwood, great and tall. My mighty branches shelter all. I'm good enough, I'm smart enough and, doggone it, people like me.'"

Now I ask you, what's that acorn going to be when it grows up? You're probably thinking an oak. I say, yes, but a really insecure oak—because all this time it has been getting the message that it wasn't okay to be who and what it was. It has been getting the message that it ought to be something else and in this case something it is not capable of becoming.

But what if that same manager takes a different approach and says, "First, let me find out what is the nature of this person." Then come the other questions, "How can I cultivate that nature? How can I find the natural gifts that this person has and then structure a growth plan around those natural gifts?" Then they might have said to the acorn, "Here's a tape on *The Power of Positive Oak Thinking.* Here are some examples of successful oaks I'd like you to learn from. Here's a sign-up for a seminar on oak skills. I want you to start networking with other oaks, and I've written an affirmation for you that is related to your oak qualities." If they had done that, the use of the same techniques would have paid off handsomely because they were nurturing the nature that was already there. The more we find the seeds that are inside ourselves and other people, the more we will value those persons as they are and help them grow along their natural lines so that they tap their true potential.

In one of Dr. Kenneth McFarland's speeches, he talks about a friend of his, Dr. Edward Rosenal, who at age 11 had seen a doctor light up the faces of his parents by alleviating the pain and suffering his brother was going through. His brother had been violently ill, and his parents called the doctor. The doctor finally arrived, and what he did and how he did it made the parents' faces shine in such a beautiful way that, at age 11, young Edward Rosenal decided to become a doctor. He went on to have a brilliant career as a physician in Cincinnati.

After I play that tape, I tell my audiences that in 1979, I spoke for a group of Dairy Queen owners and operators. I asked the question, "Why did you get into this business?" One woman raised her hand and said, "I got into this business because, when I was a nurse, the pain and suffering I saw everyday used to bother me too much. I was over at a neighboring ice cream store one afternoon, and I saw this little boy pointing at a picture of a hot fudge sundae. I swear the kid was having a spiritual bonding with that hot fudge sundae, and I decided that I would change professions so that I could put that kind of light in little faces." She left the field of medicine to put lights in faces. Edward Rosenal entered the field of medicine to put lights in faces. In each case, the person had the same ultimate goal, which was to bring happiness and satisfaction to the world and to alleviate discomfort for others. But they did it in opposite ways— by honoring the nature of the unique seed inside of them. One went into medicine and the other went out of medicine.

Years ago, a friend of mine, Bruce Belland, who is the founder and one of the singers in the group The Four Preps, said to me, "Jim, I heard your acorn principle. Let me give you an example that relates to that. When my second daughter was born, it was an emergency cesarean operation. We were very worried, and I was there at the hospital. I remember prior to going into the hospital, talking with my wife's doctor about what I did for a living. The doctor confided in me and said, 'I wish I had been a musician because I love to play concert piano.'"

"Later, after my wife had the delivery, the doctor came out with the good news that my wife was fine and I had a brand new healthy baby girl. While we're standing there and I was receiving the good news, another doctor walked up to the physician who had just delivered my child and said, 'Excuse me, doctor, I just wanted to tell you that you performed brilliantly in there, and it was an honor to have assisted you.' The doctor thanked his colleague, and the colleague left."

"I turned to the doctor and said, 'Now tell the truth. You have just brought a new life into the world, saved another life, and you've had one of your colleagues tell you it's an honor to be in your presence—for heaven's sake, can you honestly say you wish you had been a musician?'"

"The doctor grinned, nodded his head and said, 'I was pretty good in there.' We both chuckled and then the doctor said, 'I know exactly why, too—because this morning, I got up early and, for one hour, I played Chopin at the piano.'"

My observation about Bruce Belland and about his doctor is that when you make time for what you love—when you nurture your nature—it overflows. It causes an energy to overflow into the rest of your day or the rest of your life and it affects everything else you do. So the quickest way we can make our lives better is to make time for the things we love because, when we are doing what we love, we are serving the world in the way we were designed to.

OUR DEEPEST FEAR

Nelson Mandela

Our deepest fear is not that we are inadequate.
Our deepest fear is that we are powerful beyond measure.
It is our Light, not our Darkness, that most frightens us.
We ask ourselves, who am I to be brilliant,
gorgeous, talented, fabulous?
Actually, who are you NOT to be?
You are a child of God. Your playing small
does not serve the World.
There is nothing enlightened about shrinking so that
other people won't feel insecure around you.
We were born to make manifest the glory of God
that is within us.
It is not just in some of us;
it is in everyone.
As we let our own Light shine, we unconsciously
give other people permission to do the same.
As we are liberated from our own fear,
our presence automatically liberates others.

Fearful of human interaction, Sam seeks shelter in his work.

WHO WILL PLAY YOUR MUSIC?

Michael Jones

Corporate Trainer
Musician
Author, *Creating an Imaginative Life*

I lead workshops on creativity. This involves bringing in a piano and using music to help managers become more sensitive to following the impulses of their heart.

To help them reclaim their story, I have often shared one of my own. The idea that we each have a song within us that only we can sing has resonated deeply for many of them. Here is what one senior executive from a major oil company said to me after completing a ropes course as part of an executive leadership program:

"I realized that my fear of heights was a reflection of my fear of life. As I stood shaking on that platform thirty feet above the ground and looked at the rope that danced in front of me, I remembered your story about the old man and how his question to you about *Who will play your music* gave you the faith and courage to leave the security of your known life and take that leap of faith into the unknown. So I imagined that dancing rope was *my* music, and I thought, 'Who is going to play that music if I don't do it myself?' Then I felt the tears well up in my eyes, and just before they began to blur my vision, I jumped. As I swung back and forth on that rope I just started to laugh, it was such a wonderful release that I thought my heart would melt. I know that my life will be different now, but I will also always remember that moment as one of the most joyful experiences of my life."

Here's my story ...

For many years my art and my work represented separate and distinct lines of the development in my life.

My art was music. From a moment when I was two or three and my aunt picked me up and gently guided my fingers over the piano keys, I had spent at least an hour of every day at the piano.

My work was educating managers and consulting with organizations. While psychology and organizational behavior fascinated me almost as much as music, my business practice also offered a cover, a means through which I could engage directly with the world and still preserve a protected space for this inner work. Being at the piano had taught me how easy it was to feel profoundly vulnerable and self-conscious, even embarrassed when I began penetrating into the deeper layers of who I was—which our art often asks us to do—even when I knew that the qualities being released would prove to be my greatest strengths.

Sometimes, however, during management retreats the topic of music might come up in conversation over a meal. Then I would lead a small and curious group down a narrow darkened hallway behind the kitchen, where I knew a spinet piano was stored, and play it for a while. Because of this vulnerability, I was often uncomfortable performing my own music for others, with the exception of close friends. Instead, I did covers [my versions] of other people's music and relied on these arrangements when I played for these managers or in a public place.

It was one of these arrangements that I was exploring while sitting at a piano in a hotel lobby one quiet evening. I had been teaching a seminar for the last few days and we had given ourselves the night off. I had come back to the hotel early from the restaurant where we had eaten to prepare some materials for the next day.

Upon seeing the piano I decided to sit down for a few moments and play.

The hotel wasn't that empty, however. Soon an old man walked unsteadily out of the nearby lounge and plopped himself into a big easy chair beside the piano. There, he slowly sipped his wine and watched me play. I felt distracted and uneasy, trapped on the bench where at any moment he might request one of his favorite tunes, one I most likely did not know how to play.

"What's that?" he asked when I was done.

"Oh a little bit of *Moon River*," I replied.

"Yeah, I recognized that," he said. "But there was something else before it; what was that?"

"That was some of my own music," I replied. "I don't have a name for it yet."

"You should." He said. "It deserves one." He looked thoughtful for a moment. Then he said, "Your music is beautiful, but you're wasting your time with that other stuff."

"What do you mean?" I asked

"It's your music that brought me out here."

"But," I said in my defense, cutting him off, "it's the other music that people want to hear."

"Not when they hear this," he replied. "Please play some more." Then he closed his eyes and sat back in the chair.

When I finished playing, he and I sat together for a long time. Slowly he opened his eyes and sipped from his glass. "What are you doing with the music?" he asked.

"Nothing," I said. "It's just something I do for myself."

"Is that all?" he replied, surprised by my words.

Then I explained what had brought me to the hotel. "But how many others can do this consulting work?" he asked.

"Oh, perhaps twenty or thirty," I said, adding quickly, "but I don't want to give it up; my mission through the work is to change the world."

"I'm sure it is," he said. He seemed moved by the forced conviction of my words. Then he set his wine glass down on the table and looked directly at me. "But who will play your music if you don't do it yourself?"

"It's nothing special," I protested.

I was about to offer other excuses when, with fire in his eyes and a voice sober and clear, he said, "This is your gift—don't waste it."

With that he stood up, steadied himself by resting his hand on my shoulder for a moment, raised his glass in a silent toast and then weaved slowly back to the lounge.

I sat frozen on the bench. *Who will play my music?* I asked myself this question over and over again.

To do what was being asked of me here was no easy thing. I could neither push forward nor hold back. When we reach this moment of turning in our life we are often asked to go beyond our skills, to do the opposite of what has gone before. If we have been unfocused, this is time for focus; if we have been driven to succeed, this is time for space.

And our "art" may not necessarily be a special talent like writing or music. Instead it may be a quality of caring that we offer, or a capacity to listen deeply to the concerns of others or simply the wonder and beauty we awaken in the world through the attention we bring to a piece of music, a flower or a tree.

The old man reminded me that I could be of little help to others in fulfilling the vision for their own life until I had done something about fulfilling my own. In the years that followed I let go of my consulting practice to continue composing and recording the music that I played that night. One recording led to ten more and now the music that I once shared only with close friends has spread around the world.

Yet I felt a sadness for the work I left behind and I have returned to the consulting work I did before. But something is very different now. I no longer need to fulfill the expectations of others or leave any part of myself outside the door. When I set aside my consulting practice to return to music, I could not foresee where it would lead. But over time the painful doubts and uncertainties have evolved into a wonderful dance that has elegantly woven together and integrated all of the various and seemingly separate strands of my life. While finding the marriage between my intellect and my soul may have been too complex and perhaps too terrifying for my strategic mind to grasp, creating our lives so that they are a reflection of what we love is child's play for the heart.

"Don't grieve," the Sufi poet Jalaludin Rumi says to us. "Anything you lose comes around in another form. The child weaned from the mother's milk now drinks wine and honey mixed."

So now, when I join these groups, I don't bring only charts and projectors and theories as I did before. In addition, I bring myself, some stories and a nine-foot-six concert grand—and I am careful to save a place beside the piano for the old man from the lobby of the hotel.

Integrity and Self-Esteem

Nathaniel Branden

Author, *The Six Pillars of Self-Esteem* and *The Psychology of Self-Esteem*

To understand why lapses of integrity are detrimental to self-esteem, consider what a lapse of integrity entails. If I act in contradiction to a moral value held by someone else but not by me, I may or may not be wrong, but I cannot be faulted for having betrayed my convictions. If, however, I act against what I myself regard as right, if my actions clash with my expressed values, then I act against my judgment, I betray my mind. Hypocrisy, by its very nature, is self-invalidating. It is mind rejecting itself. A default on integrity undermines me and contaminates my sense of self. It damages me as no external rebuke or rejection can damage me.

If I give sermons on honesty to my children yet lie to my friends and neighbors; if I become righteous and indignant when people do not keep their commitments to me but disregard my commitments to others; if I preach a concern with quality but indifferently sell my customers shoddy goods; if I unload bonds I know to be falling in value to a client who trusts my honor; if I pretend to care about my staff's ideas when my mind is already made up; if I ask for honest feedback and penalize the employee who disagrees with me; if I ask for pay sacrifices from others on the grounds of hard times and then give myself a gigantic bonus—I may evade my hypocrisy, I may produce any number of rationalizations, but the fact remains, I launch an assault on my self-respect that no rationalization will dispel.

If I am uniquely situated to raise my self-esteem, I am also uniquely situated to lower it.

One of the great self-deceptions is to tell oneself, "Only I will know." Only I will know I am a liar; only I will know I deal unethically with people who trust me; only I will know I have no intention of honoring my promise. The implication is that my judgment is unimportant and that only the judgment of others counts. But when it comes to matters of self-esteem, I have more to fear from my own judgment than from anyone else's. In the inner courtroom of my mind, mine is the only judgment that counts. My ego, the "I" at the center of my consciousness, is the judge from whom there is no escape. I can avoid people who have learned the humiliating truth about me. I cannot avoid myself.

On Living a Lie

Richard Brodie

Former Chief Software Designer, Microsoft Corporation
Author, *Getting Past OK* and *Virus of the Mind*

The lies most devastating to our self-esteem are not so much the lies we tell as the lies we live.

Nathaniel Branden, PhD

Any path is only a path, and there is no affront to oneself or to others, in dropping it if that is what your heart tells you. Look at every path closely and deliberately. Try it as many times as you think necessary. Then ask yourself, and yourself alone, one question. Does this path have a heart? If it does, the path is good; if it doesn't, it is of no use.

Don Juan

I closed the ten-foot-tall oak door in my office, twisted shut the long, narrow strip of blinds covering the hall window and loosened my polka dot necktie. Safely hidden from the passing eyes of my employees and co-workers, I flopped face up on the Danish gray leather love seat I had purchased and let my heavy eyes fall shut.

It had been nine months since my promotion. My stellar performance as the project lead on the first version of Microsoft Word had inspired Bill Gates, Microsoft's CEO, to offer me the job of a lifetime: his personal technical assistant. That had led to this, the management of an entirely new department dedicated to the top-secret project "Cashmere." From my hopeful beginning with Microsoft as a summer computer programmer, I had been catapulted into the management of a dozen software engineers, a technical writer and a marketing planner.

I was a success by anyone's standards—I was Microsoft's most golden of Golden Boys! At the age of 26, I had written one of the world's best-selling pieces of software, worked personally with one of the smartest and most famous people on the planet and had enough stock options to make me a millionaire. Still comfortably on the green side of 30 years old, I had achieved everything I had ever hoped to achieve. My colleagues looked up to me with envy and admiration—or both.

I was unhappier and under more stress than I had ever been in my life. Depressed, fatigued, with my self-esteem at an all-time low, I lay on the leather love seat, resting my weary head on one armrest and belligerently bouncing alternate legs on the other. What had gone wrong? I beat myself up mentally. I had always enjoyed working here so much, I thought. What happened? By all rights, I should be the happiest guy on the planet, but here I was unproductive, depressed, tired. Feeling incompetent to meet these new challenges, I was essentially waiting for someone to catch me, to notice I was doing a terrible job. Someone did. It was Bill.

Bill Gates called me into his office. Everyone at Microsoft had the same size office—kind of an egalitarian thing—except for Bill and Jon Shirley, the president. Their offices were about three times the size of everyone else's. Bill's was always filled with thousands of sheets of paper: reports, computer printouts, memos, trade magazines that he never had time to read. He had a big desk at one end and a sofa with chairs around a coffee table at the other.

He flashed his famous boyish grin at me and I smiled nervously. I had developed a nervous tic in my right eye in recent months, and I was hoping it wouldn't flare up and embarrass me. It did, but he didn't show any signs of noticing.

Bill and I had become good friends over the last few years. We had traveled together, gone to movies, even spent a weekend together at a suite in Seattle's elegant Sorrento Hotel as a design retreat, just the two of us. The hotel had gone all-out, even engraving matchbooks for what anyone could have guessed were two consummate nonsmokers. I immediately noticed the ones engraved "William Gates III," and was astonished to find some with my name later on in another ashtray.

But that was all behind us now. Here I was, not a friend and an asset, but a problem to be dealt with. Unused to being in that situation, I regressed into an 11-year-old's mentality, as if awaiting a rare spanking at the hands of my father for embarrassing him in front of the neighbors.

But Bill didn't spank. Cutting straight to what he saw as the problem, he asked me to work longer hours—at least 50 per week. I agreed, hoping that would fix whatever was wrong. It was such a relief to have someone notice I was struggling that I ignored the deeper problem: that I didn't know how to do my job and I didn't know how to ask for help. So I closed my eyes, crossed my fingers and went back to my office with the leather love seat, ready to see what would happen.

I'll tell the ending of the story in a little bit, but first I want to address the central questions. I was in a situation where my self-esteem was dropping because I couldn't function effectively. But because I had such low self-esteem, I functioned even worse. How did this cycle begin? What would it take to get out of it?

For me, the main thing missing in my job at Microsoft was a feeling of competence. With no management training whatsoever, I had accepted a crucial management position and I knew neither how to perform it nor how to ask for help. I was floundering, drowning in my sea of dreams, and I didn't have the voice to cry for assistance. I was too afraid of looking incompetent, of looking foolish, of losing face.

From a job in which I was not simply competent but world-class, I had leapfrogged to a fantastic opportunity that I was completely unqualified for. I had risen not just to my level of incompetence, but several rungs above it with no one to steady the ladder. Without much delay, I came crashing down. The cycle of low self-esteem had started.

The idea of rising to your level of incompetence is well known today as Lawrence Peter's Peter Principle. We can expect people to keep getting promoted until they start having some difficulty doing their jobs. The solution is not to prevent promotions, but to recognize the problem when it occurs and find a way out.

If you're the employee, the way out begins with asking for help. It wasn't the failure that was making me sick, it was the living a lie. I was pretending everything was fine, spending all my energy putting up an image of competence, but all the time knowing that eventually I would be found out and my whole world would cave in.

When our self-esteem gets low, we start to confuse our employer with our mother. We want to be taken care of and, given that companies are designed less to nurture employees than to produce results, we are often frustrated and find ourselves with growing resentment toward real or perceived injustices. We start acting like children, doing anything from pouting to complaining to throwing a tantrum. My act was pretending—living a lie.

Not knowing how to recover or break the cycle of low self-esteem, I left Microsoft in a fury of shame and exhilaration. Not only did I quit Microsoft, but I also sold my house and car, moved across the country to Boston, broke up with my fiancee, and grew a beard. My "solution" was to seek greener pastures, which eventually led to a three year search for my purpose in life and to the writing of my first book, *Getting Past OK.*

What I found in my three year quest was what I wanted to do with my life. That's the key to self-esteem: to spend every moment of life pursuing what's most important to you. That kind of living builds self-confidence, self-esteem, and self-trust. It produces fulfillment, satisfaction and happiness.

All people have certain experiences they crave in order to feel satisfaction and fulfillment in life: experiences like belonging, acceptance, achievement or adventure. While these needs vary from person to person, each person's sense of quality of life is directly related to how well these needs are being filled. These core fulfillment needs must constantly be met in the workplace, as in all areas of a person's life, or self-esteem starts to suffer.

You're not born knowing what your core needs are. I found mine—and everyone can do the same—by asking some key questions about what types of experiences brought fulfillment in the past. What were the high points? What has made life worth living? When have I been truly motivated, juiced, moved?

Once you answer these questions, you can find common threads that tie these experiences together. These threads form your Success Checklist, a listing of what it takes for you to have not simply an okay life, but an unbelievably fantastic life! You have a decision making tool that you can use the rest of your life to bring you greater and greater satisfaction and to raise your self-esteem when it falters.

If you're an employer or manager, realize that your scared, cowering employee with low self-esteem is not making much of a contribution to the company compared with what is possible. Talk with him. Find out what makes him tick. What motivates that timid, withdrawn man in the production department? Ask the critical, resentful woman in purchasing what's great about her life.

When you are an employer or manager, the people in your organization are your customers: your job is to support and assist them. Be constantly aware of what you can do to make a difference in their lives. How can you make them more effective and productive? How can you make their jobs easier? How can you support their personal growth and development?

I did go back to Microsoft, by the way, once I had constructed my Success Checklist. Knowing what experiences I needed for fulfillment, I created my own position—a kind of special agent who came in and saved the day when all looked lost. I worked on the first version of Microsoft's hugely successful Windows database, Access, and worked longer and more effective hours than ever before. We sold a million copies the first few months. People patted me on the back and said, "Richard, we couldn't have done it without you!" Bill invited me to his wedding reception, where the Dom Perignon flowed like water and Natalie Cole sang so close I could have reached out and touched her. I had broken the cycle of low self-esteem.

If I had gone to Bill and asked for help back in 1986—said I wasn't competent to manage this team and would he please get me some training or help me find a different way to contribute—Word for Windows, which is what Project Cashmere became, would have come out a year or two earlier, and I'd probably own the Seattle Mariners now with all the riches I forfeited by quitting Microsoft rather than asking for help.

But beyond riches and achievements, the self-esteem that comes with living life authentically and with nothing to hide is its own reward.

I wake up every day now knowing that I have a world full of opportunity in front of me—an opportunity to do what's most important to me, to help people grow and develop, to help them make a splash in life, even to alter the course of human evolution for the better. And none of that would have been possible had I resigned myself to living a lie.

The fastest way to drive an employee insane is to give him or her new responsibilities and fail to provide them with the necessary instruction and training to do the job.

Ken Blanchard

Maintain Your Integrity

Source Unknown

Self-esteem is the reputation we acquire with ourselves.

Nathaniel Branden

A while back, there was a story about Reuben Gonzolas, who was in the final match of his first professional racquetball tournament. He was playing the perennial champion for his first shot at a victory on the pro circuit. At match point in the fifth and final game, Gonzolas made a super "kill shot" into the front corner to win the tournament. The referee called it good, and one of the linemen confirmed that the shot was a winner.

But after a moment's hesitation, Gonzolas turned and declared that his shot had skipped into the wall, hitting the floor first. As a result, the serve went to his opponent, who went on to win the match.

Reuben Gonzolas walked off the court; everyone was stunned. The next issue of a leading racquetball magazine featured Gonzolas on its cover. The lead editorial searched and questioned for an explanation for this first ever occurrence on the professional racquetball circuit. Who could ever imagine it in any sport or endeavor? Here was a player with everything officially in his favor, with victory in his grasp, who disqualifies himself at match point and loses.

When asked why he did it, Gonzolas replied, "It was the only thing I could do to maintain my integrity."

WHAT IS INTEGRITY?

Jack Hawley

Corporate Consultant
Author, *Reawakening the Spirit in Work*

Integrity is having the courage and self-discipline to live by your inner truth. Imagine a human life lived that way. There's great honor in it. Consider this true story:

Patrick, a consultant working with an apparently successful company, senses something is wrong. Despite the outward success, the atmosphere in the executive suite is flat and lifeless. How can this be?

He talks with senior managers throughout the company trying to get a handle on the vanished vim. Slowly the answer pieces itself together: "creative bookkeeping." They have always lived a policy of going right up to the line of legality relative to taxes; recently they have tripped over that line a few times. Finding it so easy, they have taken up residence there, and it's sapping their vitality.

What to do? Patrick knows the motivational project they hired him for won't work while this pall hangs over the place. He takes the weekend to mull it over, listening for directions from his inner truth.

On Monday he walks into the president's office and recommends a full IRS audit. "A what?!!" Yes. He tells them for their own good to call in

SOURCE: Reprinted by permission of John Grimes. © John Grimes.

the Federal Revenue agents. Is he out of his mind? What is this, Irish chutzpah? This advice all but empties the account of goodwill that he had built up with them.

But this isn't only a story of Patrick's cheek. It's about leadership heart, too. After some heavy agonizing and palpitations—and some good planning—the company leaders decide to do it: they request an audit! It ends up costing a few million dollars in back taxes and penalties. Ouch! But vitality comes home—and creativity comes with it. They soar again.

I once mentioned this story to the president of a large financial firm. His reaction was immediate. "Yeah, that was a smart move," his head bobbing forward as he said it, "not only honest but also practical!" He explained the dreadful drain of money, time and spirit that double-dealing causes—and how all this casts a cloud over everything. His multi-metaphored message: be brave, bite the bullet if you have to and breathe the fresh air of integrity.

IMPECCABILITY

Jack Hawley

Corporate Consultant
Author, *Reawakening the Spirit in Work*

There is no such thing as a minor lapse of integrity.

Tom Peters

Phil was the head purchasing agent for the first company I worked for. He was a white-haired, bulb-nosed, streetwise gentleman from Boston, much older than us recent MBA types. He wasn't fancy. His suits, with their wrong-width lapels, always hung rumpled on his stocky frame. Nevertheless, he was a wonderfully clear role model. He was responsible for buying perhaps a hundred million dollars worth of food and beverage items each year for the company. That part of the hospitality business is known for kickbacks, double-dealing and shady behavior. People shrug it off and just don't think about it.

But it wasn't in Phil to shrug. In the face of such corruption Phil squared his shoulders and was scrupulously, meticulously, impeccably honest. He wouldn't even take home one of the jillions of cocktail napkins or "free" ball-point pens he bought for the company. Phil never even accepted a drink from the many sales reps who called him friend. "I'll drink with you, but I'll buy my own," he'd smile, pointedly.

He didn't flaunt his integrity, but he always had the time to tell us how and why he was so careful about being that way, emphasizing personal impeccability. He taught us nose to nose, explaining until we understood—never a sermon, just friendly information. And he never tired of sharing this with the young people who passed his way.

Some say knowledge is power, but that is not true. Character is power.

Sathya Sai Baba

Entrepreneurs and Self-Esteem

Wilson L. Harrell

Former publisher, *Inc. Magazine*
Author, *For Entrepreneurs Only*
Columnist, *Success* magazine

I'd like to share some thoughts with a very special group of individuals: all you entrepreneurs and, equally important, the men and women who are thinking about going into business for themselves. You are very special because, in reality, our country's economic future is in your hands. During the past decade, over 90% of all new jobs have come from the entrepreneurial sector, and, given the continued downsizing of large corporations, it is predictable that there will be an explosion of entrepreneurship. So, if you're on the edge, come on in, the water's great. You'll be most welcome to our world.

As I reflected on my life as an entrepreneur and remembered all the failures and successes and the spaces in between, I came to the profound and surprising conclusion that "self-esteem" is the very essence of entrepreneurship. This mysterious source of inner strength allows lonely and terrified individuals to accomplish the impossible, then, when necessary, to rise from the ashes of defeat and go fight again.

It seems obvious to me that self-esteem is nothing more than a report card on how well we're following our conscience. Way down deep we all know right from wrong. What we didn't learn in church or school, or in our mother's lap, we received genetically from all those who went before us. Self-esteem is the mirror that our Creator installed in each of us that continuously reflects our moral net worth. We begin our lives with a "bank account" of self-esteem. We can grow the account by following our conscience, by doing what we instinctively know to be right. Likewise, we decrease the account by breaking faith with ourselves.

From early youth, self-esteem is continually under attack. Lying, cheating, stealing are the tools that chip away at our moral worth. In early years, those destructive implements may seem small and inconsequential, but repeated use makes them grow and become stronger. And throughout our lives, there is always someone standing by to give us new and better tools. We call them "peer groups"—individuals who have already depleted part or all of their accounts and want us to join them in moral bankruptcy. The invitation to join is always accompanied by great promises of instant gratification and the comfort of being accepted. Saying yes is so easy, but the consequences can be devastating. Let me give you an example:

I once had an individual working for me. Let's call him Hank. A world-class entrepreneur, at 38 he was already president of a very successful division of my company. He was one of the finest executives who had ever worked for me. "Self-esteem" oozed from every morsel of his being. When he walked into a room, somehow everybody knew it; when he spoke, people stopped talking and listened. He was simply magnificent. He had it all, including an all-American wife and two children. Plus he would have my job sometime in the future.

Then Hank got involved with a very fast-living peer group, which included a stunningly beautiful, young woman. Like Hank, she had everything, except she had a small problem—she occasionally snorted a line of coke. She persuaded Hank to join in the fun by promising instant gratification. Six months later, Hank was no longer the same person. Somehow the spark was gone. Oh, he still functioned, sales were up and on paper everything was great, but I didn't think so. I suspected that Hank's occasional "line" of instant gratification had become something a lot more insidious. We had a long discussion. Hank knew that what he was doing was wrong and promised to quit. He didn't.

During the next few months, I witnessed a horrifying transformation of another human being. At first missed appointments, and then days when he didn't show up at all. Like Jekyll and Hyde, even his appearance changed: the inner glow was gone; his positive attitude became hesitant and insecure. No matter how he dressed, he somehow looked sloppy and unkempt. His mood swings were erratic and unpredictable—highs too high, lows much too low. Our one-on-one meetings, which had always been exciting and productive, became depressive affairs that I dreaded. Hank would no longer look at me when we talked. Instead of challenging me with creative ideas, as he always had, he now kowtowed and made excuses, blaming everyone and everything for his failures, which increased by leaps and bounds. Before my eyes, I watched a shining superstar become dimmer and dimmer until it was no more.

Our relationship ended when Hank officially resigned. Two years later, he was dead. The papers gave his cause of death as a heart attack, but they were wrong. Hank had murdered his self-esteem and then couldn't live without it.

The relationship between entrepreneurs and self-esteem is amazing. First of all, it is difficult to conceive of people seriously thinking about going into business for themselves unless they have already built up a healthy reserve in their accounts of self-esteem. In fact, self-esteem is a prerequisite to being an entrepreneur. Research tells us that the principal motivating factors for entrepreneurs are to get their heads above the crowd, to be free. So if you have decided that you would be an entrepreneur, then you've already learned how to fight and win against the evil forces that challenge self-esteem.

Congratulations. But now that your self-esteem is urging you on to greater things, I have a warning. If you become an entrepreneur, you will be challenged as never before. Along your highway to success, you will meet temptations that will make all previous encounters seem like pygmies in a world of giants. The devil "greed" will always be lurking. The "honesty line" will sometimes become dim. Your handshake or word may be defused by cleverly written contracts. The obsession to succeed can easily become an excuse for compromising integrity. Let me tell you from personal experience that, when the day comes that you can't make payroll, or the bank calls your loan, or you lose your largest account—and that day will surely come, again and again—you will learn the true meaning of terror and the temptation to seek relief by drawing down on your self-esteem account by doing things you know to be wrong. So remember, terror and temptation go hand in hand. They are an entrepreneur's constant companion. When they come your way, look them squarely in the eye and "spit on them."

As an entrepreneur, you will be called on to take risks. I believe that risk taking and self-esteem are directly related. Every entrepreneur I have ever known has, at one time or another, taken incredible risks. If things go wrong, they bleed awhile, get up and go fight again. Their self-esteem may have been slightly wounded, but it was never killed. When they win, there is a flood of exhilaration that only a fellow entrepreneur can understand. And something else happens: The moral bank account receives an enormous deposit.

In closing, I would like to wish you well. Go make a footprint in the sands of time. It matters not whether the footprint you leave behind is small or large. The important thing is that it has your name inscribed on it. It's there for your children and their children to see and be proud. And let me tell you, my friends, there is no greater gift you can leave to all those that will follow, than to give them a full bank account of self-esteem to begin life with.

Over time the wise have agreed that love and work are essential ingredients for happiness and peace of mind. Many of the joys and frustrations in our lives seem to fall into either or both of these categories.

Walter Scott

VICTORY FORMULA

Lou Holtz

Head Football Coach, Notre Dame University

When challenged to describe the essential elements in his formula for winning, Holtz came up with ten principles that can produce a winning team on or off the football field. In his own words:

1. **Do right.** You know what's right, you know what's wrong. Too many people in this country talk about their personal rights. I'm still one of those old-fashioned people who believe in obligations and responsibilities.

2. **Do your best.** It is not enough to be born with the skill of an All-American. In order to succeed day in and day out, each individual must strive to do the best that he possibly can.

3. **Treat others as you want to be treated.** I have never seen a business, a family, an organization or a football team that cannot be turned around if you can generate love, mutual appreciation and fellow feelings.

4. **Set goals.** You have to have something that you wish to obtain. Everybody has to understand what we are trying to accomplish. Why are we here? There are a lot of reasons why these young players are here at Notre Dame: They are here to get an education and to win football games.

5. **Accept your role.** Not everybody can be the number-one quarterback at Notre Dame. But in order for the team to succeed, everybody from the water boy to the coach has to accept the hand that he or she has been dealt and make the best of it.

6. **Practice fundamentals.** Our whole program is based on doing little things the right way. Let little things slide, and the whole foundation of your organization will collapse.

7. **Believe in yourself.** I want a group of players that believe in themselves. You can't be a great coach, a great football player or a great entrepreneur if you don't have faith in yourself.

8. **Care about people.** Teamwork is the foundation of success. The three universal questions that an individual asks of his coach, player, employee, employer are: Can I trust you? Are you committed to excellence? And, do you care about me? If we don't care about one another, we don't stand a chance.

9. **Overcome adversity.** There is one thing in life that is universal. You're going to have problems, so be prepared for them.

10. **Don't flinch.** Believe that you're going to succeed. You cannot flinch, you cannot let people think that you are seriously in jeopardy of failure.

A Million Dollar Lesson

Petey Parker

President, Petey Parker and Associates

A cab driver taught me a million dollar lesson in customer satisfaction and expectation. Motivational speakers charge thousands of dollars to impart his kind of training to corporate executives and staff. It cost me a $12 taxi ride. It cost you the price of this book and the time to read this section.

I had flown into Dallas for the sole purpose of calling on a client. Time was of the essence and my plan included a quick turnaround trip from and back to the airport. A spotless cab pulled up. The driver rushed to open the passenger door for me and made sure I was comfortably seated before he closed the door. As he got in the driver's seat, he mentioned that the neatly folded *Wall Street Journal* next to me was for my use. He then showed me several tapes and asked me what type of music I would enjoy. Well! I looked around for a "Candid Camera!" Wouldn't you? I could not believe the service I was receiving! I took the opportunity to say, "Obviously you take great pride in your work. You must have a story to tell."

"You bet," he replied, "I used to be in corporate America. But I got tired of thinking my best would never be good enough, fast enough or appreciated enough. I decided to find my niche in life where I could feel proud of being the best I could be. I knew I would never be a rocket scientist, but I love driving cars, being of service and feeling like I have done a full day's work and done it well. I evaluated my personal assets and … wham! I became a cab driver. Not just a regular taxi hack, but a professional cab driver. One thing I know for sure, to be good in my business I could simply just meet the expectations of my passengers. But, to be *great* in my business, I have to *exceed* the customer's expectations! I like both the sound and the return of being 'great' better than just getting by on 'average.'"

Did I tip him big time? You bet! Corporate America's loss is the traveling folks' friend!

SOURCE: Dilbert by Scott Adams. Used by permission of United Feature Syndicate, Inc.

Do What You Love–
The Money Will Follow

We need to stop looking at work as simply a means of earning a living and start realizing it is one of the elemental ingredients of making a life.

Luci Swindoll

In Srully Blotnick's research reflected in *Getting Rich Your Own Way* (Playboy Paperbacks, 1982), 1500 people were divided into two groups and followed for 20 years. Group A made up 83% of the sample. These people were embarking on a career chosen for the reason of making money now in order to do what they wanted later. Group B, the other 17%, chose their career based on what they wanted to do now and would worry about the money later.

The data revealed some startling discoveries:

- At the end of the 20 years, 101 of the 1500 had become millionaires.
- Of the millionaires, all but one—100 out of 101—were from Group B, the group that had chosen to pursue what they loved!

Did you know that when you can say, "I love my work," you reduce your risk of heart disease? A study done by the Massachusetts HEW investigating the cause of heart disease asked participants two questions: Are you happy? Do you love your work? The results indicated that those who answered yes have a better chance of not getting heart disease.

Deepak Chopra, MD
Magical Mind, Magical Body

Work Is Love Made Visible

Kahlil Gibran

Author, *The Prophet*

And what is it to work with love?

It is to weave the cloth with threads drawn from your heart, even as if your beloved were to wear that cloth.

It is to build a house with affection, even as if your beloved were to dwell in that house.

It is to sow seeds with tenderness and reap the harvest with joy, even as if your beloved were to eat the fruit.

It is to charge all things you fashion with a breath of your own spirit,

And to know that all the blessed dead are standing about you and watching.

…

Work is love made visible.

And if you cannot work with love but only with distaste, it is better that you should leave your work and sit at the gate of the temple and take alms of those who work with joy.

For if you bake bread with indifference, you bake a bitter bread that feeds but half a man's hunger.

And if you grudge the crushing of the grapes, your grudge distills a poison in the wine.

And if you sing though as angels, and love not the singing, you muffle man's ears to the voices of the day and the voices of the night.

Reverence in the Workplace

Jack Hawley

Corporate Consultant
Author, *Reawakening the Spirit in Work*

Christmas trees are cut without prayers. We need to respect Mother Earth and care for the planet.

Franklin Kahn
Navajo Elder

I'm in the boardroom of a new client company, I walk to the chalkboard and draw a horizontal line, planning to use it for showing a range of behavior in organizations. I say, "There's a reverence continuum in organizations." I'm a little surprised when the word reverence comes out and notice a few brows wrinkling and some quizzical looks. How did I get into this?

A few months previously a woman from India had come to stay with us and our five teenagers. She was a bright shining lady, a woman who had gained some extra capacities to "see" in ways that many of us don't. There was something special in her ways: a veneration of seemingly worldly things that brought learning to others.

She told us how her father taught her and her siblings to treat all things—not only people—with deference and respect; he even included objects that form part of one's household. Little acts, like opening a door, for example: "Don't just yank it and barge through," he taught. "Turn the knob slowly, swing the door along its arch carefully, have reverence for it." Reverence for a door?! I noticed our offspring exchange glances behind their politeness.

"Even eating an apple," she said on another occasion. "We were taught not to gobble it, but to hold it lovingly in both hands and give thanks for the gift of sweetness and nourishment it so freely offers." At that, son Alec, who usually inhaled apples, wrinkled his brow and glanced at the waxy Macintosh in his hand.

Our airy kitchen enchanted her and her cooking soon cast a spell over us. It didn't take long for her to sweep the meat and eggs from the fridge, but she did it so sensitively and with such a logic that we welcomed it. After preparing delicious vegetable stews (curries), she would quietly chant the prayer and set aside her first morsel as an offering of gratitude. Her subtle examples began to seep into us all.

Christmas season came and enveloped the family. We were all, as was our custom each year, dancing to the stressful strains of the holiday hustle-bustle, scurrying our separate ways, meeting only on rare occasions. One day I walk in, breathless as usual. Louise is also there, having just arrived with a new Christmas wreath. "Nice," I say. "We've got five minutes. Let's hang it." I grab hammer and nails. She grabs the wreath. We zip out to the front door.

Our Indian lady is there with us, totally enthralled with the wreath. "Oh, it's so beautiful, so green," she gushes, "such a wonderful symbol. Oh, see how the leaves and berries exist together ... oh, how gorgeous."

"Yeah," I say, motioning for Louise to hold it in place on the door. Bang, bang. "There, done," I smirk. I pivot to return to the house and Oops!, almost trip over the Indian lady. She's doing a namaskar (kneeling on the patio, forehead to the cement, hands joined out in front of her), intoning a special blessing toward the wreath!

What do you do when a friend is kneeling at your feet directing prayers at your holly? Do you ignore her and tiptoe away, step over her and risk stumbling? Do you kneel with her? Having never encountered the issue before, we just stand a little self-consciously, waiting for her to finish. And we wait, and wait—one minute, two minutes, three. While positioned there, waiting, I come down a little from the frenetic pace and the world becomes a little quieter. Indeed, now that I notice it, she's right about the wreath: it really is a beautiful thing, and what it represents is even more so.

What's more, as we stand there, her blessing seems to work! The wreath becomes imbued with something more significant than simply being a decoration. For four full minutes (a long time nowadays) I stand there; the wreath is on the door at my shoulder. As I do, I begin to feel something more from it—a specialness, a power that I was unaware of before.

And that power lasts throughout the holidays. Gradually the family pace becomes less hurried. As the calm grows, so does our appreciation of the season. And each time I pass the wreath, I feel that "something" reach out and touch my shoulder.

Mine Are the Small Initials

Mildred Brown Duncan
Medical Secretary

Every time I type a letter for the physician I work for, at the bottom of the page I put his initials in capital letters and, alongside them, mine in lowercase.

"The small initials are mine," I commented to a new employee one day checking over some back correspondence. Afterward I got to thinking about that phrase. What did it mean? The busy, important physician as contrasted to the insignificant secretary?

No, that's not at all the way I look at my job. There are many rewards and satisfactions in being a secretary to a doctor. In his office the physician writes a prescription that will ease pain, and through diagnosis he can effect a healing.

But many of the rewards are on my side of the door. I'm the first to see the smiling face of one who, leaving the office, clutches hope and assurance as tightly as he holds a sample of medication or a prescription.

Often I'm the link to the doctor, and by simply saying, "You'll like him very much; he's easy to talk to," I see jaw muscles relax and eyes lose a little of the anxiety that often comes with meeting a new doctor.

It comforts a patient to know that even when it is impossible for the doctor to come to the phone, the secretary has time to listen and can be trusted to deliver the message. I try to keep in mind that that's the reason I'm here—and also the reason I'm often behind in my typing!

I have been given messages so important, and at times so frightening, that I could concentrate on nothing else until they were safely delivered. By answering the phone, I may hear something as routine as the news that a hospital bed we requested is now available—or something as spine-chilling as a terrified voice screaming, "He's tried it again," meaning suicide.

I have received some special gifts. Three I cherish. The first is a cardboard angel taped to the wall behind my desk. It was laboriously colored by a little hand whose muscles wouldn't follow directions very well, and given to me at Christmas time by a mentally retarded child.

The two others are intangible, but no less real. One came from a new patient. The years had ringed her neck as faithfully as a tree trunk and given her eyes the look of deep softness that comes from suffering. We finished with my routine questions. When I said, "You can come into the doctor's office now," she arose from the chair slowly and replied, "I thought you were the doctor."

The last gift came from a gracious elderly man with a mahogany face crowned with gray-white hair. He pushed a stub of a pencil and crumpled envelope toward me as he started to leave and said, "Miss, would you put your name on this paper?"

"Certainly, but why would you want it?"

"Because you've been kind and I'd like to know your name."

He shuffled out, and I stored his compliment on the shelf in my heart that I reserve for very special things. Our paths crossed again one day. This time the crisis was in my life, not his. While tears cascaded down my face, he said softly, "I'll pray for you."

In a single day's mail I have sent a letter to a worried mother instructing her how to adjust the medication to better control epileptic seizures, a letter to a man advising him to seek legal counsel, a letter stating that an ambitious young person, derailed from normal living by years of mental illness, has now sufficiently recovered to have his inherent civil rights restored.

At night when I cover the typewriter and stack beside it the charts still waiting to have progress notes typed in, I can't help thinking that they are much more than ink and paper pages. They are records of pain and its being relieved, of sorrow and its being endured, of problems and their being either solved or met head-on and courageously accepted. In short, they represent human lives I've been privileged to touch. And some of them have a special something I can't define, something which makes me know that even if I never see the person again, the impression he made in a single visit will be forever indelible.

At the end of the day I turn out the light, pick up my keys and walk out of the office, leaving a part of myself there, and taking with me the knowledge that though the service, like the initials, is small, I too have served.

Dedicated to Libby Miller and the lives she has touched in the medical arena, including my own. Thanks, Mom.

JLM

Learning a Lesson

Susan Cunningham Euker
Classroom Teacher

I am a teacher. I don't think I actually knew that until spring of last year, even though I have been in the classroom for over 20 years.

Until I met T.J., I was an educator. Not that there is anything wrong with being an educator—it is just different from being a teacher. It is perhaps more academic, more accountable to standardized state tests, more necessary to Scholastic Aptitude Test scores. Teaching is listening to the small voice in your heart that validates children the world has dismissed. It is sharing a part of yourself and in the process, receiving back far more than you give.

T.J. changed it for me—big, blond, unkempt, antisocial, quiet, forgotten T.J. He taught me much about what I value about myself and how those values transfer to my students. He showed me what my profession is about.

T.J. sat in the very back of my classroom alone, isolated for one entire semester and, in spite of my efforts, did nothing—no assignments, no tests, no class work, no participation, no interest in much of anything. And he failed—flat.

I was curious about this unusual young man, and after checking confidential records in the guidance office, I discovered information that made the pieces of T.J.'s puzzle fit. He had lost his father by the seventh grade and had great difficulty getting along with his alcoholic mother throughout his teenage years. He had a brother who was severely limited, and there was indication of possible abuse of both children. T.J.'s mother was so verbally abusive to the school administrators that they had almost given up dealing with T.J.'s truancy.

T.J. lived in a painfully dysfunctional family. His low self-esteem became understandable to me; his reason for hurrying home each day after school became clearer and his missing school frequently even became justifiable. I hurt for him. Because my course is required for graduation from high school and because for some reason T.J. wanted to graduate, he was back in the spring semester of his senior year for one final try. I had my doubts. So did everyone else.

Things began that semester with T.J. withdrawing as he had done previously. But then as the class discussed self-esteem one day, something changed. I had my students tape blank pieces of paper on their backs, and I gave them five minutes to circulate around the room, find five people they did not know particularly well and write one positive thing they had noticed about that person on the sheet. After we sat down and discussed anxieties and feelings about completing this exercise, I asked them to read silently what was written on their papers. I next asked them to write a paragraph describing themselves as others saw them and how they felt about what they had read. T.J. did as he was directed. I wondered why.

The next day, T.J. approached me after class and asked if he could present his "personality collage" to the class. I was agreeable, even though the collage had been due more than a month before and had been presented by the other students on a day when T.J. was truant. Frankly, I was curious, and I told T.J. that we would be delighted to see his collage.

When T.J. came to class the next day, he had his collage with him and was prepared to explain it to the class. The other students had presented elaborate posters with pictures, words and mementos arranged artistically on various sizes and shapes of tag board. T.J.'s collage consisted of only one thing: three farming magazines connected to one another by a piece of baling rope. T.J. explained that farming was his family's business and the baling twine was what held his life together. At the bottom of the three magazines was taped the piece of paper T.J. had worn the day we had done the self-esteem activity. Written on it were "kind," "funny," "pretty hair," "a nice person" and "caring."

I silently hung the collage in the front of the room for all to see. As T.J. returned to his seat that day, he moved his chair up close to the last row of students. I fought back the tears and continued the lesson of the day. Sensing the privilege of experiencing T.J.'s presence, perhaps for the first time, the class remained silent. For T.J., it was the beginning of a connection.

T.J. graduated last June. Not only did he pass my class, but he also somehow passed 12th grade social studies, the bane of every graduating senior. During the graduation ceremony, there was only one time when I felt the joy of that small voice in my heart—when T.J. received his diploma. I remembered the gift he had given me and my fourth period class that semester, and I cried. As he passed me in the recessional that night, with his robes flying, his mortar board askew and his diploma held high in joyful celebration, he smiled, reached out, shook my hand ... and winked.

I knew then that I was a teacher. T.J. had taught me.

THE QUESTION

Bob Moore

Author, *You Can Be President (or Anything Else)*

Keep away from people who try to belittle your ambitions. Small people always do that, but the really great make you feel that you too can become great.

Mark Twain

Several years ago I was invited to hear an important speaker address the student body of a small college in South Carolina. On the appointed day I entered the auditorium and found it filled with students excited about the opportunity to hear a person of her status speak.

After the governor of the state gave the introduction, the speaker moved to the microphone, looked at the audience from left to right, and began with the following words: "I was born to a mother who was deaf and could not speak. I do not know who her father is or was. The first job I ever had was in a cotton field." With that statement a beautiful smile shone forth as she said, "And I stand before you today as the Treasurer of the United States of America. My name is Azie Taylor Morton."

The audience was spellbound. She continued, "Nothing has to remain the way it is if that's not the way a person wants it to be. It isn't luck, and it isn't circumstances and it isn't being born a certain way that causes a person's future to become what it becomes." She softly repeated, "Nothing has to remain the way it is if that's not the way a person wants it to be."

"All a person has to do," she said in a firm voice, "to change a situation that brings unhappiness or dissatisfaction is answer the question: 'How do I want this situation to become?' Then the person must commit totally to personal actions that carry them there."

"I am aware of this," you may be thinking. I understand. Yet, isn't it amazing, when work dissatisfaction or unhappiness appears, how few people ask themselves the question, "How do I want it to become and what personal actions will carry me there?"

What we need is more people who specialize in the impossible.

Theodore Roethke

LOOK WHERE YOU WANT TO GO

Jim Donovan
Author, *Handbook to a Happier Life*

We go where our vision is.
Joseph Murray

If you ask race car drivers how they are able to get through those tight places without hitting anything, what you will hear is, "Look where you want to go, not where you don't want to go." If you look at the wall, chances are, you will hit it. We can use this metaphor in our lives as well. Focus on what you want in your life rather than what you don't want. All too often people spend most of their time and energy thinking about what they want to get rid of—I want to lose ten pounds—or what they don't want—I wish I didn't have these bills. Try instead to focus on what you do want. I was talking about this with a friend recently and learned that the way sky divers are able to "link up" in midair is that they look into the eyes of the person they want to connect with. Their bodies then follow and *automatically move toward each other!*

I was thinking about this one day when our cat (Ming) came into my office. He likes to sit by the window ledge behind my desk and fantasize about catching a bird. I watched him as he began his ritual for getting to the window ledge. First, he sits looking intently at the top of my desk. It's like he is focusing on being there. He then jumps to the desktop, a distance 20 times his height, easily and effortlessly. I realized that this is the same principle in action. Advance confidently in the direction of your goals.

This practice works whether your goal is to get what you want in your life or simply to jump to the top of a desk. The other element that cannot be overlooked—it was appropriately pointed out to me—is faith. Ming has faith and trusts that he will not fall flat on his face, and so should we!

All who have accomplished great things have had a great aim, have fixed their gaze on a goal which was high, one which sometimes seemed impossible.

Orison Swett Marden

Fired

Mary A. Long

Excerpted from *Guideposts*

I was a 56-year-old widow who desperately needed to work. And this was my first full-time job in 30 years.

It came without warning, like a mugging on a dark street. The assistant supervisor had given no indication that anything was wrong—she'd simply asked me to meet her in the conference room. But when I walked into the large, stark room, furnished only with a long table surrounded by chairs, I saw that the head supervisor was there, too. Suddenly I felt apprehensive, as if I were the defendant in a courtroom. The two women sat sphinx like, not smiling, not greeting me.

"Wh-what's the matter?" I stammered.

"Mary, we're going to have to let you go," said the older woman. She looked straight at me, without blinking.

Involuntarily I took a step backward. She might as well have slapped me. "But I only transferred to your department five days ago," I managed to protest. In fact, I'd asked to be transferred, after seven months in a more diversified area where I felt I couldn't keep up.

Her reply was crisp and to the point.

"You just don't come up to company standards for learning the job. You're too slow and you make too many mistakes."

She paused briefly, but I was too stunned to say anything. Clumsily, I fished in my purse for a handkerchief that wasn't there.

"I'm sorry," the supervisor went on. "Your dismissal checks are waiting for you in Personnel."

So the decision had already been final at least a day earlier! There was no court of appeals. The meeting was over.

Moving like a sleepwalker, I picked up my checks, gathered a few personal belongings and went to the employee parking garage for the last time. In the privacy of my car, I exchanged my glasses for dark lenses that would hide my red, swollen eyes. Then I slumped forward on the steering wheel. Fired. Dear God, what's to become of me?

I was in debt and without savings. At 56, I was too young to collect on my late husband's Social Security—and apparently I was too old to make a success of working. And I'd been so proud to have found that job! It had been 30 years since I'd worked full time, and I had only a high school education.

Oh, God, it's so humiliating. Is this what I get for all my faith and prayers and effort?

Finally I composed myself enough to drive through the somber February afternoon to my apartment.

As soon as I unlocked the door, Duchie, my pet beagle, sprang forward with the wagging tail and happy wiggles that meant "I'm so glad you're home!" I scooped her up to absorb the comfort of her warm little body. She licked my cheek. Suddenly, intensely, I felt like a child again. I wanted to feel my mother's arms around me and hear her loving voice: "There, there, dear, you're going to be all right."

For a while I went about familiar tasks: giving Duchie her dinner, making a pot of coffee. Then I sank into my recliner with the dog in my lap. I wanted to relax, close my eyes and pretend the events of a few hours before had not happened. Instead, I relived the humiliating scene. I felt so ashamed and weak and helpless.

Who would hire a virtually unskilled 56-year-old woman who had just been fired? I couldn't afford to go on renting this apartment without a job. And living with any of my three married children was out of the question; they had all they could do to raise their own families.

Nevertheless I had to let my children know what had happened. But I dreaded it. They'd shared my pride in getting a job. I wanted them to think of me with joy and respect, not pity.

Reluctantly, I picked up the phone and dialed my daughter Donna, who lived a few miles away.

"How come you're home so early, Mom?" she asked at once.

"I just got fired," I said, trying to sound matter-of-fact.

"Are you joking?"

"No, it's true," I replied.

We were silent. I knew she, too, was fighting back tears. "Mom, they can't fire you."

"But they did." I gave her the details.

After another painful silence, she spoke, her tone angry and sardonic. "I just hope you can find something good in this, Mom!"

I flinched. I understood that the bitterness reflected her feelings about the situation, not about me. But I realized something else. Donna was challenging the "preaching" she'd heard from me so often in the past. When her father was alive and my circumstances were more secure, it had been easy for me to claim that God helps us find something worthwhile in every experience if we work at it and keep faith in Him. I'd had a kind of sunshine faith.

Now a stormy day had come.

I hesitated. And in that split second I saw something more frightening than having no job. I was letting my faith be undermined along with my self-esteem. And faith was all I had to help me.

My answer to Donna was a manifesto for myself (even if delivered in a wavering voice): "God is sure to lead me to something better if I just don't lose faith."

All that evening I reminded myself over and over: I lost my job, not my faith. I prayed long and hard, asking God to help me think clearly and honestly about my situation. And I slept.

The next morning I woke up with a surprising sense of purpose. I did have a job: to put my faith to work and show my family its power. Instead of wistfully yearning for a comforting mother, I would be the strong mother, determined that my actions and reactions in the time ahead would have a positive influence on my children and grandchildren.

During the weeks that followed, I worked not only at job-hunting, but also at keeping an upbeat attitude. I tried to recognize and avoid any thinking that in essence defrauded me. Instead, I concentrated on what God would have me think:

Fraud thought:	I don't deserve unemployment checks.
God thought:	You earned them, just like any other worker.
Fraud thought:	I'll never find a job.
God thought:	You will if you keep trying.
Fraud thought:	I can't handle the worry and doubt.
God thought:	With faith and prayer, you can.

It was a long, difficult struggle—a matter of months, not weeks. I filled out application forms and answered "help wanted" ads that didn't lead to interviews. I went to interviews that didn't lead to jobs. Bills piled up, and I had to borrow money from an understanding brother. I failed a civil-service test and had to take it again.

But with God thoughts I passed that test the second time around. With God thoughts I made a good impression during an interview at Ohio State University. With God thoughts I've worked there for three years—even though my boss had to put up with a lot of mistake-making and slow work while I was polishing my secretarial skills.

I've accepted the fact that I'm not goof-proof; I simply keep right on aiming for that bull's eye of perfection, and forgiving myself when I fail. Just as god forgives me if I try and fail.

I've learned the difference between humiliation and humility. Humiliation is telling yourself that being fired makes you a worthless person. Humility is knowing you lost your job simply because you needed time and training that the company couldn't expend.

As for pride, I know what that is, too. It's calling your daughter and saying, "Guess what, Donna, I found another job! An even better one!"

And hearing her say, "Oh, Mom, thank God!"

THE WOMEN OF AHMEDABAD

Gloria Steinem

Author, *Revolution from Within: A Book of Self-Esteem*

Let no one be discouraged by the belief there is nothing one man or woman can do against the enormous array of the world's ills—against misery and ignorance, injustice and violence ... few will have the greatness to bend history itself, but each of us can work to change a small portion of events, and in the total of all those acts will be written the history of this generation ... It is from numberless, diverse acts of courage and belief that human history is shaped.

Each time a person stands up for an ideal, or acts to improve the lot of others, or strikes out against injustice, he sends forth a tiny ripple of hope, and, crossing each other from a million different centers of energy and daring, these ripples build a current that can sweep down the mightiest walls of oppression and resistance.

Robert F. Kennedy

In modern India, the women who sell vegetables in the street, roll cigarettes or weave baskets for sale while they nurse their babies, carry construction materials on their heads in human chains at building sites and perform a thousand other individual, piece-work jobs are called "self-employed women." They are the bottom rung of the labor force, but their work is indispensable. In addition to making and distributing many small products, they also mend and resell cooking pots, collect paper from offices and garbage dumps and pound used nails straight enough to be used again: a human recycling system in a country where everything is used many times.

Not only are they the poorest of India's workers, they are also subject to the special punishments of living in a female body. Girl children are considered so much less valuable than boys that two thirds of the children who die before age 4 are girls—the result of infanticide, plus saving scarce food and medical care for boys. Girls are so much less likely to be sent to school that the national female literacy rate is less than half that for males (among these workers, often much less), and their humanity is so minimally acknowledged that killing a wife in order to take another wife—and get another dowry—is one of the major sufferings addressed by the women's movement.

In a world that so devalues them, they have little reason to value themselves—which is why there is so much to learn from their successes.

For years, journalists and government officials in industrial cities like Ahmedabad have been condemning the fact that women do such hard physical labor—but nothing changed. Then in 1971, a young Gandhian labor organizer named Ela Bhatt did something new: she asked the women themselves what they wanted.

As it turned out, they had long been amused and angered by experts with soft hands who said women shouldn't do such work. It helped feed their families and gave them a small measure of independence, and they were not about to give it up. What they wanted were better conditions in which to do it: safe places to leave their children; higher wages for their handmade or recycled products and construction jobs; an end to the bribes they had to pay the police for the privilege of selling their wares in the street; and relief from moneylenders who charged murderous interest rates for the few rupees they borrowed to buy vegetables or raw materials each morning and then paid back at the end of each day. Finally, they wanted a secure place to keep their few rupees from husbands who otherwise considered women's earnings their own.

But even as they wished for these things, they also said nothing could be done. They had no faith in each other, no trust in Ela Bhatt, no reason to believe in change. Who would listen to poor and illiterate women?

By the time I first met Ela and some of these women in Ahmedabad in 1978, their Self-Employed Women's Association, whose acronym SEWA also means "service," was about 6 years old. They had exposed the corruption of police who demanded bribes, started child care centers and infant crèches and even persuaded the Bank of India to let them open a special branch for their small loans and hard-won savings. They themselves pounded the streets for members, put two improvised teller windows in a small room and literally created a bank. (The problem of illiteracy had been overcome by putting a photograph of each woman on her passbook. "Maybe we can't read," as one of them explained with a smile, "but we can think.") To the surprise even of Ela Bhatt's sponsors, a Gandhian textile workers' union that had considered these women too passive and disparately employed to organize, they were doing better than many more educated workers in traditional unions.

What made the difference? First, an organizer who had lived the problems of being a woman herself, and who listened to each woman as a sister. For the first time, they felt worth listening to. Second, their mutual support and their small but growing list of successes when dealing with corrupt police and dishonest employers. As a lawyer and a skilled organizer, Ela knew the importance of both listening and explaining new alternatives in using demonstrations, the media and even the courts.

But Ela Bhatt herself thought there had been one crucial turning point.

After the work of forming SEWA, Ela suggested the founding group celebrate by taking a holiday together. The women had never done anything separate from their families and children before, but other workers took holidays. Why shouldn't they?

After a discussion, they decided to visit Hindu holy places that were nearby, but farther from home than most of these women had ever been. After much planning and preparation to free them from family obligations, which were not easy to do even for a few hours, Ela hired a rickety bus and they set off.

Everything was fine until they neared a temple that could be reached only by boat. Menstruating women were not allowed in temples, and inevitably, some of the women had their periods. They were sure that if they crossed the river, the boat would capsize to punish them for defying tradition, and since they couldn't swim, everyone would drown.

By appealing to every emotion from curiosity to defiance, Ela finally convinced them to get in the boat and consign themselves to the wide river and fate.

They crossed—and nothing happened. After placing their offerings of fruit and flowers in the temple, they crossed back again—and still nothing happened. For the first time in their lives, they had defied the rules that denigrated them—and they had won.

Somehow, everything was connected to that first defiance and victory. If women's bodies were not so "unclean" and inferior after all, perhaps their work was not so inferior either.

Now, a dozen years later, SEWA is the most powerful women's trade union in India, and one of the largest in the world, with independent grass roots organizations in nine other regions. It offers revolving loan funds to help women farm, set up small businesses and carve out a small security in a system that offers little hope to those at the bottom. As for Ela Bhatt, she is consulted by the World Bank on grass roots economic development and served for a while in the Indian Parliament. But at heart, she is an organizer and still spends most of her time helping to develop strength and leadership among poor women.

SEWA itself has become a model of self-help and economic empowerment for women throughout the Third World. And even in our own industrialized nation, SEWA is often mentioned as an example to follow wherever poor or otherwise powerless women gather to organize.

But these least valued of women should inspire anyone, anywhere, female or male, who is devalued so deeply that inferiority seems to be inherent in the reality of her or his own body—whether for reasons of race or appearance, disability or age or anything else.

If feelings of unworthiness are rooted in our bodies, self-esteem needs to start there.

The Kingdom of Heaven

Thich Nhat Hahn

Author, *Touching Peace*

We do not have to die to enter the Kingdom of Heaven. In fact we have to be fully alive. When we breathe in and out and hug a beautiful tree, we are in Heaven. When we take one conscious breath, aware of our eyes, our heart, our liver and our non-toothache, we are transported to Paradise right away. Peace is available. We only have to touch it. When we are truly alive, we can see that the tree is part of Heaven, and we are also part of Heaven. The whole universe is conspiring to reveal this to us, but we are so out of touch that we invest our resources in cutting down the trees. If we want to enter Heaven on Earth, we need only one conscious step and one conscious breath. When we touch peace, everything becomes real. We become ourselves, fully alive in the present moment, and the tree, our child and everything else reveal themselves to us in their full splendor. The miracle is not to walk on thin air or water, but to walk on Earth.

I don't know ... somehow I thought it would be different.

2 The Basic Principles of Managing for High Self-Esteem

Coaching is a profession of love. You can't coach people unless you love them.

Eddie Robinson
Head Football Coach, Grambling University
(one of only four football coaches
to win over 300 games)

You can buy people's time; you can buy their physical presence at a given place; you can even buy a measured number of their muscular motions per hour. But you cannot buy enthusiasm ... you cannot buy loyalty ... you cannot buy the devotion of their hearts. You must earn these.

Clarence Francis

Early management techniques.

Positive Self-Esteem at Work: The Eight Behavioral Keys

Kathy L. Indermill

Principle Consultant, By Design

How do you humiliate and demean someone and then expect him or her to care about product quality?

Tom Peters

As much as Theory X managers resist the notion, as gleefully as Garry Trudeau lampooned the California Task Force on Self-Esteem, as contented as major stockholders are with management for profit tactics, the secret is out. People like working for companies that take an interest in their personal and professional development—that support them in feeling good about themselves. People don't like working for companies in which they feel unvalued and manipulated by a "we vs. them" management style. When the labor shortage of 2000 arrives to put the big squeeze on competition for competent employees, then perhaps we will remember the prophetic words of Rosabeth Moss Kanter, former Editor of the *Harvard Business Review*: "The companies that are the best at creating a good quality of work life will be able to attract and retain the most skilled workers." Hello, corporate America, it's the 1990s. Is anybody listening?

For those companies who are listening, the message is clear. It's time to weed out working conditions that contribute to feelings of alienation, frustration and discontent. It's time to implement training programs that teach executives, managers and employees alike how to create work environments that enhance self-esteem. The business community is in a position to take a socially responsible role in addressing societal ills related to low self-esteem, such as alcoholism and chemical dependency. After all, the majority of us spend a minimum of eight hours a day, five days a week for most of our lives attempting to fulfill our achievement and affiliation needs. That's an eternity to spend in a place where the work culture and climate breeds fear, anger, cynicism and resentment, instead of positive self-esteem.

One of the reasons self-esteem has gotten such a bad rap in the workplace is that no one seems to know for certain what it is, where it comes from or how to get more of it. Since there is no generally accepted definition of self-esteem yet, for purposes of this article, self-esteem is defined as: The attitude one has toward oneself based on the sum of:

- Self-respect (an assessment of personal worth)
- Self-confidence (an assessment of personal competency)
- Self-responsibility (an acceptance of accountability for one's actions and acting responsibly toward others)

According to Nathaniel Branden, practicing psychologist, psychotherapist and pioneer in the field of self-esteem, a person with high self-esteem is better equipped to deal with life's problems, is resilient, is more likely to be creative and ambitious, is more likely to form supportive relationships, is more inclined to be respectful of others and experiences more joy in living. Given the obvious benefits of self-esteem, is there anyone among us in the work force who wouldn't want more rather than less of this elusive elixir? The question is, "How do we go about manufacturing the stuff for ourselves and developing it in others?"

For starters, we can look to people in the trenches whose pioneering efforts may lead the rest of us to follow suit. Kay McCleery is one such activist promoting self-esteem in the workplace. As Training Director, Franchise Opening Manager and Franchise Service Consultant for Hobee's Franchising Corporation, and founder of her own consulting firm, Hospitality Systems International, West, McCleery is well-positioned to practice what she preaches. As she says, "Whether corporate America wants to deal with it or not, the majority of personal and interpersonal problems in the workplace are linked to low self-esteem. We have a big problem on our hands, and we are it."

Eight Keys to Enhancing Self-Esteem in the Workplace

Although we can't raise anyone's self-esteem but our own, we can take action in the workplace that nurtures and supports the growing of others' self-esteem. The following eight behavioral keys are useful in enhancing self-esteem. McCleery has found that the restaurant managers who use these keys consciously and consistently have the happiest staff—which puts money in the bank instead of into training employees who become turnover statistics.

When these eight behavioral keys become second nature or a knee jerk "reaction" instead of merely good ideas, then our workplaces will be true breeding grounds for positive self-esteem. But, let's not get ahead of ourselves. Each individual key represents a set of specific behaviors that must be learned, practiced and used conscientiously for best results.

1. Respect Others. Aretha Franklin was right; everyone wants a little R-E-S-P-E-C-T. Each of us has an inner need to be seen and understood by others. Managers can demonstrate respect by being courteous, listening attentively and empathetically and maintaining eye contact, as well as by avoiding giving advice, lecturing and using a condescending or sarcastic tone.

The problem is, in far too many cases, we haven't been the recipient of our fair share of respect in life, so we aren't overly skilled at giving it to others. Worse yet, those of us with Type A behavior patterns and low self-esteem tend to become controlling, impatient and downright verbally offensive in stressful situations, thus amputating whatever communication skills we have cultivated. Regardless of the circumstances, the truth is, no manager will elicit exceptional performance from employees by treating them with hostility, contempt or lack of respect.

A restaurant is a perfect testing ground for practicing self-esteem enhancing behavior because a restaurant is one of the most performance-oriented, stressful business environments there is. McCleery emphasizes, "In a typical Hobee's Restaurant there are an average of 375 customers a day whose needs must be satisfied or they may walk out the door and never come back."

One of the "star" managers in the self-esteem enhancing work arena is Kathy Gunn, Manager of Hobee's Restaurant in Cupertino, California. Kathy is one of those consciously competent managers who is in the trenches on a daily basis, creating a work environment that regularly produces positive examples of each of the eight keys introduced in this article. Kathy's management style is built on a foundation of respect for her employees. "When someone has an issue, I immediately arrange a one-on-one meeting. We usually go to a private spot outside, as opposed to the office, which feels more open. I begin by saying, 'Tell me what's on your mind,' then I listen closely and don't interrupt until the person is finished."

The greatest motivational act one person can do for another is to listen.

Roy E. Moody
President, Roy Moody and Associates

2. Enable and Empower. To enable is to give people the knowledge and skills they need to be successful on the job; to empower is to support people in taking self-responsibility. Without training, people can't achieve and without self-responsibility, people tend to become doers instead of thinkers. Enabled people feel good about themselves because they have the opportunity to excel. Empowered people feel good about themselves because they accept responsibility for their lives, accept their power (their gifts, talents and resources) and demonstrate that they can impact their lives in important ways.

Kathy Gunn enables her staff by giving them excellent, performance-based training for each position. Every month she and her staff receive evaluative feedback on how well they've met established performance standards. "There is a 'Be the Best' contest between all the Hobee's Restaurants and each store is rated every month on how well it's doing." It's no surprise that Kathy's store has won first place honors.

She also empowers her people by encouraging them to take initiative, ask for what they want and solve their own problems. For example, her restaurant is in the process of switching from Styrofoam to paper cups, and she explained to her staff that it was too expensive to have paper cups for personal use. Their solution was to bring cups from home, and they asked her for a safe place to put them. Kathy agreed that the solution was viable, but told them that they would be responsible for creating a place in the restaurant where the cups would be safe. Another example was the day a server came to her with an interpersonal "I can't work with 'so and so' problem." Kathy helped the server get to the root of the problem, then offered solution alternatives (e.g., that she would be a mediator if asked). The employee chose what to do about the problem, they both agreed on a plan and then Kathy gave the plan a time frame. She took follow-up action by observing behavior and talking to both parties about how their meeting went.

Man's self-concept is enhanced when he takes responsibility for himself.
Will Schutz

3. Act Congruently and Consistently. Behavior is congruent when what we are feeling on the inside matches what we are doing and saying on the outside. Behavior is consistent when it is in character and in alignment with personal and organizational values.

As Branden has said, "The lies most devastating to our self-esteem are not so much the lies we tell as the lies we live." And many of us have become quite good at covering up our real feelings. Unfortunately, "quite good" is not good enough. In *The Cynical Americans*, Kanter and Mirvis indicate that confidence in business and business leadership has fallen from approximately a 70% level in the late 1960s to about 15% today. According to their recent study, "... 43% of the American working population fit the profile of the cynic, who, to put it simply believes that lying, putting on a false face, and doing whatever it takes to make a buck are all part of our basic human nature." So, why aren't people more authentic and real? Because it takes a lot of courage to be honest.

Employees are at best confused and at worst cynical and distrusting of incongruent, inconsistent management behavior. Managers can create trust with employees by being real and telling the truth. How can we expect employees to be honest and open with us when we never directly communicate to them what we're really feeling and thinking?

Kathy Gunn tries to help each employee to feel more open and comfortable with her by being real. One day, she was at work when she found out her cat had been diagnosed with feline leukemia. Her staff was in a collective good mood, so there was the usual joking around, but Kathy was uncharacteristically quiet. At some point during the bantering, she said, "Hey, you guys, if I seem in a quiet mood today it's because I just found out my cat has leukemia." The staff rallied and somehow she made it through the day. As Kathy says, "I don't like to leave any gray areas."

Modeling may not only be the best way to teach; it may be the only way to teach.

Albert Schweitzer

4. Create Safety. A "safe" work environment is one in which people feel they can give input openly without fear of ridicule or reprimand. They feel safe to say, "I made a mistake." In his book, *Talking Straight*, Lee Iacocca advises, "Only the boss can set a tone that lets people feel comfortable enough to say those magic words, 'I don't know' followed by, 'but I'll find out.'" When people feel safe, they are naturally inquisitive and creative. When people don't feel safe, they may become defensive, over-controlling, fearful, timid or resentful—none of which produces peak performance. In general, our society is not a particularly "safe" place to live, but managers can learn how to create safer work environments that promote initiative, creative problem solving, open communication and greater teamwork.

Kathy Gunn builds "safety" into the fabric of her work culture one interaction at a time. She frequently asks for employee input, and consequently her staff feels valued. She's also tolerant of mistakes. "I give my staff lots of self-responsibility and control over their own destiny, so I make a concerted effort not to be critical about the decisions they make that turn out to be mistakes."

Feelings of worth can flourish only in an atmosphere where individual differences are appreciated, mistakes are tolerated, communication is open, and rules are flexible—the kind of atmosphere that is found in a nurturing family.

Virginia Satir

5. Teach Personal Limits. Most of us were never taught how to set our personal limits with other people—we were never taught how to tell someone respectfully that his or her behavior feels abusive and is therefore unacceptable to us. Abuse of any form (e.g., verbal and nonverbal), as well as exploitation in the name of being "open, honest or assertive," should be considered unacceptable behavior. Everyone, no matter what the position or title, has the right to set personal limits. As managers, we have the opportunity to teach by example. By taking care of ourselves, our own needs and time requirements, we serve as role models for others. Sometimes it is necessary to say to a verbally disrespectful employee, "Your behavior is completely unacceptable to me and continuing it will demonstrate your choice to accept the consequences." Our challenge as managers is to set personal limits using a neutral tone, without resorting to character assassinations, dictatorial commands or indirect nonverbal behavior that is intended as punishment.

> *No one can make you feel inferior without your consent.*
>
> Eleanor Roosevelt

Kathy Gunn has also had to set her share of personal limits, but perhaps the most pointed example would be the time her boss/owner called her during a rush hour and began giving her feedback about a decision she had made. She clearly and concisely set her limits by saying (in a neutral tone), "I'm here to be with customers. If you have things you need to talk to me about, call me back after we've closed and I'll be glad to discuss them with you."

6. Investigate Performance Discrepancies. We managers cannot understand an employee's actions until we understand why the actions made a kind of sense to that person. As Branden suggests, all actions, inappropriate or not, are always related to an attempt to satisfy needs, to our efforts to survive, to protect ourselves, to maintain equilibrium, to avoid fear and pain, to nurture ourselves or to grow. When an employee is behaving unacceptably, first make an effort to understand what is causing the performance discrepancy—the difference between actual and expected performance. Help yourself and your employee to discover how he or she views the situation before determining what actions can be taken to correct the problem.

One day Kathy Gunn realized the phone near the cash register was ringing too long before someone picked it up. She observed that a newer employee in the Host position had walked by without answering the phone, so she made a mental note. Later that morning, she took the person aside and inquired, "Have we made you feel that you weren't supposed to answer the phone?" The employee said, "No, I just wasn't paying attention, and I will from now on." Kathy followed with, "Good, it's important to cue into the phone because every call is a prospective customer."

Good treatment of workers results in similar treatment of customers.

Todd Englander
Incentive

7. Observe Behavior, Then Provide Constructive Feedback. One of the best training methods is immediate, constructive feedback about performance. However, giving constructive feedback is a learned skill. We all know how we like to be given feedback, but somehow we forget about that when giving it to others. Whenever possible, managers should be specific about an employee's performance strengths, then provide specific performance improvement feedback. They should avoid labeling employees, assessing their character or giving extravagant compliments. People feel resentful when judged and feel less worthy when they know the praise is unrealistic.

Catch people in the act of doing something right.

Ken Blanchard

With her employees, Kathy Gunn prefers to give performance feedback as she's working side by side. Then, she says, "I have an opportunity to notice the positive things they do in the moment. If I notice a performance problem that requires training or coaching or if it's something that cannot be corrected in the moment, I arrange to get together at the end of the shift. People say I have eyes in the back of my head when someone forgets to garnish an omelet with chopped parsley, but I just laugh and tell them I notice when it's there too!"

8. Nurture Potential and Recognize Desired Performance. This is McCleery's favorite topic. "See the gold!" she encourages. "Develop champions and refuse to see someone as incapable of 'star' performance." People with low self-esteem are often as frightened of their virtues as they are of their shortcomings. Shortcomings can create feelings of inadequacy, whereas virtues can create fears of having to take self-responsibility or of social alienation. The more people resist their own potential, the more a manager's patience can be tested. But, as Dr. Robert Ball, former Executive Director of the California Task Force on Self-Esteem and author of *Walking on Water,* implores, "Be kind. Everyone you meet is fighting a hard battle."

Kathy Gunn tells the story of one young busser who lacked self-confidence, asked an endless number of questions and required more feed-

SOURCE: Reprinted by permission of John Grimes. © John Grimes.

back than most of her staff. After two long years, Kathy's patience and his persistence finally paid off because he is now one of her "star" servers. She also proudly recalls the day the mother of two young employees came in just to let Kathy know how much her sons had grown and matured while working at Hobee's.

> *If you treat an individual ... as if he were what he ought to be and could be, he will become what he ought to be and could be.*
>
> Johann Wolfgang Von Goethe

> *The trouble with the rat race is that even if you win, you're still a rat.*
>
> Lily Tomlin

A Call to Action

If Kay McCleery's and Kathy Gunn's experience with the eight behavioral keys has challenged you, then perhaps you will take it upon yourself to heed the call to action. The notion of enhancing self-esteem in the workplace is not an impossible dream, but to make it a reality, individuals and chief executive officers of every corporation must commit to learning new skills and creating workplaces that breed positive self-esteem. Hello, corporate America, is anybody listening?

Self-Esteem and the Managing of Others

Ken Blanchard
Management Consultant
Coauthor, *The One Minute Manager*

People who feel good about themselves produce good results.

The One Minute Manager

People who produce good results feel good about themselves.

The Power of Ethical Management

I first became interested in the whole area of self-esteem when my wife Margie worked with Mark Tager, an MD and health expert, on a book entitled *Working Well*. They wanted to find out what made a healthy work environment. One of the questions they asked people around the country was: Can a bad boss make you sick? And, of course, everyone said, "You better believe it!" Then they started mentioning migraine headaches, ulcers, sleepless nights, heart attacks and even cancer.

When I thought about it, I realized how right they were. After all, bosses are really important to people's lives. For example, you can talk to people at one point and they will tell you how excited they are about their work and their job. And then you see them three months later and they are miserable. In nine out of ten cases, the only significant change in their work environment is that they have a new boss. In most instances, their old boss, who had been supportive and made them feel good about themselves, had been replaced either by a person who jerked them around and made them feel unimportant or by a "do-nothing boss" who was never around and avoided conflict at all costs.

What fascinated me was to find out what made people like that. That curiosity led me to study the field of self-esteem and eventually do an audio tape program with Jennifer James, a cultural anthropologist and wonderful speaker, entitled *Inner Management: The Power of Self-Esteem*. I found out two things. First, self-esteem is a choice. Second, lack of self-esteem is an ego problem.

Self-Esteem Is a Choice

According to Jennifer James, we develop our sense of self-esteem from four places. The first source is *fate*. We have no choice about who we are born to, where we are born or what race or sex we are, but these factors have been shown to have an effect on our self-esteem.

The second source is *family* or other significant adults in our early life: how we were raised or treated at school; whether both parents, a single parent or no parents lived with us; how we were treated and how the family operated together. Did we have any influential teachers in our early educational experience? In other words, the most significant people in the early part of our lives help to shape what we think of ourselves then and now.

The third source of self-esteem consists of *life experiences*. The successes and failures that you have in life all add up to influence how you feel about yourself today.

The fourth source is your *perception* of the first three sources. As you can imagine, this is the most important source of self-esteem. Why? If you interpret the first three sources of self-esteem in a positive way, chances are you will have a positive self-image of yourself today. For example, if you feel lucky to have been born into your family, if you believe they loved and encouraged you and if you tend to focus on the positive experiences in your life, you are likely to have a positive self-image. If, on the other hand, you didn't like your family circumstances, were constantly put down when you were growing up and tend to focus more on your negative life experiences, you will likely have a low self-esteem today.

Lack of Self-Esteem Is an Ego Problem

Where does ego fit in here? If self-esteem is a choice, then you need inner strength to deal with the ups and downs of life. Most people would interpret that to mean you need a strong ego. That's exactly what you don't need.

In our book, *The Power of Ethical Management*, Norman Vincent Peale and I said: "People with humility don't think less of themselves, they just think of themselves less." What we were suggesting in that quote is that it's healthy to feel good about yourself—but don't get carried away. The problem is with the ego.

Someone once told me that ego stands for "edging God out." When we start to get a distorted image of our own importance and see ourselves as the center of the universe, we lose touch with who we really are as children of God. Our thinking blurs, and we lose the sense of our connection with home base, others and our true selves.

It's interesting to see how self-doubt and false pride play out in managers. When they are addicted to either ego affliction, it erodes their effectiveness. Managers dominated with self-doubt are the "do-nothing bosses." They are described as "never around, always avoiding conflict and not very helpful." They often leave people alone even when they are insecure and don't know what they are doing. They don't seem to believe in themselves or trust in their own judgment. They value others' thoughts more than their own—especially the thoughts of those to whom they report. As a result, they rarely speak out and support their own people. Under pressure they seem to defer to whoever has the most power.

At the other end of the spectrum are the "controllers." These are managers dominated by false pride. Even when they don't know what they are doing, they have a high need for power and control. Even when it's clear to everyone that they are wrong, they keep on insisting they are right. These folks aren't much for supporting their people either. If everyone is upbeat and confident, the controller throws out the wet blanket. They support their bosses over their people because they want to climb the hierarchy and be part of the boss's crowd.

If any of this sounds a bit too close for comfort, don't be alarmed. Most of us have traces of both self-doubt and false pride, because the issue is really ego. We are stuck, all alone, focusing only on ourselves. The good news is, if we can accept God's unconditional love, we set the stage for a time when results or approval from others are no longer the most important thing in life.

In recent years I ask people in my management seminars, "How many of you have children?" Many hands go up. Then I ask, "How many of you love your children?" They laugh as the same hands go up. Then I raise the key question: "For how many of you does your love of your children depend on their achievements? If they are successful, you will love them. If they aren't, you won't." Not one hand ever goes up. "So love of your children does not depend on what they achieve or how much power or influence they gain," I continue. "And yet, why won't you and I accept that kind of unconditional love from our Father?"

If we can begin to accept the unconditional love that is available to us, our focus no longer has to be out there with results, accumulation, power, acceptance, control or other earthly things. Now we can focus on our journey—how we live our life and how we help others. Now our self-esteem is assured. We cannot achieve enough, control enough or accumulate enough to get any more love. We have all the love we'll ever need. This was the theme of my book *We Are the Beloved*.

So the choice is up to you. Accept your own okayness and you can hear feedback, accept criticism and praise without second-guessing the intentions. At the same time, you are not afraid to support or praise others because you realize it doesn't take anything away from you. You can redirect or reprimand someone who is off base without putting that person down. After all, the people working with you are the children of God too. As Spencer Johnson and I said in *The One Minute Manager,* "people are okay, it's just their behavior that is a problem sometimes." In dealing with poor behavior, remember you want to get rid of the behavior and not the person. That's why we insisted that a reprimand—negative feedback—always end with an affirmation like, "The reason I am upset with you is that you're good—you're better than that." If you can't reaffirm a person, then a reprimand is not appropriate. It's not an attitude problem, it's an ability problem. Now redirection and coaching from you are needed.

The big picture from my viewing place is that the greatest problem in organizations today is the human ego. If we are to empower people and make our organizations customer-driven, cost-effective, fast, flexible and continuously improving, the people who are running organizations in the traditional sense—those who are at the top of the hierarchy—have to get out of their own way. The only effective way I know of doing that, besides a near death experience, is a spiritual awakening and realization that God did not make junk. Our okayness and self-esteem are givens. As a result, my own personal mission statement is, "To be a loving teacher and example of simple truths that help myself and others to awaken the presence of God in our lives." God loves you and so do I. Effective managers accept that love and spread it out to others. Go for it!

SOURCE: ETTA HULME reprinted by permission of Newspaper Enterprise Association, Inc.

The Basic Principles of Managing for High Self-Esteem   **65**

The Worth Ethic

Kate Ludeman, PhD

Author, *The Worth Ethic, Earn What You're Worth*
Coauthor, *The Corporate Mystic*

Love is the most powerful force in the world, and that includes the world of work. Nevertheless, nobody talks much about love at work. It's as taboo as sex was 20 years ago. We act as if somehow we would doom our business to failure if we once admitted that we love our work team for its skilled performances, love our products for their genuine usefulness or love our managers for the productivity they inspire.

We expect work to reward us with a meaningful life that engages our emotions as well as our minds and bodies. Naturally, we want to care and be cared about at work. We want to believe we are worth as much to the company as our bosses are. We want to perform meaningful work, and we expect a similar commitment from our co-workers and bosses.

This is especially true because we spend the majority of our lives at work. Our work week, which shrunk to just over 40 hours per week in 1973, is back up to around 46 hours per week today. We have ten fewer hours of leisure time each week than we had 15 years ago. Work consumes two thirds of our day and dominates our lifestyle.

All these factors contribute to our growing need for the Worth Ethic. The Worth Ethic is a belief in your indelible self-worth and the fundamental and potential worth of others, and it is especially for those of us who will work in the last decades of the 20th century and beyond. People who live by the Worth Ethic don't follow directions without thought or interest. They take responsibility at work and put forth their best efforts. Worth Ethic managers commit themselves to help employees develop, to use their skills and talents and to reap the just rewards of their efforts. The result is a multitude of personal contributions that create worthy products and services.

Fortunately for us, the Worth Ethic benefits employers as much as it benefits us. When people find their worth affirmed at work, productivity skyrockets. Why is that? One reason, according to the senior vice-president of Federal Express, James A. Perkins, is that employees treat customers the way they themselves are treated by management. "When you take care of people," Perkins says, "they will deliver service in a courteous and efficient manner. When that happens, profits will be forthcoming." In just 15 years, Federal Express has grown to a $4 billion company and is listed as one of the top companies in *The 100 Best Companies to Work for in America*.

Then there is the Worth Ethic example of Florida Power & Light, which organized 10,000 employees into teams to focus on employee involvement and innovation. One Florida Power & Light team saved the company $26.6 million in one year. At Frito-Lay's plant near Bakersfield, California, teams working in open systems with lots of communication and little supervision brought the plant up to full production in one week (typically, "ramp-up" takes 6 to 13 weeks). At Goodyear Tire & Rubber Company's Lawton, California, plant, people involvement is the secret to "producing 50,000 tires a day where at a comparable sized plant they do 25,000," says Goodyear executive vice-president Stanley J. Mihclick.

Bosses can share power, rewards and praise to create the "WE" of the Worth Ethic, but today most don't. Companies approve of open communications and honest disagreements between employee and boss, but that's as close as they come to encouraging a free exchange of feelings in the office, shop, company halls or parking lot.

A few forward-looking managers use this new approach to leading people. They recognize that everyone in the company wants to be capable and powerful. They empower their employees to make significant personal contributions at work by training every person to maximum potential, offering challenges at each level of responsibility and managing employees with flexible organization and caring systems. Greg Steltenpohl and Gerry Percy, cofounders of the Odwalla Juice Company in Davenport, California, expanded their company from 4 to 75 people, from squeezing fresh juice by hand for a few local restaurants to selling millions of bottles a year, using the firm's philosophy, "Juice for Humans." Steltenpohl says that means "trying to run Odwalla as a human-oriented business, both for the customers and for our employees."

At Morrison & Foerster, a nationwide law firm, young associate lawyers use report cards to rate the senior partners on their strengths and weaknesses. According to James Finberg, coordinator of the program to evaluate the thirty lawyers at the firm's San Francisco office litigation department, the program "gives us the sense that the partners respect us and consider our comments about how the firm should be run to be important." That's important, says Peter Keane, president of the Bar Association of San Francisco, because, "if a firm doesn't want to be raided, it's going to have to be more responsive to associates' ideas and desires."

How do you, as one person, move your boss toward caring about you? After all, the idea of caring about employees hits at the quick of what managers have been taught not to do—get involved with employees and empathize with their feelings. Most don't listen to our complaints or dreams unless they are forced to. And if your boss is more adversary than collaborator, inclined toward workaholism rather than a balanced lifestyle, you can't expect such a person to superimpose new caring behaviors on top of his or her old attitudes.

People change behavior in a lasting way only if they are willing to change their attitudes first. That's where you come in. Eleanor Roosevelt wisely observed, "No one can make you feel inferior without your consent." To change the way you are treated by your boss and co-workers, change your own attitudes first. Begin with a shift in your attitude toward telling the truth, sharing visibility, speaking up when you have a good idea or getting clear on your life priorities.

Can you, as one individual, put the Worth Ethic to work? Yes! The Worth Ethic shows up in your personal integrity and how you use your personal power. It shows up in your willingness to find deep meaning in your work, to use your intuition, to develop your talents and to approve of yourself. It shows up in your success at balancing your life so that you reward yourself for work well done and at managing stress and time so that they work for you.

The Worth Ethic is conceived in self-esteem and nurtured by your own accomplishments and self-satisfaction. Once you have it inside, you will be surprised at the frequency with which your boss will compliment your work and give you more opportunities to shine. The reasons for this are twofold: (1) with greater feelings of self-worth come increased abilities to hear and accept the good things people say to you, and (2) as you accomplish more and show your self-satisfaction, people will begin to ask you about the change they see. "What's happened to you?" they'll ask. Then you can tell them, "The Worth Ethic!"

Six Ways You Can Personally Develop a Worth Ethic

1. Move to Meticulous Standards of Integrity and Trust. Somewhere a lot of people got the idea that if they told the truth they wouldn't get what they wanted. Once I took on a boss, confronting him with my version of the truth about how we should develop our products. He didn't agree and neither did my co-workers. But I kept hammering away until eventually he heard me out and tried one of my ideas. It worked, and the next time I offered an idea, I was listened to right off.

Too often, we operate out of expediency when we should be more concerned about building trust. Over the long run, expedient actions create distrust and suspicion. Joint problem solving efforts are nearly impossible without mutual trust. That's why, when managers decide whether to promote a person from individual contributor to first-level manager, they place heavy emphasis on the person's ability to build trust and get people to work well together. Earn the respect of others by holding yourself accountable for what you say and do.

2. Find Meaning and Purpose on the Job. Meaning comes from making a solid connection between your core values and your job tasks. To find where your own deepest values connect to your job, think of the times when you most loved your work. Think about whether your company's products and services relate to your values. For example, do they make the world healthier, happier or safer? Consider how your personal values and your job connect to the company's short and long term goals.

In my first corporate management position, I was asked to present a program explaining how performance evaluations were done at our company, how jobs were coded and graded and how the salary system was administered. Boring, I thought. But three days later, after I thought about it some more, I realized the program told employees how their salaries related to levels of responsibility and education, how managers evaluated their performance and how their salary increases were financed and justified. Properly presented, the program would give employees a new understanding of money and what they needed to do to earn more of it on the job. Suddenly I had considerable enthusiasm for my new assignment. And eventually the program became very popular because it did, in fact, help people gain control over an area that is tough for many of us: money.

3. Empower Others by Sharing Your Own Power. Create a productive partnership on any project you lead by encouraging others to make identifiable contributions. Then make identifiable contributions. Then make sure you share the credit for your group's accomplishments. When you focus on people, you increase their opportunities to participate, build their commitment and encourage their creativity.

Most of us see at least one of our peers as a competitor for the next promotion we want. But sharing power sets us up for success faster than hoarding visibility can ever do. Research shows that organizational competence comes from participation, commitment and creativity. After the Ford Motor Company's design staff was trained in positive behavioral techniques and learned to involve employees in daily problem solving and decision making, its score in these areas improved about 70%. If you are viewed as extremely competitive, the top management is more likely to bring in an outside manager than promote you when an opening occurs. Why? Because the next strongest person is likely to quit rather than be managed by you. People who can't build strong relationships don't get promoted.

4. Recognize the "Winner" in Everyone—Including Yourself. Praise people in as many ways as you can. Smile, look and speak directly at the person, use the person's name. Then say exactly what the person did to earn your respect. Does your next quarter's bonus depend on how faithfully the phones are answered and how quickly and clearly the messages get relayed to you? Words such as "You're terrific because you found out what the customer wanted, figured out where I was, got in touch with me and, in the long run, contributed to reaching our sales target this quarter," make an assistant feel great—and give him or her specific ways to repeat the performance and earn more praise.

Listen. Giving people—your boss, your co-workers, your assistants—the gift of your full attention is a very strong way to show you value their ideas. Heed the words of J. W. Marriott, Jr., chairman and president of Marriott Corporation: "If we treat our employees correctly they'll treat the customers right. And if customers are treated right, they'll come back." Listening is high praise and good for your career.

Most importantly, praise yourself. Sure, you fail sometimes. R. H. Macy failed seven times before his New York store took off. Babe Ruth struck out 1330 times in pursuit of his 714 home runs. Praise yourself and others for good attempts. It's true that we tend to treat others very much as we treat ourselves. If you don't pat yourself on the back, you'll find it almost impossible to praise others.

5. Get Comfortable with Your Creativity. Daniel Yankelovich, editor of *Psychology Today*, says "Younger and better-educated jobholders … have made the momentous discovery that work, rather than leisure, can give them what they are looking for—an outlet for self-expression as well as material rewards."

Support yourself with positive "self-talks" about the worth of your ideas even when others do not. No doubt you've heard the response of the Yale University professor who first read Fred Smith's management paper on providing overnight delivery services (Smith later founded Federal Express): "The concept is interesting and well-formed, but in order to earn better than a C, the idea must be feasible." And Spencer Silver, whose work led to the adhesive used for 3-M's Post-Its, admitted that "if I had thought about it, I wouldn't have done the experiment. The literature is full of examples that said you can't do this."

To develop confidence in your creativity and intuition, make a list of the times they have worked well for you already. The more you see how they have helped in the past, the more it will occur to you to trust them in the future. Encourage others to share their creative ideas too. Don't get so attached to your own ideas that you can't see the value of integrating the ideas of others. Admit your own mistakes and tolerate others'.

6. Clarify Your Priorities to Balance Your Work and Home Life. Many of us are convinced that, to get promoted, we have to work long hours. Some of us go so far as to stay late and return on weekends to put in "face time." Gary Cooper, professor of organizational psychology at the University of Manchester, England, studied the work habits of over 1000 executives in the United States and Britain and concluded, "Any manager who works over 50 hours a week is turning in less than his best performance."

Good health is critical to sustain peak performance in any endeavor—including work. This means we all need to eat healthily, avoid alcohol and drugs and get plenty of sleep and exercise. Lack of sleep, for example, diminishes your ability to think creatively and to cope with unfamiliar situations. British psychophysiologist Dr. James Horne has found that losing even one night's sleep disrupts a person's ability to think divergently.

Work without resentment, putting your energies into the task at hand, but don't use work as an excuse to justify the lack of an outside life. In a study of 37,000 people, researchers in the United States, Finland and Sweden found the health risk of living alone is as great as the risk of smoking. People without close friends and a strong social network are twice as likely to die prematurely as those with these supports.

If you believe you can't have both a work life and a home life, you are setting yourself up for a self-fulfilling prophecy. This is a particularly relevant point since almost half of all workers today are women—who are usually required to juggle both a career and family—and *American Demographics* magazine predicts that women will fill 64% of the new jobs created between now and the year 2000. The question is not whether we can have work lives and home lives, but how we will manage them.

Here Are Some Proven Time Management Tips

Watch for your personal patterns of productivity: do you do better work early in the morning or later in the day? Can you take care of paperwork before or after official hours? Do you work more efficiently at your desk in the office or at home? Firms such as Pacific Bell, Travelers Companies and J. C. Penney have found worker productivity increases up to 25% when people work at home.

Use calendars, schedules and lists, of course. But if you are a "left-brain" person, also schedule "joy breaks" during the day, and plan your play as carefully as you plan your work.

Set specific, worthwhile, challenging goals. Goal setting is the single most reliable way to become more productive when you work.

Begin installing the Worth Ethic by treating yourself more caringly and then treating others as you treat yourself. You will greatly increase your own and others' job satisfaction as you inspire high integrity and meaning in work, share power, praise and recognize, support people's creativity, development and growth, pay for productivity and wellness and serve as a role model for a balanced work and home life.

You will also lead your group to new heights of productivity. Groups managed by Worth Ethic values consistently outperform groups led by managers who are competent but uncompassionate. For example, at Transco Energy in Houston, President George Slocum holds "bragging sessions" to let his employees boast about their cost cutting schemes. Based on past experience, he expects to save $18 million over the next two years simply because departments want to be recognized at these meetings.

These heights of job satisfaction and productivity will not go unnoticed. People around you will want to follow your lead and make their own internal changes. Now, you know as well as I do that change is almost never a simple matter of attending a training session or watching a demonstration, and then putting it into effect when you get back to the office. But as you support people with your long range strategies, external changes will show up in the systems, procedures and structures that help your organization operate. In the end, the Worth Ethic will create broad success for you and your company. You can be sure of this, because the Worth Ethic works.

Self-Esteem and Work

Will Schutz

Corporate Consultant, Trainer
Author, *The Human Element* and *The Truth Option*

Emotion is the chief source of all becoming—consciousness. There can be no transforming of darkness into light or of apathy into movement without emotion.

Carl Gustav Jung

*P*icture this situation:
From a large group I take six volunteers to another room. I select a trio of the six and, out of earshot of the other three, give them a private communication. I then take the trio back to the whole group and ask them to clean up the front of the room. They are sluggish, uncaring, clumsy, sloppy and slow. I thank them and ask them to sit down in the large group. I then return to the other room and give the remaining three volunteers another private communication. I escort them back into the room and ask them also to clean up the front of the room. They attack the task with vigor, divide the labor, go swiftly and seem proud of their work. Question: What did I tell each trio? No, I did not tell them to go fast or slow, to be eager or slovenly, to be efficient or inefficient. In fact, I did not tell them anything at all about how to do the job. What then did I tell them? At the end of this section the answer will be revealed, although it may be obvious before then.[1]

After 15 years of working with organizations, I have concluded that a positive self-concept—self-esteem—is the bottom line, the key to increasing productivity and the quality of the workplace. This conclusion led me back to many thoughts I had beginning in the 1960s about this topic. I always had trouble understanding the criticism of the "me" generation. Tom Wolfe and others called it narcissistic, conceited, self-absorbed, selfish and prideful. From where I stood, near the center of the human potential movement, these descriptions were bewildering. With few exceptions, the people I knew who were successful in finding who they were had none of these traits. As each person came to "know thyself," they seemed to me to be calmer, stronger, more real, more honest, more successful in their relationships and genuinely caring and helpful people. I am certainly not saying that the "me" generation or some self-esteem advocates are entirely guiltless of the charges made. I am only speaking of the great majority of the people I experienced. From my vantage point, self-esteem advocates are exactly right. Self-esteem is, indeed, the heart of the matter.

An answer to my puzzlement came from the dictionary. "Self-esteem" is defined in two ways and they are, in one sense, contradictory, which may help explain my dilemma. *The Random House Dictionary* defines self-esteem as:

1. An objective respect for or favorable impression of oneself.
2. An inordinate or exaggeratedly favorable impression of oneself.

Apparently self-esteem advocates assume the first definition, while critics use the second meaning. The confusion may be a result of this paradox: if I have high self-esteem in meaning one (let us call it *self-respect*), I do *not* have an exaggerated sense of myself as in meaning two (call it *arrogance*). It is when I have *low* self-respect that I become arrogant, brag, and act conceited as a way to try to convince others—which means basically myself—that I am really all right.

What Is Self-Esteem?

Self-esteem is the feeling I have about my self-concept. When what I want for myself matches what I perceive myself to be, I have a positive self-concept, which in turn helps me feel as alive, self-determining, self-aware, significant, competent and likable as I want to be. Self-esteem comes from choosing successfully to be the type of person I want to be.

Self-esteem is both conscious and unconscious. It begins in childhood, and it is developed as I create my self-concept through internalizing (or rejecting) messages about me that I receive from my parents and others, and from my own experiences of what I can and cannot do and what I am and am not. I compare myself to others, or to an idea of the type of person I want to be or to others' definitions of an ideal.

I am not aware of some parts of my self-concept. I choose them to be unconscious because I am uncomfortable with them, or I feel I cannot or do not want to deal with them. For example, I may have assumed that I was basically a bad boy, therefore not lovable by those who knew me well. I made this feeling of being unlovable unconscious: it was too painful to acknowledge. To hide this feeling from myself, or to defend myself against having to experience it, I may become arrogant; that is, I exaggerate my own importance, or I brag about my accomplishments or I act too ingratiating. This behavior arises out of unconscious low self-esteem and unconscious low self-respect. I demonstrate self-esteem by being flexible, able to express myself fully, in charge of myself, and having accurate perceptions and learning to make all my perceptions conscious.

At the height of the McCarthy era in the late 1940s, I was a graduate student at the University of California at Los Angeles, supporting myself through the G.I. Bill and my salary as a teaching assistant. As a university employee I was required to sign a loyalty oath in order to retain my job. I took the position that I would not sign because I felt people should be judged on the basis of their performance, not their political beliefs. I became very active in opposition to the oath. My father heard of what I was doing and flew out from the Midwest. He spent three days with me discussing the situation and the position I was taking. His attitude was, as always, very logical. "Of course you are right in principle, but you will jeopardize your future. You are an untested teaching assistant. No one knows you, and once you have your degree, others will be hired first. They are less risky for an employer."

His arguments persuaded me. I went to lunch with my fellow nonsigners and told them I had decided to sign and "fight from within"—a euphemism we used for dropping the fight. When I left the restaurant and walked into the bright sunlight of Los Angeles, I felt as if I weighed three tons. My muscles were stiff and heavy, and I felt totally dark. At that point, a little voice whispered in my ear: "What kind of person do you want to be?"

"Be quiet," I said. "Can't you see I'm busy being miserable?" But the voice persisted, and I finally got the point: signing or not signing was not a matter of logic. Most people could think of many excellent reasons for taking either position. The decision depended on what kind of person I wanted to be. I decided not to sign the loyalty oath. My body lightened. I felt as if I weighed three ounces. I felt wonderful. My body was telling me what kind of person I wanted to be. When I followed that picture, I felt good. Looking back, I can see that this was my first experience of realizing that my self-esteem depends on how close I am to being the kind of person I want to be.

To the degree that I experience myself as being like my ideal, and as being unlike the self I want to avoid, I have positive self-esteem. Similarly, the more I fall short of my ideal, the more disappointed I am in myself, the more anger I feel toward myself. Feelings of disappointment in and anger with myself reduce my self-esteem. Why do I feel these inadequacies in my self-concept? How can I heighten my self-esteem? The answer to these questions lies in the concept of choice: I assume I choose my feelings and behavior because, ineffective as they may seem, I believe they will lead to a payoff. When I choose low self-esteem, it is because I get a payoff for it.

For example, suppose I want to be funny but am not. I am dour and ponderous. What do I get out of being humorless? On reflection, I find that it feels safer to me. I suspect that people are laughing at me anyway, and I fear that if I take something as a joke when it is meant to be serious, I will be caught off guard and feel hurt. Therefore, I assume that everything is serious, so I can avoid painful surprises. My fear prevents me from being the humorous person I want to be, and that lowers my self-esteem.

When I am not feeling good about myself, compliments and support from other people are pleasant to hear but do not make me feel better for very long, if at all. I dismiss compliments because I believe the complimentors do not know all my faults, all the thoughts and feelings I have and all the things I have done. If they knew they wouldn't feel the same way about me. I may even perceive other people's praise or liking for me as a threat. What if I do something to disappoint them? They may withdraw their liking, so it is risky for me to feel good when they say good things about me. There are other payoffs for choosing not to like myself more: "It is arrogant to like myself ... If I appear modest, people will like me better ... People will not expect much of me if I appear unsure of myself ... I will not be impertinent enough to think that I am better than my parents or siblings ... I would be ridiculous to like myself if no one else did."

How Can the Organization Make Use of Self-Esteem?

Here is a new twist on an old saying: *If I give a hungry woman a fish, she won't be hungry. If I teach her how to fish, she'll never be hungry. But, if I create conditions within which she teaches herself how to fish, she'll never be hungry and she may have enhanced self-esteem.*

Self-esteem is at the heart of all human relations and productivity in organizations. For example:

- **Teamwork** difficulties arise from rigidities and defensiveness which come not from differences among members, but from low self-esteem and fear of exposure.

- **Conflict resolution** similarly depends on dissolving rigidities and getting people to see conflict as a logical puzzle for team members to solve together.

- **Problem solving** is blocked when a person is anxious about being exposed, or is determined to be right or shows other kinds of defensive behavior that stems from low self-esteem.

- **Leadership** relies centrally on self-awareness, which in turn requires sufficiently strong self-esteem to acknowledge weaknesses and feel comfortable being known to others.

- **Performance appraisal** is successful to the extent that each person feels acknowledged for his or her strengths and weaknesses and for who he or she is and, through healthy self-esteem, being willing to give up blame in favor of mutual problem solving.

- **Injury- and illness-free workplaces** may also be attained through self-awareness.

- **Quality** programs succeed when personal agendas based on low self-esteem are handled effectively to free the team to truly work out content issues.

- **Diversity** may be celebrated when threats to the self-concept from "different" groups are alleviated.

Since productive and efficient functioning depends on high self-esteem, the organization can capitalize by enhancing self-esteem. From this standpoint, the goal of the ideal organization is to bring about the greatest self-esteem for the largest number of employees. If all employees have high self-esteem, the organization will inevitably be productive and successful.

But the organization cannot give people self-esteem. Providing jobs or food or money is sometimes equated with increasing a person's self-esteem. Virtuous as these acts are, they are not necessarily related to increased self-esteem. A hungry man given food is no longer hungry, but does not necessarily have any better feeling about his own ability to feed himself. This is *not* to say we should not be generous. It is only to point out that these acts do not inevitably lead to increased self-esteem.

Too widespread is the notion that helping you means giving you something *I* think is of value. Many of our failures of relationships result from giving you what *I* want to give you and being amazed at your resentment. Such a result follows from not bothering to find out what is of value to you. Giving because I want to be seen by others as generous is not true generosity. Typically, it comes from feeling low self-esteem. If I feel truly generous, I bother to find out what will be seen by you as helpful. My focus is on *being* helpful, not on being *seen* as helpful.

For a social or personal action to be effective for increasing self-esteem, it must be carefully thought through. *Helping is a fine art.* If I want to help you increase your self-esteem, I must be inventive enough to create conditions within which you will develop your own abilities and overcome your fears of not being adequate (recall the fish story above). It is my experience of doing and being something I formerly did not feel capable of that leads me to feel increased self-esteem. So, although the organization cannot give employees higher self-esteem, it can create conditions within which it is easier for them to enhance their own self-esteem. The following table describes these conditions.

Atmosphere Goals of an Ideal Organization

To achieve the goal of having individuals feel ...	The organization facilitates an atmosphere of ...
Alive	Participation
Self-determining	Freedom
Self-aware	Openness
Significant	Recognition
Competent	Empowerment
Likable	Humanity

The table lists the specified links between individual self-esteem and the organizational atmosphere conducive to bringing about those individual feelings. More detail on these dimensions follows.

For the *individual,* the goal is to continuously enhance the six dimensions defining self-esteem.

- **Aliveness.** I'm fully alive. I use myself well. I'm energetic. I'm not bored.
- **Self-determination.** I choose my own life. I'm self-determining and autonomous. I feel free and not coerced. I'm responsible for myself.
- **Self-awareness.** I tell the truth to myself and to others. I'm aware of myself. I'm aware that I have an unconscious and constantly strive to be more conscious. I don't deceive myself.
- **Significance.** I feel significant. I'm an important person. I make a difference.
- **Competence.** I feel competent. I can cope with the situations presented by life.
- **Likability.** I feel likable. I enjoy my own company. I like the person I am.

For the *organization,* the goal is to create an atmosphere that fosters all employees' self-esteem, specifically by means of the following factors:

- **Participation.** The organization offers full participation in its business. I, the employee, do not want (nor am I required) to participate in all activities, but I do have the opportunity and am invited to do so. I'm kept informed of company activities and included in the appropriate activities I wish to pursue.
- **Freedom.** I'm trusted to determine my own best courses of action.

- **Openness.** The organization and I are fully open with each other. We keep no secrets (except certifiable industrial or security secrets) and do not withhold. All questions are answered truthfully and completely.
- **Recognition.** I am known and recognized by the organization. As a policy, the organization routinely acquires an understanding of the worth and abilities of each employee.
- **Empowerment.** I am fully empowered and do everything voluntarily. I participate in final decisions on all the issues that I know the most about and that most affect me.
- **Humanity.** The organization appreciates and knows me as a person and encourages social contacts.

How Can I Increase My Self-Esteem?

If the organization, or anyone, can't increase my self-esteem, how can I do it myself? Five methods are described here for beginning a process of improving self-esteem.

1. Affirmations. The first approach is at the behavior level. Although it does not get at the root of low self-esteem, it is helpful to practice more positive behavior while the pursuit of causes—the next four methods—is progressing.

At the level of behavior, these behaviors may be practiced as a method of increasing self-esteem:[2]

- Tell my truth; let myself and others know what my truth is.
- Be aware that I am always choosing and accept responsibility without blame for everything happening in my life.
- Seek deeper self-awareness, read, discuss, ponder, improve my awareness of old programs and deeper levels of being.
- Give up blame, postpone judgment, listen and understand before defending or attacking or making others wrong.
- Envision my ideal self. Keep in mind I am choosing the way I want to be.
- Don't lie, don't blame, don't withhold, don't deceive myself.
- Question my limiting beliefs. I am aware that any time I tell myself I cannot do something, I am right.
- Be in touch with my body, listen for ever present cues.
- Treat my growth and myself with respect and patience, rather than irritation and judgment, and maintain the larger perspective of developing along my own path.

2. Ideal Self. This method converts the concept that self-esteem depends on how much I am like my ideal self into a measurement.[3] It helps pinpoint which aspects of me are unsatisfactory and therefore prevent me from feeling better about myself. Once I find the unsatisfactory parts, I can discover my payoff for not being more the way I want to be. By taking the difference between what I am and what I want to be, I get a measure of my self-esteem.

Examples of items are:

- I act more competently than I really feel.
- I don't feel alive enough.
- I prevent people from seeing that I am as significant as I am.

3. Choice. Now, I use the concept of choice, or self-responsibility, to take the next step. Rather than simply promise myself to "just change" those items I feel are unsatisfactory, I assume I choose to have these deficiencies because I get a payoff for it. To find the payoff, I remind myself that this is not an exercise in judging myself as good or bad. I must allow myself to see myself better without judgment, in the spirit of exploration and understanding. After bringing my payoffs to my awareness, I am in a position to make a conscious decision about what I want to do. For each of the most unsatisfactory items I write down my payoff for feeling this way. The payoff must be positive and not flippant. I keep in mind that the payoffs are rewarding enough to prevent me from esteeming myself more; so they must be potent.

Example of a payoff: I act less competently than I am able to because I don't want people to be disappointed in me because they expect too much.

4. Childhood. The next approach to improving my self-esteem is through exploring the origins of these unsatisfactory feelings and opinions about myself. Where did I get my ideas about who I am? As with the other approaches, this is not a panacea. It simply points me in directions that are relevant and potentially valuable for increasing my self-esteem. All of these approaches are even more valuable if I can gather another person, or even a group of friends, who will complete these exercises with me and participate in a discussion after we have finished.

Part I. I explore how my feelings about myself may have started in each area of behavior and of feelings. One of the early sources from which I derive my picture of myself is the inferences I drew about myself from my parents' actions around and toward me. This is not an exercise in blaming parents. It is an attempt to understand myself better. I keep in mind that these were always my interpretations of what they did. Examples:

How did my parents react when I asked, said, implied or felt:

... I want to be included? (Examples, "Can I go with you? Can I sit at the table with you? Can I come into your room? Can I go to the store with you? Can I go visiting with you?")

... I want to be in control? (Examples, "I want to do it myself. I won't do what you told me. I want to do it my way.")

... I want to be open with you and have you be open with me? (Examples, "Tell me how you really feel about me. Tell me your real feelings about other people, events or about yourselves. I want you to know how I really feel, what I am afraid of, what I like about myself.")

Part II. Using the results of this inquiry may help me find the origin of the decisions I made about myself that I am now not satisfied with. To explore where the decisions that determine my self-esteem originated, for each unsatisfactory item listed above I ask myself,

- When is the first time I recall acting or feeling this way?
- Did I ever act this way toward a parent or close relative?
- Did any close relative act or feel this way toward me during my childhood?
- What is my payoff now for acting or feeling this way?
- Is this what I really want?
- What am I willing to do about it?

5. Essence Imagery. The fifth technique uses a method to contact the unconscious and bring it under conscious control. Here are the instructions:

Please shut your eyes. Think of three things you like most about yourself. Pause. Now rank these three traits from the most important, number one, to the lesser important, numbers two and three. Pause. Now imagine yourself having traits one and two, but not three. Feel what that would be like, and get a picture of that situation. Pause. Now imagine yourself with trait one, but not two or three. Pause. Now imagine you have none of these traits. Notice how you feel. What pictures come into your head? Pause. Now please open your eyes and notice your feelings as you open your eyes. Pause. What is it that is left after you have eliminated all three traits?

Participants have a variety of reactions from elation and freedom to fear and desolation. It is valuable to assume that what remains is your essence. You are not your traits. By reaching your essence in a tangible form, it is possible to alter it consciously. Participants may now go back to the picture of their essence and work with it. They are encouraged to strengthen it, if they wish, by talking to it, touching it, feeding it, seeing other people there to help them strengthen it, or whatever else they wish to do. In other words, they have an opportunity to reshape their own self-concept in the directions they wish. This is the deepest level of work with self-esteem.

Back to the Original Exercise

My communication to each group was very simple. To the first group I said, "You have very low self-esteem. By that I mean you don't feel alive, you don't control your life, you are not aware of yourself, and you feel insignificant, incompetent and unlikable." To the second group I said, "You have very high self-esteem. By that I mean you feel alive, in charge of your life, aware of yourself, and you feel significant, competent and likable." And that is all.

This exercise illustrates that the feelings about self-esteem govern a vast amount of behavior. To bring about a poor or an excellent job from the trios, it is not necessary to be specific about what behaviors to perform. Their condition of self-esteem determines morale, efficiency, relationships and other important aspects of human functioning. A change in self-esteem is so fundamental that it automatically changes a myriad of specific behaviors, as demonstrated by the dramatic difference between the two teams.

ALL YOU HAVE TO DO IS ASK!

Stephen Boehler

President, Mercer Island Consulting
Former Division President, Weyerhauser
Former Advertising Executive, Procter & Gamble

When Procter & Gamble expanded Pringle's Newfangled Potato Chips nationwide during the 1973–1975 period, the product was an immediate and enormous success.

But within a year, the business began a precipitous and long term decline, with sales off roughly 25% per year from 1975 through 1980. The result, from the standpoint of a proud and successful Procter & Gamble, was most unsightly. P&G simply wasn't used to a secondary market position, much less such a public failure. The business lost a ton of money; some outsiders estimated losses as high as $250 million on Pringle's. P&G's confidence and image was also shaken; after all, this was the consumer products company with more market leading brands than any other. Nothing short of market leadership was considered a success, and Pringle's had become Procter's single greatest, and most public, corporate failure.

A great deal of time, energy, resources and investment was thrown at the Pringle's business in an attempt to turn it around. Very senior P&G executives were brought in from around the company to lead turnaround efforts. Efforts were driven from the top down, allowing the most senior officials the opportunity to set policy and tactics. A new advertising agency was tried. Yet nothing worked.

Why couldn't the best and brightest at the venerable P&G, with vast resources at their beck and call, turn around Pringle's? Ironically, after bringing senior executives from all over the company to study and attempt to "fix" Pringle's, a small group of junior executives discovered the truth: the answers were readily available all along; we simply needed to ask "the people." And, this is the first law of the business turnaround: the people always know the score, but are underutilized assets in our top-down, hierarchical business world. The system of big business in the United States is largely set up in ways that fundamentally prevent the work force from contributing. This results in a demoralized work force, one that "checks its brains at the door" (to borrow a 19th century business dictum).

And yet, in perhaps as structured a work environment as there is in the United States, a group of junior executives turned around the Pringle's business by creating an environment that fostered teamwork, personal involvement and individual contribution. In a matter of little more than a year, the Pringle's product was improved, costs declined dramatically, the package was changed, the price decreased, new flavors were introduced and Pringle's Light became the nation's first "light" chip.

How did all this happen? In the incessantly paternal environment at P&G, senior management simply let the Pringle's executives alone; it actually appeared as if the senior executives were tired of hearing about Pringle's and decided to simply ignore it for the time being while they worked on greater issues.

At this time, a 25-year-old brand manager visited the plant in Jackson. During this visit, he asked a 25-year veteran line worker what was working and what wasn't, and perhaps most importantly, what could be done to fix various problems. The line worker became immensely animated in describing possible solutions: arms waving, voice rising, eyes alight. When the young brand manager asked why the line worker was becoming so excited, the worker simply replied, "Well, I've been working here for 25 years, and no one has ever asked me my opinion before." And, of course, the young brand manager saw the single greatest truth in business: the people doing the work know what's going on; all you had to do was ask!

In this vacuum, the junior Pringle's executives formed a business team, one of the first of its kind in a consumer goods business in the United States. This team quickly created its own charter and mission, and operating goals and business strategies followed. These were all on target, as the people closest to the business were the ones creating them. In team meetings, people working on the Pringle's business got to share their opinions on everything and anything, as long as it pertained to Pringle's. The resulting discussions and exchanges fostered creation of marketing and product plans that had the imprint of an entire team, and that were shaped from the consumer up as opposed to from the top down. No topic was off limits, and no issue was too sacred to challenge.

The Pringle's story is a well-known turnaround. It's been written about in numerous business periodicals, MBA case studies have been developed around it and many current and former P&G employees can look proudly on their own role in that great turnaround. What isn't well-known is not only that the turnaround itself was led by a hard working and hard listening team of junior executives, but also that its success helped spawn an entire movement toward business teams and the evolution of Procter & Gamble's heralded brand management system. Hard working became hard listening, and the people spoke and worked with an amazing passion for the business.

Radical Reliance on Self-Esteem

Bud Seith
CEO, Catalyst Group and former vice-president and CIO, Xerox

With Jacklyn Wilferd, PhD
CEO, Internet Marketing and former marketing executive, Xerox

A fully functioning employee with a healthy self-image is money in the bank.

Marilyn Ferguson

It's no secret there is trouble in the American workplace. Profits are up, but people are down. We embrace technology for higher productivity while we ignore employees' basic concerns about the future. A cloud of uncertainty hangs over even highly skilled "knowledge workers" as employers seek a competitive edge in the race for profits in a global economy. Wall Street dictates what qualifies as a strong position at the starting line—stock prices, credit ratings, patents and record profits. What about the people?

Are people still our "greatest asset"? More importantly, do they believe they are valued in their organizations and companies? What message are we sending the work force? Just ten years ago, good employees were offered secure benefits, training and advancement opportunities. These have been replaced by reductions in force, strategic outsourcing and, in some cases, unabashed downsizing for short term gains. People are viewed as a burden to the bottom line and a liability for the future. With such a disparaging view influencing business decisions, is it any surprise that eroding self-esteem in the workplace has become a portentous issue?

As business leaders, our concern must be for the viability of the enterprise as a whole. Too often we develop numerical myopia—a nearsighted focus on business metrics that blurs our creativity. It's what enables people to perform with vigor and self-renewing energy. Get that right in your company or organization and all the numbers improve simultaneously. The entire enterprise flourishes.

In all my business experience, I have never met a manager so meanspirited that he or she would want—even unintentionally—to undermine the self-esteem of employees on the job. But I have worked with many, including CEOs of vast corporations, who do not understand the leadership principles involved in creating work environments where high self-esteem thrives.

In my practice as a Power Coach^{SM}, I teach executives and business professionals how to apply leadership principles in the most diverse situations. The ideas are not hard to grasp. On the contrary, they are intuitively simple. Yet the results they yield are consistently beyond anything my clients anticipate.

My faith in these principles grew over a 25 year period as I applied them in my management career at Xerox Corporation. I call them "principles" because they are ideas that can be repeated and duplicated. I found I could rely on them in practically any circumstance. They get results even when nothing else does. I have used them in dealing with executives in boardrooms around the world. I have used them to influence multimillion-dollar corporate decisions. And I can tell you, they work.

One of the most important principles of leadership I have discovered is that it is the leader's job to create and hold a vision of what will be for the organization. Leadership is a powerful force, especially when it gives a new sense of purpose and high self-esteem to people.

Business metrics are important but not a substitute for leadership vision. Can you replace a visionary leader with an indifferent management team? I don't think so. The reason, of course, is that people enthusiastically follow leaders with a vision. We may not completely understand why, but an ineffable something about them attracts us to follow them to extraordinary ends.

Successful leaders are experts at getting us to experience reality in a new way. They are indeed powerful because they give purpose and meaning to people and change the way people value themselves. Yet we can all create and sustain vision, once the concept is understood. As business managers, we'll want to learn how this works if we are serious about leading our companies and organizations to their full potential.

In 1980, I was asked to take over the management of a failing Information Systems organization at Xerox Corporation in Rochester, New York. The vice-president of Human Resources had personally flown to London on a Sunday to visit me at my home in the English countryside and recruit me for the job because I had a track record of transforming weak areas of business into successes. Xerox did not necessarily understand the principles of leadership I was using, but they were impressed with the results I got from them.

Having decided to accept the challenge, I soon found myself on a transatlantic flight to New York, scouring a full report by the Information Systems group managers. Xerox sales were booming, but this organization was hopelessly off track. Data centers across the country had huge backlogs in customer billing and major bottlenecks in administration. System breakdowns, bureaucratic procedures and demoralized employees were the norm. The management team had no idea how to reverse the trend. The recommendations in their report were uninspired—another $5 million here, 70 more people there and so on. They really believed these were the right answers.

Performance in this organization was so poor it was impairing core Xerox businesses. It was being blamed for manufacturing delays, revenue shortfalls and customer complaints in all regions and product sectors. Vice-presidents were decommitting from important targets as a result. It was a huge problem with major business impacts.

Friends and supporters had warned me it would be difficult. Even my best friend said, "Congratulations, Bud. You've finally taken on a job you cannot succeed at." My predecessor had tried everything to no avail—time, money, the latest technology and new work processes. Exhaustive efforts had not done the trick.

Senior management decided there had to be a problem with the people. So they brought me in and fully expected me to replace a good part of the staff.

I knew the people were not the problem. It was crystal clear to me that the solution lay with the people. They would ultimately transform the organization into what it needed to be, but I also knew they could not do so in the existing environment.

What was missing was an environment that inspired innovation, creativity and invention. We needed an environment that allowed people to really contribute off-the-board, improbable, fabulous changes. I needed it to happen fast. There was no time for evolutionary problem solving processes. I knew I had to do something revolutionary.

The third day of my new job, I had an unscheduled visit from the vice-president of Human Resources. "How does it look?" he asked tentatively. I smiled and replied, "We're going to be in great shape." I had an approach that I was certain would work. It was unproved, but I was absolutely sure the performance would be fabulous. How could I have known this after only three days? How could I have been so sure?

I had a vision that I believed in—a very common-sense clear view of what would be. To begin with, I was absolutely certain I could rely on what I knew to be true about human nature. I knew that people are dying to contribute, that people want to be creative and that they need to express their creativity in their work. I knew, too, that if they had an environment that encouraged them to show up in this way, the business issues we were facing would be resolved. I had absolute trust in the people. They were working on things I could not even pronounce and were far more competent in these matters than I was.

So the vision I created for the organization was the realization of an environment where the people were expected to be who they truly were, where self-esteem thrived, where every person and every contribution was honored, where everyone achieved remarkably more than they thought possible. I saw this as a reality that they could not yet see.

Over the objections of practically everyone with whom I shared my plan, I made some announcements consistent with my new vision for the organization. I told them that, effective immediately, everyone was now a consultant to me in addition to their regular duties. As consultants, they each reported directly to me—all 500 of them. It was a startling change. I expected each of them to tell me how they could make specific improvements to their work function. They knew I was dead serious about this. No kidding.

Then I established three ground rules. First, every idea is a good idea. There will be no criticism of the ideas you give me. Ideas will be assessed but no one will make an idea wrong. These people were accustomed to an environment where most of their suggestions were put down and summarily thrown out. So they had ceased offering new thoughts. I had to put a stop to judgments about ideas and people, period. Judgment has no place in building an environment of high self-esteem.

Second, I expected that every idea would be implemented. I trusted that their recommendations had value; so the onus was on them to prove me right. They held themselves accountable for contributing ideas that would actually work, which brought a whole new level of realism to their proposals.

Third, managers were responsible for making it happen. They could ask for additional budget or resources, if necessary, but they were not at liberty to just criticize, ignore or reject our people's ideas. Managers had a new standard to live up to, and the organization had my guarantee on that. As it turned out, the managers enjoyed this role; however, most of them protested at first.

I wasn't just looking for loose suggestions. I needed 500 consultants performing at a professional level. The people needed some basic training in workflow analysis, formulating recommendations and evaluating business impacts. So I arranged a training program for everyone. It took a half day every week for six weeks to complete. Then every person prepared an individual presentation for me, just like a real consultant.

Every presentation was an honoring experience for them and a learning experience for me. The people delighted me with bright ideas and thoughtful preparation. I was grateful for everything they brought up. They were now beginning to reflect the trust I'd placed in them.

The high point of all these efforts was when four of our professional people offered a new strategic direction that would save over a half million dollars a year, including a proposal to eliminate their own jobs. Now that showed high trust in me! Of course, I accepted their plan, rewarded them with sizable bonuses and made certain they got even better jobs in the organization.

Remarkable things began happening at our operations across the country in the weeks and months that followed. The impact was utterly amazing. Teams began making improvements faster than I could imagine. They gained the respect of the rest of the company. People were excited about their work. The business metrics took a sharp turn for the better.

To sustain the phenomenal spirit of creativity, I had all managers set aside some money in their budgets for what I called "broken glass." At first, some complained they didn't know how to spend the budget for broken glass. "That's because you haven't broken any yet!" I'd say. Later they would call and proudly announce, "I broke some glass today."

"That's great." I'd ask, "What did you do?" I still love hearing stories about broken glass because I know it means there is a work environment out there where people are honored for taking risks.

People loved the work, loved what they did and had fun doing it. The next employee survey showed improvements beyond the bounds of statistical validity. In less than a year, attitudes had changed from passionless boredom or repressed rebellion to the extreme high end of the scale. "We love it here and we are pleased with ourselves" was the new consensus. Within the corporation, we became known as a major source of talent for the rest of the business.

The organization produced results beyond what had been thought possible. All performance objectives were overachieved. Backlogs were cleared, complaints stopped. In a four year period, the output of the organization increased by over 300% while operating costs were reduced by nearly 50%. Performance metrics led industry standards. Our data centers and national telecommunications operations became a showcase to the world for Xerox Corporation.

All the credit goes to the people who accomplished this work. My role was focused on creating and sustaining an environment where creativity and high contribution abounded. I simply made it safe for them to show up.

Today's competitive business climate calls for higher productivity, improved quality, innovative products and business solutions—all at reduced costs to the bottom line. Achieving the results is possible through radical reliance on our human resources driven by a leadership vision of self-esteem.

TREATED WITH RESPECT

Robert Levering and Milton Moskowitz

Coauthors, *The 100 Best Companies to Work for in America*

We need to have respect and love for all things and all people.

Don Doyhis

Former Chairman of Morrison & Foerster, the largest law firm in San Francisco, Carl Leonard, pointed out to us that treating the support staff well is not just some "nice California granola kind of warm fuzzy thing," but makes economic sense: "It doesn't matter how great a brief you've written, if you are dependent on a messenger and at 5 P.M. or 5:30 P.M., that messenger says, 'I've done my job and I don't have to do this,' that great brief never gets there on time. This is hardheaded economics, running a law firm. And if these people feel like they are part of a team and treated with respect, they will outperform their counterparts in other places who aren't treated that way."

It may be hard economics but it also reflects a warm heart. And Morrison & Foerster values glue people together. Lynn Azevedo, a litigation secretary, said: "I think that our salaries are above what some of the other larger firms are paying, but in addition to that, it is the way they treat you as people. I came here from a very large firm, and if a secretary there, for instance, didn't care for the people she was working for—attorneys, legal assistants or whatever—she had no say in the matter. You were just let go. Here that never happens. You can talk to your floor supervisor, you can talk to your attorneys about it. I have been in situations where that has come up and everybody listens."

Robin Rouda, who works in recruiting, said the firm makes it "very clear" to law students who work as summer interns that "our staff is like gold to us and are not to be treated any less preciously. In fact, anyone who is found to be speaking down to somebody or mistreating them verbally, or in any other way, is really out on their ear. We just will not tolerate it." Janice Sperow, an associate (law firm lingo for a lawyer who has not yet made partner), added this confirmation: "We have had people who have all the credentials, top of their class from Harvard Law School, they're on the law review, they have clerked for so and so, they have done all the right things and then they came here as interns and acted like a jerk to their secretary—fetch me this, fetch me that, run my personal errand—and they did not get an offer to come back here."

The Value of Respect

Chérie Carter-Scott, PhD
Author, *Negaholics* and *The Corporate Negaholic*
Chairman of the Board, The MMS Institute

There are countless ways of attaining greatness, but any road to reaching one's maximum potential must be built on a bedrock of respect for the individual, a commitment to excellence, and a rejection of mediocrity.

Buck Rodgers

One fundamental common denominator cuts across cultures, nationalities, races and religions and that is respect. Regardless of personality types, learning styles, orientation, strengths or weaknesses, respecting an employee transcends all differences. Differences are the basis for judgments, separation and prejudice, and judgments are the cancer cells of relationships. Respect allows for differences. Respect is accepting others as they are without wanting them to be more like you. If you respect people, then you honor their areas of expertise, competence, preferences and strengths as well as their shortcomings. In this fashion, you empower them with a sense of positive self-regard, or self-esteem.

Preserving employee self-esteem is a delicate issue. It requires clarity in communication. Communication involves several aspects: roles and responsibilities, expectations, opportunities and consequences, monitoring of performance, consistent feedback, positive reinforcement, recognition and appropriate and timely rewards. In addition to communication, other important aspects of respect are compassion, empathy, support and tactful directness. In a world where one out of four people experiences a health crisis with someone close to them, coupled with the pressures of raising a family, nurturing a primary relationship and earning a living, human relationship skills play a very important role.

Employees are people. An obvious statement? Perhaps not, when you consider bosses who expect workers to perform like machines. If a boss views employees as a means to an end, then he/she may not be willing to invest the time, energy and concern for the employee's overall well being.

Employees are people who grew up in families. The family environment treated them in ways that imprinted them for life. These imprints led to decisions and behaviors about life. The decisions and behaviors allowed them to survive then and are still operative now.

Individuals bring their unresolved issues from their family of origin to the work environment and then act those issues out in the larger family—the corporate family. Whether someone was raised in a functional or dysfunctional environment, he/she brings talents and abilities, as well as personal issues to the job situation. They may have issues about authorities, sibling rivalries, the only child syndrome or low self-esteem manifesting in a variety of ways. If these issues were never adequately addressed in childhood, they will surely surface and be acted out in later life in the workplace. When the issues are acted out, they can provide the subject matter for criticism, isolation, ostracism, negativity and finger pointing.

For instance, if a child is teased on the school playground, he may make the decision that people are cruel, that to survive he must keep others at a distance and therefore he would rather be on his own. This decision may manifest in an adult who shies away from groups and is a loner, and who may very well end up being labeled a nonteam-player.

All forms of low self-esteem stem from the "Hole in the Soul" syndrome. The "Hole in the Soul" is the experience of insufficiency. The individual feels that he/she isn't or hasn't enough of what is required to meet the expectations of the task or role. For instance, if a young woman had difficulty with math in school, and avoided jobs requiring skill with numbers and then was promoted to a job that required managing a budget, dealing with quotas and utilizing statistical data, she could very well feel overwhelmed, fearful and insufficient to meet the new requirements.

The person who frequently broke things and was labeled "clumsy" as a child, when presented with the opportunity to expand their literacy into computers, may experience a huge internal "no" response to the invitation. This may be interpreted as unwillingness to grow or resistance to change. *But if you understand the stimulus, the response makes perfect sense.* If you are only privy to the response, the tendency may be to label, criticize or pigeonhole the person with a judgment. Given the fast pace of the 1990s work environment, there isn't always time to get to the core of issues which appear one way on the surface. Therefore, individuals' issues from their family of origin may become exacerbated in a situation that reinforces their experience of insufficiency or low self-esteem.

During a conflict resolution seminar I was conducting in Namibia, Africa, a short stocky black man, named Five, a union leader for the postal service, passionately lamented the work conditions. "Management doesn't care. They just say the right words. They don't walk their talk."

Ronnie, a tall, lean, blond, well dressed phone company manager tilted his chair on the back two legs and rebuffed, "It's not all that bad!"

Five, glaring at Ronnie, exploded, "You don't know, you are removed, you don't see what is really happening."

Ronnie, with cool demeanor offhandedly remarked, "You come work for me, things are different where I work."

Five fumed with disdain, "Come work for you?"

"Yeah, you'll have a positive experience, I'll make sure of it. Everyone who works for me has a good attitude," Ronnie said glibly. The temperature in the room rose with the collision of cultures, racial tension, corporate stratification and discrepancy of life experiences.

"Time out!" I declared. "Can we seize this moment as an example of real conflict and examine it in front of the group? If you are both willing, let's analyze the interaction, and learn from the conflict." They agreed. Both people were feeling disrespected. When he said that Ronnie didn't know the situation, Five insinuated that Ronnie was out of touch or minimizing conditions; Ronnie felt discredited.

When Ronnie said, "Come work for me," Five felt diminished. Instantly, Five reexperienced all the white men in his past who had said the words "you work for me." The hierarchy of race in politically charged Africa restimulated old wounds. The stigma of color was a constant issue in Five's life. Even if Ronnie had the best of intentions in offering Five a job, he said the very words that ignited Five's short fuse.

An incident like this triggers judgments on both sides. Judgments are coupled with belittling statements, backstabbing, colluding, case building, division of the work force into two opposing camps, subtle sniper attacks, border skirmishes, sabotage, withholding of vital information and covert operations. In short, others are set up for failure.

The opposite of respect is diminishment. This escalation of events results from an initial misunderstanding. The antidotes are acknowledging everyone's feelings and apologizing. It takes a big person to admit to being wrong. In this situation each man had to unearth the judgments and feel what the other one felt in order to find the other's humanness. The barbs of the hurtful words had to be withdrawn. In recalling the words, it was evident that the misunderstanding had escalated and the respect that was discarded needed to be reestablished. The broken connection had to be repaired. In the end, Five said to Ronnie, "I'm sorry I didn't give you credit."

Ronnie said, "I am sorry, Five, for what happened. You've had a rough go of it." It was important for Five to hear these words because he was the fifth born in his family and that is how he got his name.

The 21st century has many challenges for leaders who want to reinforce self-esteem in their employees. Self-esteem is fragile, precious and easily damaged, but difficult to reconstruct. Having employees participate in the choice, strategy and implementation of changes demonstrates respect, invites and encourages their input, and reinforces their self-esteem. *If you empower employees to take charge rather than merely take orders,* you not only build self-esteem, you develop leaders rather than followers.

The enlightened leader or manager needs to perceive workers as assets that require attention, nurturing, training, developing, informing, interacting, truth telling and feedback. Employees need to be honored as the most precious asset the organization has. Therefore, leaders must look at a long range plan that respects employees, their uniqueness, their families, their futures and their ultimate well-being. The following is an overview of the seven rules for reinforcing respect.

Methods for Reinforcing Respect

1. Requirements for Relevant Relationships. Most CEOs, leaders and managers fail to stipulate to the group of people they are leading what it is they stand for. It is a sign of respect for yourself and your employees to specify where you are coming from—your values, your expectations and your requirements for a fulfilling relationship. You may value and *require* honesty, integrity, a commitment to excellence and a compassionate management style. You may require timely and detailed written reports or projects.

Likewise you may request things such as that people submit three proposed solutions along with every problem or complaint, and you may refuse to stand for behaviors such as lying, stealing or divulging company secrets. These behaviors are grounds for immediate termination, with no second chance offered.

I suggest you set aside time and make your three R's list:

- What I *require* from people who work here.
- What I *request* from people who work here.
- What I *refuse to tolerate* from anyone who works here and is a cause for their termination.

This list is rarely, if ever, addressed in a job interview or an orientation program, but it is critical for true success and satisfaction on the job.

2. Responsible Management. After employees are hired, ask them, "What management style works best for you?" For some people it's, "Tell me what you want, leave me alone and I'll be fine." Other people may request or need daily interfacing. Still others may require a lot of coaching. You may want to ask, "What has worked well for you in the past? Under what kinds of conditions do you flourish? What do you need from me to be successful—freedom or structure, autonomy or accountability, to work in a team or to be left alone?"

You may also want to ask them about their learning style: "How do you learn best? Do you like to read about it, go to a seminar, receive hands on instruction or be shown step by step?"

I once coached a boss named Erica and her subordinate, Jan, in Texas.

Erica said, "I don't know what's the matter with this person. I give her what she wants and she doesn't do it. She doesn't act on it. For instance, she keeps telling me she wants to learn about computers. So I give her the books and she doesn't learn anything."

Later, when I met with Jan, she said, "You know, I don't know why my boss doesn't help me. She never gives me what I want. I asked her to help me learn computers and she gives me a stack of books." As I probed a little deeper, I found out that Jan's learning style was that of a hands-on experiential. She needed to put her own fingers on a keyboard and be coached. She didn't learn anything from books. It didn't work for her.

3. Relevance. Find out what is relevant to employees in terms of *their* values, their needs, their wants, and their proclivities.

Let me illustrate this with a story. My sister, Lynn, turned 50 last year. Lynn doesn't have a significant other in her life so I, as her sister, business partner and lifelong companion, took it upon myself to make her 50th birthday memorable.

I kept thinking about what would be enough for someone who was my sister and my business partner who was turning 50—a very significant moment in her life. What would be sufficient?

I came up with a trip to Greece. It turned out that I had enough frequent flier miles so that I could put it together. I rented a house for a couple of weeks on Mykonos. I did a house exchange with a family in London and took the whole family on my frequent flier miles. Lynn flipped over it. It wasn't very expensive; it was just creative. She felt that there was such a noticing of who she was, an honoring of what she valued, and a creativity to put together something that she would never forget for her whole life. It was just somehow going outside the norm and finding something that would really hit her at such a deep level. I am not advocating that you give employees trips to Greece, but that you find out what really makes them twinkle and sparkle and provide that.

4. Recognition and Reinforcement. Recognition is noticing and paying attention. Reinforcement is stimulating the behavior you want to promote. Some people like written notes. Others like verbal face-to-face recognition. One manager I know keeps a stack of cards in her drawer and writes numerous appreciation notes every day, such as "What you did today with customer X was so special and means a lot to me and the company. It's the kind of thing I really value and appreciate."

Some people prefer to be recognized privately, others prefer recognition in front of others. The way to find out what they prefer is to ask.

5. Realization. Find out what people need and want to realize their own goals. Ask them, "What are your ultimate career goals? Where do you see yourself in five years? If you were doing absolutely what you want, what would it be?"

If someone is looking at her job as temporary and really wants to go on to become an artist, and you are operating with the assumption that the employee is in this job for life, then you two are not on the same page. So you want to find out what is in her heart, what she ultimately wants to be doing, what is her purpose, what drives her and where she wants to be focusing her attention—what I call her "spiritual DNA." You can only discover this spiritual DNA by asking enough questions to really find out who somebody is on the inside. First you have to make conditions safe for somebody to tell you. Otherwise, they will tell you what they think you want to hear for fear of being fired because they are not committed for the long term.

The other day I told my bookkeeper, Tren, "I have this strong feeling that you are not doing what you want to be doing. I feel like you are doing this as a job and your heart is somewhere else. If it's true, we need to talk."

He said, "The truth is I really want to be an interior designer. I'm doing it on the side, but I want to be doing it full time, and I really want to stop being a bookkeeper."

I said, "When the truth is spoken, we can take action and we can support you in following your life's desires and dreams, but until you tell me the truth, I'm just going to get mad at you for not doing a great job at bookkeeping. It's not what you want to be doing anyway, and then you get mad at me because I'm mad at you. This destroys a relationship that could be healthy and productive."

Getting underneath what people do for survival reasons, for security, to maintain the status quo or because they have a belief system that says they can't really do what they want—they have to do one thing to earn money and do what they want to do on the side—is the kind of thing that really supports people in honoring their truth, living their dreams and allowing their spiritual DNA to unfold.

Ultimately you want your company to be filled with people who want to be there. Your job as a manager is to help anyone who really doesn't want to be there come to terms with that fact, and support them in getting to where they want to be. If you truly support somebody, you let go of the survival needs of your organization. You let go of the warm body syndrome. Managers often think, "I need this warm body to do this job, and I can't let go of them." Well, if you let go, someone will show up who *wants* to do the job.

6. Reasons for Rejection. Every employee has a list of "never do's." Ask each employee, "Are there any things that would really upset, annoy or hurt you that I should never do—screaming, touching, off-color jokes, teasing, reprimanding in front of others and so forth?"

I have an employee who is a very good technician, enters data at wizard speed and can be counted on to repair a lot of our computer problems. He is also a very shut-down individual who doesn't communicate a lot and my sister can't stand him. I have to be a buffer between the two of them. She says, "He doesn't talk to me, he doesn't respond, he doesn't do this." I say, "Leave him alone; he's an extreme introvert." A few months ago she said to him, "You have been so much nicer to me lately. Can you tell me what happened?"

He said, "Well, I'm not exactly sure, but I just don't like being touched. I can't have anybody touching me, and you used to touch me all the time. It used to make me crazy."

Lynn just automatically touches people. She is a very tactile person. For him, it's the worst possible thing she could do, but he never told her. In two years, he had never mentioned it. She didn't know it and he wouldn't say it, and it was a constant source of irritation that was never addressed. It's important to know what works and what doesn't work for people.

7. Rewards. Find out from employees what kind of rewards work for them, when they want to receive them and at what frequency they need to be rewarded. Rewards are the little treasures in life. Rewards don't have to be huge. They just need to be something that is meaningful to that person. For example, we have an answering service, and every three months or so, we bring them a huge box of donuts because they happen to like donuts. It's one of the things that motivates them. A friend of mine is a publicist and one of her clients sends her a huge bouquet of flowers every month. Just the other day she told me, "These guys send me flowers every month. I love it!"

One person is motivated by donuts, another by flowers. These little gifts communicate to the receiver, "Somebody knows I'm around. Somebody cares that I exist. Somebody values what I do." These little gifts are the jewels that we can give our employees and associates on a daily, weekly or monthly basis to let them know how much we value them.

When you utilize these seven "Rs of Respect," employees will feel understood and honored, self-esteem will be enhanced and peak performance will be released. Spirits and productivity will both soar because everyone in the organization can put their full energy into the tasks at hand and produce breakthrough results.

Respect, Caring and Big Loving

Jack Hawley

Corporate Consultant
Author, *Reawakening the Spirit in Work*

Love all, serve all.

Pocket logo
Hard Rock Cafe sweatshirt

Isaac Tigrett, cofounder of the Hard Rock Cafe, had pledged that if he ever got the opportunity to run a business, he wouldn't do it like any he had ever seen. "I was the third- or fourth-youngest person in the place and knew nothing about the restaurant business, so I had to follow my heart," he says. "There simply weren't any guidelines for creating the kind of place I had in my mind and heart."

He personally hires every one of the employees. "My rainbow collection," he calls them. "We had twenty-five native languages on the staff." He holds daily, and then weekly, "family meetings" with the entire staff. "Teach me this business," he tells them, "and I'll provide the resources and the rudder."

The staff meetings are wild and full of energy. "We train and train some more," he says. "Every week, we talk about kindness, about quality through politeness, and about our themes: classlessness and 'aggressive American friendliness.' We have to work to offset the usual English reserve. We want the place to exude love."

Isaac institutes the first profit-sharing plan in a restaurant company in England. Profits are doled out to every employee based on a scoring system that includes friendliness, helpfulness and fitting into the "family," as well as more conventional work performance items. Everybody is treated equally. Normally, women in the 1960s were paid exactly half of men's wages; at the Hard Rock they're paid exactly the same.

"You won't find a more *dharmic* manager than me," he laughs. "I knew everybody at the restaurant by name and everybody knew me. And they all had my phone number and knew they could contact me directly at any time. I spent 70% of my time on the phone. The employees and I had a special relationship. Later I even put Fax machines in each of the employee lounges, direct to my office. Every employee in every Hard Rock Cafe in the world knew he or she could contact me personally any time.

"I empowered certain people as 'management' or 'supervisors,' and then helped them not abuse that power. I held them responsible for business matters—and accountable as human beings, too. Whether through ego or ignorance or simply habit, if their actions went counter to what we were aiming for in our work environment, it became an opportunity for me to provide some 'special help' to them! They absolutely knew where I was coming from.

"I gave the personnel manager power to overrule the general manager, for example, in matters of heart and common courtesy—pay shortages or advances before a holiday, things like that. These people are restaurant workers, they don't make much money; the least we can do is be sensitive and stretch a little for them. Respect was the key. We respected people and expected respect in return.

"And the same goes for customers," he continues. Then he explains that because of his own aversion to waiting in lines, he felt a special concern for the people in the long lines always outside the front door. "I hated seeing people in a queue in bad weather," he laments. "But what can you do? We talked about it a lot in our meetings and finally hit on an elegant idea.

"We decided to extend the boundary of our restaurant to the end of the waiting line, wherever that was, and sometimes it was way around the park. We didn't consult lawyers or any of that stuff, we just proclaimed it. We appointed a Queue Maitre d'. He was constantly out there making people more comfortable. He would bring out umbrellas in rainy weather (and we never lost one); when it was hot, iced tea, and when it was icy, cocoa or soup. That sort of captures how it was," he says. "Everybody loved the place!"

Isaac's eyes light up when he talks about the company. "Being one of the Hard Rock Cafe family was therapy for people. Even if they came from a violent home life, here they were loved, and they loved back in return.

"People always do. I could hire those no one else would take, and in six or seven months they'd be new people. I called it my 'High School' and I told 'em I wanted everyone to graduate. I realized early on that we were creating habits, that's all, just habits. That's what success or failure in life comes from: habits. So I determined to create good ones. We graduated some great souls."

One day, it struck him: "If we're so famous, if people love the Hard Rock so much, why not take that and reflect it back at them with a message?" So he started printing epigrams on paychecks, T-shirts, sweatshirts and such. They were little aphorisms: "Start the day with love," "Do good, be good, see good" and so forth. "I sold millions of sweatshirts to lots of different kinds of people—some of them pretty rough," he says with an impish gleam, "and on every one of them was that sign: Love all, serve all. That must've done some good!"

Here we have Isaac talking dharma, love, spirit and energy—all huge ideas, all dumped into the same mixing bowl. Also in the bowl, of course, are the qualities of integrity, courage, inner truth, affection, politeness, caring, respect, intensity and power, to name but a few. This matter of reverence is obviously a huge, important subject, and also a disorderly one.

"Everybody loved the place," he repeats, beaming, "everybody felt bigger working there. We were famous. Just walk into the place and this great energy hit you immediately. Employees were proud of the place, from the dishwasher on up." He uses the words spirit, love, dharma and energy as though they are interchangeable.

Isaac successfully sold the Hard Rock Cafe and is enjoying continued success with The House of Blues, which he founded in Los Angeles with Dan Ackroyd.

The Screamer

Joe Black

Professional Speaker and Trainer
Author, *The Attitude Connection—Focus on Quality*

A young lady, recently hired by the hotel where my company was conducting a Continuous Improvement Seminar, pulled me aside and asked if she could talk with me. She told me she had been listening to my presentation on quality awareness for the past two days while she was preparing refreshments for our breaks. She wanted my opinion about a problem.

"What do you do when your boss is constantly screaming at you and cursing day in and day out? It's so unfair because no one has given me any training in how to do my job."

"What a sad but common problem," I thought. No one is born knowing how to do a job. He or she must be properly trained and educated as to the best way to accomplish the assigned tasks. Since no one comes to work wanting to make mistakes or wanting to have a bad day, mistakes are usually caused for two reasons:

1. A lack of proper education/training.

2. The lack of attention or an "I don't care" attitude.

The second reason is often but not always closely related to the first. Both are typically due to management not focusing on, and investing in, the proper training for their associates.

This young lady was obviously intelligent, and she wanted to do her best. I asked if she had talked with her boss about the problem.

"No," she responded. "I'm afraid of him."

Wanting to know more about her, I inquired if she felt comfortable sharing a little of her background. Carolyn told me about her family, where she was from, her educational background and work experience. Although she was a very smart person, she had not enjoyed many of the benefits you and I have received in life. Her self-confidence was low. Rather than blooming, she was wilting under her boss.

I explained that no person has the right to yell or curse at another, that she was a unique human being and deserved respect. If she allowed people to treat her with disrespect, she would contend with it all her life. How others treated her was her decision to make, not theirs.

She looked as though a revelation had dawned. "I really never stopped to realize that this is true." She thanked me, said she appreciated my time, and went on her way.

Two days later, I was in my hotel room when the telephone rang. It was Carolyn. "Mr. Black, could you meet me in the lobby? I want to talk with you ... I must talk with you."

I said I'd be right down. Several possible scenarios ran through my mind as the elevator whisked me down to the lobby.

There was Carolyn—all smiles. "Mr. Black, I've thought a lot about our conversation and I've read your book, *The Attitude Connection*." She continued, "I have just come from my boss' office. He began screaming at me again this afternoon and I asked him to sit down. To my surprise, he did. Then I told him, 'Stop screaming at me; you're hurting me. Please stop.' To my amazement, he replied, 'Why didn't you tell me before? I scream at everyone who works for me until they tell me to stop.'" She then assured me she would never again work for anyone who yelled at her.

"Carolyn, I'm proud of you. I hope things will be better between you and your boss now."

"Oh, he's not my boss anymore. I quit. After our conversation two days ago, I went to visit my friend at the Marriott Hotel. She's so happy there; she told me the Marriott folks all treat each other with respect. When I learned they had a position open, I applied. They hired me to start next week. I'm a smart person, Mr. Black. I don't have to take verbal abuse. I know that now." She thanked me and invited me to come to the Marriott to conduct our seminars next time we were in the area.

When she left, I felt like a million bucks! Isn't it amazing the positive influence we can have on other people's lives when we take the time to care?

Two events conclude this story:

1. The screaming boss stopped me the next day in the hall and said he understood I was the reason one of his best employees had left. "No, sir," I retorted, "you're the reason!"

2. I moved our next seminar to the Marriott Hotel. They truly are a quality organization and they don't scream at their associates!

A Master of Human Relations

Source Unknown

I will pay more for the ability to handle people than for any other talent under the sun.

John D. Rockefeller

Dale Carnegie used to tell a story about Charles Schwab, who was paid a salary of a million dollars a year in the steel business. He told Mr. Carnegie that he was paid this huge salary largely because of his ability to handle people.

One day as Schwab was walking through one of his mills, he discovered a group of men smoking directly under a "No Smoking" sign.

Instead of pointing at the sign and saying, "Hey, what's wrong with you guys—can't you read?" Schwab chatted casually with the men and never mentioned the fact the they were smoking under a "No Smoking" sign.

At the end of the conversation, he gave the men some cigars, and then, with a twinkle in his eye, he said, "I'd appreciate it if you'd smoke these cigars outside."

That was all he said—no lecture, no shaming, no demeaning put-downs. Surely the offenders knew that he was aware that they had broken a rule, and they most likely admired him for his approach. I am sure that, because he had been such a good sport with them, they were willing to reciprocate by being good sports with him.

The Fun Minute Manager: An Interview with Ken Blanchard

Joel Goodman
Director, The National Humor Project
Author, *Laffirmations* and *Playfair*
Coauthor, *Chicken Soup for the Laughing Soul* (forthcoming)
Editor, *Laughing Matters*, from which this interview is excerpted

Ken Blanchard
President, Blanchard Training and Development
Coauthor, *The One Minute Manager, Putting the One Minute Manager to Work*
and *The Power of Ethical Management*

People rarely succeed at anything unless they are having fun doing it.

La Rochefoucauld

I believe that the ultimate in self-actualization is when a person is confused about the difference between employment and recreation.

Ken Blanchard

Joel Goodman: Do you have any early memories about the role of humor in your life?

Ken Blanchard: In the sixth grade elementary school basketball championship, our school got to the finals. We played Lincoln, and they had this big guy who in sixth grade seemed he must have been well over six feet tall. All the kids on the team called him Meatball. I had one of those days you dream about—everything I tossed up went in. People couldn't believe it—we won.

At the end of the game we went in to change. Meatball was sitting on the bench. As I walked by I just patted him on the back and said, "Good game, Meatball." He jumped up, grabbed me by the shirt, threw me against his locker and said, "Only my friends call me Meatball." I don't know where I got the composure, but I said, "Well, then why don't we be friends!" He laughed like crazy, and thought it was the funniest thing he ever heard. He put me down and said, "You're all right, man."

JG: And that's why you're here today! Are there any other people from early in your life who played a role in your developing your sense of humor?

KB: My dad had the tremendous capacity to take a situation and find humor in it. During the Second World War, he was in the Marshall Islands in the Pacific, and 70% of his men were killed or wounded. Later, the guys I met said that one of the things that really kept them going was my father using the intercom system and finding humor in things.

When I went to junior high, I was nominated for president of the class, and I had to give a speech. Dad sat down to help me with the speech and he said, "The first thing you've got to recognize to give a speech is you need to get humor in here and you have to make people laugh."

On the day of the speeches, I got up in front of the entire seventh grade and said, "As the cow said to the farmer when the milking machine broke down, thanks for that warm hand." People got a big kick out of it. By the way, Meatball served as my campaign manager.

JG: Did you continue to receive a "warm hand" later in school?

KB: People just got to expect that humor was part of my style, and that I could find some humor in most any situation. I gave the graduation speech at both junior high and high school in front of thousands of people. What I noticed was that many other people gave talks and the audience looked very bored. I realized that I couldn't let people go more than a couple of minutes without a good laugh, or I knew I'd start to lose people.

So my quotient is to get in your serious points in about that two minutes that you've got them, and then you'd better hit 'em with some more humor.

JG: So that was really honed early on then. Down the road a bit, where else did you find humor ... or did humor find you?

KB: At Ohio University, I was teaching a Business Policy course. Using humor, we just had a marvelous time. I had never imagined that I would ever be in front of students with everybody laughing and enjoying. The ratings on the class were fabulous, and so I decided then to move into teaching, because the students said, "You're just not like any of the other professors because you're not dry." This was especially wonderful for me to hear, because I had known what it was like to be bored in class—most of my professors never really could see the funny side of anything.

So I started to use humor, and what's really interesting is people began to call me with stories that I could use. I like to look at reality and just call it the way it is. With humor in stories, people can laugh because they say, "That's just like my mother," or "That's just like me," and they become part of the thing.

JG: From my own experience in doing corporate consulting and in-house programs on the positive use of humor in management and organizations, I have bumped into people who say, "What are you talking about, humor, let's get down to the bottom line," or "Let's cut out the funny business." Any words of wisdom to managers who might find humor to be an effective tool?

KB: One of the classic concepts that we all learned in school was the difference between process and product. Product is the end result, what you're trying to accomplish, while process is how you go about doing it and the interaction. I heard this marvelous quote when I was in Japan: "Managing for profit or bottom line only is like playing tennis with your eye on the scoreboard and not on the ball." People who keep on saying "Let's get back to business," are forgetting the whole process piece, and the ball.

Through the use of humor and laughter you permit people to self-heal. Another quote that I really love is "In life, what you resist persists." Humor can be a wonderful release for people, because if you deal with what's bothering you, in the very process of dealing with it, it will go away. One of the neatest ways to deal with it is through humor—then everybody knows what you're doing, they all laugh and you don't have to say anything more.

Humor and laughter in organizations can increase the amount of feedback you can get, the honesty, and the capacity for people to tell you good things. All the solutions to problems in organizations are within your own people, but the problem is that half of them don't want to say anything, because they usually get zapped—you kill the messenger.

It's through humor that you can open up the lines of communication. People in our organization are willing to tell me things that they don't tell other people, because they know that I will receive it well, that I can and do laugh about the challenges we face.

JG: One of the tenets I put out in a number of the programs I do is that there's a difference between being a solemn manager and a serious manager. It's very appropriate to be serious about your job, but not to take yourself too seriously.

KB: That's the pride issue. False pride means you can't laugh at yourself. When you have self-esteem and things are in perspective, you laugh at yourself and your foibles. You're not up for grabs. As Norman Vincent Peale says, "You know that God did not make junk," and that you're okay.

It was interesting, on one of my birthdays, my staff threw a party for me. A whole bunch of them got together one night, and came up with 21 different skits that they could do on my behaviors. They finally picked about seven or eight and it was hysterical. I have pictures of me with tears coming out of my eyes. And my wife, Marge, said, "Watching that whole process I realized what a real character I was living with."

And I said, "Well, everybody's really a character—it's just that you wouldn't kid most people about their characterness, because they're too serious about it."

For my father, on his death bed, humor was still his main way of dealing with people. I'll never forget. He had a stroke, and was on a life support system. He was trying to tell me something I couldn't understand. A nurse came up and said, "Admiral, why don't you write your son a note." He handed Dad a clipboard. My father started to write, and I said with a laugh, "I couldn't even read his handwriting when he was feeling good!" So the nurse then wrote the alphabet in big letters, A-B-C, and suggested that my Dad just point to what he wanted to say. My father looked at me, got this twinkle in his eye, and pointed S-H-I-T. Looking at the funny side can get you through all kinds of things.

It's like Yogi Berra being asked, "Why did you win today?" He said, "We didn't make any wrong mistakes." Then somebody asked him, "If you had to divide 100% in baseball, what percent is mental and what is physical?" He said simply that 90% is mental and the other 50% is physical.

JG: Do you have any other favorite stories that you use in your programs to illustrate ideas or concepts?

KB: A famous playwright sent Churchill a note: "I'm sending you two tickets to my opening night. Bring a friend if you can find one." Churchill wrote back saying, "I really appreciate the invitation. I'm sorry I can't go the first night, but I'd like to go another night, if there is one."

Then there's the one about the little guy who's a clerk in a grocery store and this big Texan comes in who says, "Son, I want a half a head of lettuce." The clerk says, "Well, sir, I don't think we sell a half a head of lettuce." The Texan retorts, "Son, I don't think you heard me. I want a half a head of lettuce." The clerk says he'll go back and ask the manager. So he heads to the back of the store, not seeing the big Texan following him step by step. The clerk tells the manager, "There's some big jerk out there who wants a half a head of lettuce." All of a sudden, seeing the Texan behind him out of his left eye, he wheels around and blurts out, "And this nice man wants the other half."

JG: A brilliant example of aikido and rolling with the punches. Speaking of rolling with the punches, what about humor on the home front?

KB: I get a lot of letters about what I do concerning marriage. People ask me what's the number one criteria in marriage, and I say it's got to be humor. If you can't laugh at what you're doing in your relationship, you're really in bad trouble, because it can be a pain in the tail living with somebody else.

I've heard people say to Marge, "What's it like living with Ken?" The number one thing she describes about me is my humor. It's not in front of a crowd, it's just the two of us. One of my great joys is to hear her starting to giggle over something where I'll just take it and …

JG: Be merciless.

KB: It reminds me of my uncle who was a real character. People used to line up for him, because as a pediatrician, he made the parents so calm about their kids. I was reading recently that it's really clear doctors with good bedside manners have less chance of being sued than competent doctors with lousy bedside manners. "Malpractice insurance" is to know something about getting along with people and using humor effectively.

My wife recently had an operation, and she had a fabulous doctor. I can't imagine anybody ever suing him. I watched him come onto the floor of the hospital, and the nurses looked differently, the orderlies looked differently, everybody did. He came in with a smile and he had information on everything and he would kid. People just loved to be around him.

JG: Competence and inspiring confidence can go hand in hand. Do you think there's hope for us? Can we learn to develop these humor skills?

KB: We did some consulting in some school districts recently. The number one thing we found is that nobody in school was having fun anymore. The kids didn't want to be there, the teachers didn't want to be there, the principal didn't want to be there; even the janitors who used to do most of the counseling down in the boiler room didn't want to be there. Laughter is a lost art. Nothing in schools can be that serious, I mean, we're dealing with kids' lives—we need to laugh.

No situation can be dull if you're looking for the humor in it. And so everything is a potential learning experience.

FROM WHO TO WHY

James O'Toole

Author, *Leading Change: Overcoming the Ideology of Comfort and the Tyranny of Custom*

Don't find fault. Find a remedy.

Henry Ford

When James Houghton took over the Corning Glass Company, he knew he had to turn things around. New technologies and global competition demanded innovation.

Blocking his way was the company's tradition of being run as a dictatorship. Houghton had to eliminate its "management by fear" culture.

So he launched a quality program based on respect for individuals.

One critical event, early in the quality program, signaled the change.

Someone made a very costly mistake. On hearing the news, Houghton blurted out, "Who did it?"

Then he caught himself. His face reddened with embarrassment, and he rephrased his line of questioning:

"Why did it happen?"

"How can we fix it?"

"How can we make sure it doesn't happen again?"

From that defining moment of leadership "the successful transformation of Corning was assured."

SOURCE: Dilbert by Scott Adams. Reprinted by permission of United Feature Syndicate, Inc.

Taking Responsibility

Michael J. Wyman

Acknowledgment and Empowerment Consultant, Trainer and Coach

Everyone is responsible and no one is to blame.

Will Schutz

As a corporate consultant, I was asked to assist a company that had low morale and had been deeply in debt for the first three years of its existence. When I met the owner, all he talked about was how it takes a minimum of three years to break even and how his unsympathetic staff of part-time actors cared only about their salaries and bonuses and couldn't care less about his financial state or personal well-being.

I listened to his whole "victim drama"—as I had so often done with other CEOs—and then said, "If you want to turn your company around, you're going to have to take total responsibility for your situation." Then I asked, "Who or what do you believe is creating your financial failure, lack of success and low morale?"

He immediately said, "My staff, the economy and the competition."

I asked again, "Who or what do you believe is creating your failure or success?"

He paused, then said, "My staff, the economy and the competition."

I finally said, "If you want to turn your company around, you're going to have to accept that consciously or unconsciously you are responsible for creating your reality exactly the way it is."

With a look of surprise, he said, "How can that be?"

I said, "The powers of your beliefs, thoughts and feelings are all creating and attracting to you the people, experiences and events that are showing up in your personal and business life. The bottom line is that whatever you continue to acknowledge as your truth—be it positive or negative—continues to manifest. When you change your beliefs, thoughts and feelings, you will change your reality. As a matter of fact, the low morale, low self-esteem and low sales and income are all due to the negative attitude and limiting beliefs of you and your staff. Most people have no idea how powerful their acknowledgment of what they perceive reality to be really is."

Finally, he woke up, realized that what I was sharing was true and decided to work with me to change his beliefs about business and his attitude toward his staff. Once he consciously chose to go from the beliefs of "It takes three years to turn a profit, the economy stinks, my clients are disloyal and my staff doesn't care" to "My amazing new business now produces extraordinary and tangible financial results, the economy is great, my clients are loyal and my wonderful and creative staff really care about me and the company," his entire company transformed itself within one month.

One of the important ingredients within that unbelievable month was confronting the entire staff and waking them up to the fact that "There are no more free rides, and if you want a salary and bonuses, you are going to have to make sure the company at least breaks even, and better yet, makes a profit." No longer were they going to threaten their boss with leaving if he did not meet their demands. No longer was it going to be victim against victim—us against the boss. Now it was time for them to take total responsibility—along with the owner—to make sure that their attitudes, beliefs and feelings were aligned, positive and empowering, or they could leave the company immediately.

Those who accepted this truth raised their self-esteem higher than it had ever been and prospered greatly as did the company. Those who chose to continue to be victims, to be negative and to look for a free ride eventually quit or were asked to leave by the rest of the staff who had changed.

An amazing phenomenon takes place when CEOs or owners take total responsibility and change their core beliefs, attitudes and feelings about their staffs and their companies—the universe rearranges itself to accommodate and align with it to create this new reality. Those employees who are out of alignment or stuck in the past reality usually leave to find new places where they can be comfortable, which is usually with other victims. The cocreators stay on to become champions and victors.

Very shortly after this transformation took place, the company doubled its business and turned a profit, morale and self-esteem soared and the owner spent most of his time acknowledging his wonderful staff for their positive contributions to the great success of the company, the economy for being fantastic and his clients for being loyal and caring. He was a very happy man, and his employees were a very happy staff.

A few months later, after achieving even greater and greater success, the CEO unfortunately died, leaving the company up for grabs, but because the employees had all become so empowered by the extraordinary results they had produced together, they raised the needed money and bought the company from his family. To this day the company has become more and more successful in every way.

LET COMPLAINERS SOLVE THE PROBLEMS

Excerpted from the Pryor Report and based on
Maverick: The Success Story Behind the World's Most Unusual Workplace by Ricardo
Semler

Ricardo Semler, CEO of the successful Brazilian manufacturing firm,
Semco, is a strong believer in participative management.

He extended this philosophy, therefore, to an element in his plant
that fueled strong passions—the cafeteria.

Employees felt it had the worst food of any institution without bars.
So he encouraged them to form a cafeteria committee that took responsibility for selecting a supplier, monitoring quality and setting prices.

Jair Pinto, a clerk in accounting, who had been with the firm for 25
years, was elected its head.

Jair was known for his persistence. He would stalk a customer who
fell behind on his bills like a Doberman greeting an unannounced visit at
midnight.

But he wasn't being assertive about the food, so the workers decided he needed some motivation.

One day, the dessert served was a substance barely identifiable as
pudding. When Jair sat down with his meal, a worker at his table got up
and nonchalantly dumped his pudding into Jair's tray, and then walked
out without saying a word. Moments later, another worker did the same
thing. Then another. In ten minutes, Jair's tray was a mountain of pudding.

The next day, Jair began to monitor the food. He weighed the steaks
to make sure they met the 125 gram standard specified in the contract. He
was all over the kitchen staff, too. Soon the quality of the food ceased to
be a source of complaint.

The next issue was cost. Semco subsidized 70% of the meals served.
The cafeteria committee, however, instituted a "Robin Hood Meal Plan"
under which employees paid on a sliding scale based on income. Managers and engineers were asked to pay 95% of the cost of their food, for
example, while floor sweepers paid just 5%.

A few supervisors felt unfairly treated and responded by bringing
their lunch from home. The committee did nothing, waiting for the supervisors to realize 95% was cheaper than 100% of their food costs. After
a few weeks, they did.

Today, those supervisors defend the Robin Hood plan. They realize
what it means to their lower wage colleagues.

Editor's Note: When people complain, turn the problem over to them to solve.
They'll find ways you had never considered or wouldn't dare propose.

The Bridge Between Self-Esteem and a Changing Work Environment

Bob Moawad

President, Edge Learning Institute
President, National Association for Self-Esteem
Author, *Whatever it Takes*

If there was a time in your organization when the only constant was change, have you noticed recently that even change is changing? Your organization may be one of the many that is going through restructuring, reorganization, rightsizing, etc. You may have recently implemented continuous improvement processes, which means a new way of working together, changing job descriptions, layoffs and perhaps job eliminations. Organizations continue to seek that irreducible core of permanent employees that will allow them to be competitive. Have you been asked to do more with less? Have you been asked to change your management or leadership style that did you well for many years but is not part of a participative management and employee involvement culture?

Many people feel a loss of esteem when they're asked to question their 15 to 25 years of learning and doing something and are told to do it another way. Many have defined competence as expending the minimum energy for the maximum outcome. We've developed habits of working and managing. We've mastered something and now we're being asked to do it differently. We need to unlearn old habits. The doing of things in a new way is a lot more effortful and comes with feelings of unfamiliarity, uncertainty, loss of control and surprises galore.

How do you feel about total quality management, self-directing work teams, downsizing, empowerment, a changing culture and competing globally? While the organization is shrinking, midmanagement responsibilities are changing drastically. Team decision making is becoming a norm. If you have tied your entire sense of worth to your job description, then there's no doubt, your self-esteem may be on thin ice.

During these changing times you want to reaffirm your capability to learn new skills. Recognize that learning is not a task to be completed but a process to be continued. You can learn to operate a laptop computer and change your "old" ways of doing business.

I'm reminded of Ed Stitt of Trenton, New Jersey, who at 87 was enrolled full-time in a community college. Ed's comment was, "It keeps my brain alive and keeps me from getting 'old-timer's disease.'" Gladys Clappison is enrolled full-time at the University in Ames, Iowa, living in a dormitory at age 82, working on her PhD. When asked what she was studying, Gladys responded, "History—I've lived most of it, I may as well get credit for it." Selma Plott completed her bachelor of arts degree at age 100 at the University of Toronto. You can keep learning and growing too!

A person with high self-esteem and a sense of self-efficacy has the confidence to be retrained and develop an "I can do it" attitude in any situation they may face. A person with high self-esteem will tackle new ways of doing things with the belief they had when they were small which was that anything worth doing is worth doing poorly and uncomfortably—for at least a little while.

If you believe your self-esteem is based on what you do, then when you don't, you aren't! That could leave your sense of self-esteem in a very precarious position during these changing times. You are not your job description; you are not your almost vested pension; your worth is innate. Self-esteem is not egotism, nor is it an intellectual inventory of your favorable characteristics and assets. It is, however, how warm, loving and appreciative you feel toward yourself in spite of your mistakes, your weaknesses, your changing job description and your human frailties. If you have high self-esteem, you know you're good and you wear it well.

Try affirming, "I am the one and only and the very best me there ever was. I'm always growing in wisdom and in love. No one in the entire world is more or less worthy, more or less important than I am. We differ in innate talents, etc., but not in worth. I'm glad I'm me. In spite of the many challenges I face in my professional and personal life, I'm the kind of person with whom I'd love to spend the rest of my life." You may as well. Consider the alternative.

A few guidelines and "personal ad campaigns" you may want to keep in mind during these changing times are:

- Recognize that you're beautiful and unique just the way you are—the one and only and the very best there ever was.

- Get away from believing you have to stack up to others. You're only in competition with your own best self. Competing with others is not only a key to mediocrity, it can also be very damaging to one's esteem level.

- Recognize that your self-worth is innate and not determined by actions and decisions. You may lose a job, but you're not a loser. You may fail in a project, but you're not a failure.

- Accept 100% accountability for your choices and decisions. Recognize and accept the fact that you create your own tensions, positive or negative, with your reactions or responses to what is happening in your world. Circumstances and other people do not make you tense; only you can make you tense. (Are you comfortable with that idea, or does that idea make you tense?)

- Recognize that mistakes are stepping stones to achievement. If you are laid off or displaced from your job, give yourself the opportunity to make and learn from your mistakes as you seek new employment—go back for an advanced degree, etc. During changing times it may well be that your attitude quotient (AQ) is more important than your intelligence quotient (IQ). The late Buckminster Fuller said, "All of my advances were made by mistake. You discover what is by getting rid of what isn't."

- Perhaps it would be wise to adopt the attitude of Thomas Edison when asked if he felt like a failure after 25,000 unsuccessful attempts to store electricity in a box, which was ultimately to become the electrical storage battery. His response was, "We never perceive ourselves as failing at Edison Inventions, Inc. We have false starts, temporary setbacks, learning mistakes. Basically, our approach to these 25,000 attempts is that we've discovered 25,000 different ways, so far, not to store electricity. We must be getting close to a breakthrough." That attitude will bode you well.

- Enjoy each day one day at a time, recognizing that life is a journey to be embraced moment by moment. There are twin thieves that will rob you of your effectiveness today and damage your esteem. Those thieves are (a) yesterday, which is ancient history, and (b) tomorrow, which is a promissory note and guaranteed to no one. I hope you didn't buy into the pop psychology of the 1970s that attempted to convince us that today is the first day of the rest of our lives. Should you have ever taken a logic or epistemology class, you're aware that the fatal flaw in this theory is that none of us is guaranteed the rest of life. Learning to live in the now and celebrating each day with an attitude of gratitude is very esteeming. Mark Twain once said, "Live each day in such a way that if you were to die today even the undertaker would be sad." Stop and smell the roses.

- Give yourself plenty of praise for the effort. Praise pays even when things are not going well.

If you are in a period of transition, here are some additional guidelines:

- Talk to yourself gently with affection.
- Trust your inner voice and intuition.
- Be committed to developing your full potential and creativity.

- Forgive yourself. Get over that guilty feeling.
- Have fun. If you don't feel like smiling, smile anyhow. You'll think of something.
- Know when to say yes and when to say no.
- Take in the affection and compliments of others. Allow others to be your friends during these challenging times. You have the right to expect others to treat you with dignity and respect, but first begin by treating yourself that way.
- Choose not to be a complainer. It's harmful to you and those around you.
- Raise your moment-to-moment joy in living without anything special having to happen.

Remember, attitudes are contagious, and there's nothing more attractive (or employable) than a naturally happy, fulfilled, alive human being. The difficulties of life are intended to make us better, not bitter.

- Think and act positively.
- Give yourself credit for jobs well done.
- Talk daily to your favorite people.
- Plan ahead but be flexible.
- Exercise and relax.

I hate these employee motivation seminars.

- Choose not to waste your precious present with guilt over the past or worry about the future. Remember, we move toward and become like that image of our world we hold uppermost in our mind.

- It takes less energy to complete an unpleasant task "right now" than to worry about it all day.

- Choose not to associate with negative people.

- Watch your diet. Maintain proper nutrition.

- Realize that holidays, vacations and hobbies are important.

- Plan to do something today that gives you energy—something you love to do, something just for you.

- Be a "good finder" versus a "fault finder." Catch yourself and others in the act of doing things right.

3 The Importance of Caring

Everything starts with the manager. Does he care about people?

Jim Treybig
President and CEO, Tandem Computers

People don't care how much you know until they know how much you care.

John Hanley
President and CEO, Lifespring

SOURCE: In the Bleachers by Steve Moore. Reprinted with permission: Tribune Media Services.

Threads

James Autry

Former President, the magazine division of Meredith Publishing
Author, *Love and Profit: The Art of Caring Leadership*

*We lead by being human. We do not lead by being corporate, by being
professional or by being institutional.*

Paul Hawken
Founder, Smith & Hawken

Sometimes you just connect,
like that,
no big thing maybe
but something beyond the usual business stuff.
It comes and goes quickly
so you have to pay attention, a change in the eyes
when you ask about the family, a pain flickering behind
the statistics
about a boy and a girl in school,
or about seeing them every other Sunday.
An older guy talks about his bride,
a little affectation after twenty-five years.
A hot-eyed achiever laughs before you want him to.
Someone tells you about his wife's job
or why she quit working to stay home.
An old joker needs another laugh on the way
to retirement.
A woman says she spends a lot of her salary
on an au pair
and a good one is hard to find
but worth it because there's nothing more important
than her baby.
Listen.
In every office
you hear the threads
of love and joy and fear and guilt,
the cries for celebration and reassurance,
and somehow you know that connecting those
threads
is what you are supposed to do
and business takes care of itself.

WHAT'S IN A NAME?

Robert Levering and Milton Moskowitz

Coauthors, *The 100 Best Companies to Work for in America*

The simple act of paying positive attention to people has a great deal to do with productivity.

Thomas Peters and Robert Waterman, Jr.

First Federal's chairman and CEO, Bill Mortensen, knows virtually everybody by first name. Penny Resnick started at FirstFed as a temporary worker. "My very first day here," she told us, "I was sitting up here on the 12th floor at the desk when some man walked by me and said, 'Good morning, Penny. How are you?'

"And I said, 'Fine, thanks.' He walked away and I looked at the receptionist, and I said, 'Who was that?'

"And she turned back to me and said, 'That was the CEO.' And I thought, 'The CEO took the time to find out a temporary's first name? That must be a wonderful man to work for!' Here I am seven years later and he is a wonderful man to work for. This company is a wonderful place to work."

This seeming informality, ironically, is a formal policy. On the first page of "A Personal Guide to Success at First Federal," it is written: "At First Federal, we operate on a first name basis. We go about our work in a businesslike way, but we feel that work should be enjoyable and that we can all be friendly and cheerful while we are accomplishing the tasks which are assigned to us. We believe that EVERYONE in our organization is important and that each activity is as important as another."

Mortensen explained the policy: "I try to be on a first name basis with everybody. There is nothing that makes you feel worse than to have been at a place for a certain period of time and people don't know your name.

SOURCE: Dilbert by Scott Adams. Reprinted by permission of United Feature Syndicate, Inc.

We all love to hear somebody call us. And if the person looks at you and they can't remember who you are, it's very deflating. In some ways I think management has an ability to deflate more than they have an ability to motivate. I don't know how much you can really motivate, but I do know you can demotivate. We assume people want to do a good job, work hard, be proud of where they work and be proud of their own work."

A Most Important Question

JoAnn C. Jones

During my second month of nursing school our professor gave us a pop quiz. I was a conscientious student and had breezed through the questions, until I read the last one: "What is the first name of the woman who cleans the school?"

Surely this was some kind of joke. I had seen the cleaning woman several times. She was tall, dark-haired and in her 50s, but how would I know her name? I handed in my paper, leaving the last question blank.

Before class ended, one student asked if the last question would count toward our quiz grade. "Absolutely," said the professor. "In your careers you will meet many people. All are significant. They deserve your attention and care, even if all you do is smile and say hello."

I've never forgotten that lesson. I also learned her name was Dorothy.

CONSISTENCY AND EQUITY

Dr. Timothy Johnson
Chair, Obstetrics and Gynecology
University of Michigan at Ann Arbor

The one thing you've got to do is have respect for people if you are going to function or participate as a leader. You've got to have a lot of respect for everybody. You've got to have respect for the janitor and for the president of the company because neither one can work without the other one. That kind of respect as a team player and multidisciplinary is very, very important.

"Consistency" and "equity." Those are two of my favorite words. I think people really do well if they know that you are going to be there in a consistent fashion. They know how you are going to respond to a situation. It's very empowering for them because then they know how to prepare things. If you are not consistent in your responses to situations, people never know what to expect or how to do the work that needs to be done before it gets to your level. I think people know well how I'm going to respond. Since I do it in a consistent fashion, they feel pretty comfortable with what they give me in terms of work product or with the issues they bring me in terms of questions or challenges. Usually these are things they can think out before coming to me.

When I came to this department, women who were doing exactly the same jobs as the men were being paid $40,000 to $50,000 a year less.

Women with exactly the same background and exactly the same training were being significantly disadvantaged economically. So when I talk about equity, it's not just workplace equity but there has to be financial equity, there has to be work load equity. And it works both ways. One of the first things I did was to spend two years getting financial equity into the system so that the people felt like they were being paid in a fashion they could understand, that they were being fairly treated, with equal pay for equal work type opportunities.

The Invisible Sign

Mary Kay Ash

Founder and Chairman Emeritus, Mary Kay Cosmetics
Author, *Mary Kay on People Management* and *You Can Have It All*

Every person is special! I sincerely believe this. Each of us wants to feel good about himself or herself, but to me it is just as important to make others feel the same way. Whenever I meet someone, I try to imagine him wearing an invisible sign that says:

MAKE ME FEEL IMPORTANT!

I respond to this sign immediately, and it works wonders.

Some people, however, are so caught up in themselves that they fail to realize that the other person wants to feel important too.

I once waited in a long reception line, and when I finally got to shake hands with the company's sales manager, he treated me as if I didn't exist. I'm sure he doesn't remember the incident; in fact, he probably was never aware of how much he had hurt me. Yet, after all these years, I still remember—so it obviously had a powerful impact on me. I learned an important lesson about people that day, which I have never forgotten: *No matter how busy you are, you must take time to make the other person feel important!*

Many years ago I wanted to buy a new car. It was at the time when two toned cars had just been introduced, and I had my heart set on a black and white Ford. Since I never liked to buy what I couldn't afford, I had saved up enough money to pay cash. The car was going to be my birthday present to myself. With money in my purse, off I went to the Ford dealer's showroom.

Obviously the salesman didn't take me seriously. He had seen me drive up in my old car and assumed that I couldn't afford to buy a new one. In those days women couldn't get credit as easily as a man could, so very few of us ever purchased cars for ourselves. We weren't what salesmen considered "live prospects." The Ford representative would hardly give me the time of day. If he was trying to make me feel unimportant, he couldn't have done a better job. At noontime he simply excused himself, saying he was late for a lunch date. I wanted that car in the worst way, so I asked to see the sales manager. But he was out and wouldn't be back until after one o'clock. So, with time to kill, I decided to take a walk.

Across the street I strolled into a Mercury dealer's showroom—just to look, for I still intended to buy that black and white Ford. They had a yellow model on the floor, and although I liked it very much, the sticker price was more than I had planned to spend. However, the salesman was so courteous and made me feel as though he really cared about me. When he found out it was my birthday, he excused himself and returned a few minutes later to talk to me again. Fifteen minutes later a secretary brought him a dozen roses, which he handed to me for my birthday. I felt like a million dollars! Needless to say, I bought a yellow Mercury instead of a black and white Ford.

That salesman got the sale because he made me feel important. It didn't matter to him that I was a woman driving an old car. I was a human being—and in his eyes that meant I was somebody special. He had seen the invisible sign. Every manager should understand that God has planted seeds of greatness in every human being. Each of us is important, and a good manager can bring these seeds to fruition! It's unfortunate that most of us go to our graves with our music still unplayed! It's been said that we use only 10% of our God given ability, and that the other 90% is never tapped. Look at Grandma Moses, who started painting at the age of 75. She went on to become a world renowned artist, but certainly she must have had her talent at an earlier age. Wouldn't it have been a pity if Grandma Moses had never realized her God given artistic ability?

Make People Feel Important.
They Are!

I believe every person has the ability to achieve something important, and with that in mind I regard everyone as special. A manager should feel this way about people, but it's an attitude that can't be faked. You've got to be honestly convinced that every human being is important.

This is a basic lesson, one that you have probably heard many times before. Yet I remind you of it because many business people become so involved in their work that they forget to apply it. "Business is business, Mary Kay," they tell me. "You don't have to treat employees that way. My workers shouldn't expect me to make them feel important. That's not what I'm paid for."

But they're dead wrong. Making people feel important is precisely what a manager is paid for—because making people feel important motivates them to do better work. It was John D. Rockefeller who said, "I will pay more for the ability to deal with people than for any other commodity under the sun." High morale is a significant factor in increasing productivity, which means that a good manager should continually strive to boost the self-esteem of every individual in his or her organization.

My experience with people is that they generally *do what you expect them to do!* If you expect them to perform well, they will; conversely, if you expect them to perform poorly, they'll probably oblige. I believe that average employees who try their hardest to live up to your high expectations of them will do better than above average people with low self-esteem. Motivate your people to draw on that untapped 90% of their ability, and their level of performance will soar!

How does a manager make people feel important? First, by *listening* to them. Let them know you respect their thinking, and let them voice their opinions. (As an added bonus, you might learn something!) A friend of mine once told me about an executive of a large retail operation who told one of his branch managers, "There's nothing you could possibly tell me that I haven't already thought about before. Don't ever tell me what you think unless I ask you. Is that understood?" Imagine the loss of self-esteem that branch manager must have felt. It must have taken all the wind out of his sails and adversely affected his performance. When an individual's self-esteem is deflated, his level of energy is decreased. On the other hand, when you make a person feel a great sense of importance, he or she will be walking on cloud nine and the level of energy will skyrocket. You'll start the adrenaline flowing—and a kitten will become a tiger!

Responsibility without Authority Can Be Destructive.

People also feel important when they're given responsibility. But responsibility without authority can destroy a person's self-esteem. Have you ever noticed a little girl's reaction when she's been given her first babysitting assignment with her younger brother? She bubbles with excitement, because she has received the status of a grown-up. But if she is given the responsibility to watch after him, she should also be given the authority to send him to bed early if he misbehaves. That retail executive not only failed to listen to his branch manager, but he stripped him of all authority to make decisions. Consequently the branch manager developed low self-esteem and left the company for a major competitor. When given authority as well as responsibility in the new job, he began to feel good about himself and contributed innovative retailing concepts to his new employer. His contributions were so valuable, in fact, that he was rapidly promoted to a higher position than his former boss.

An attorney told me about a meeting his firm conducted for the officers of a local bank. One of his partners was in charge of making the arrangements for a luncheon and had sent out for cold cuts from a nearby deli. The law firm didn't make a very good impression. Several weeks later a female law clerk was given the responsibility, along with the authority, to arrange a luncheon meeting with another bank—with a slightly higher budget.

Knowing how important the luncheon was to the firm, the clerk felt honored to be responsible. She prepared delicious cold hors d'oeuvres at her home the night before and had some hot foods delivered from a restaurant in the building. The clerk acted as hostess, greeting each banker as he or she walked into the firm's offices. She did a wonderful job because the responsibility of being in charge of the luncheon made her feel important. The affair was a huge success. Several notes were received from the bankers commenting on the lovely luncheon, and shortly thereafter the bank began giving some of its law business to the firm.

Let People Know You Appreciate Them.

I recommend that you frequently let your people know how much you appreciate them. I've never yet met a person who didn't want to be appreciated—and if that's the way you feel, you should express your appreciation. Even if it's only for showing up for work on time let the person know that you value punctuality. "I think it's great, Jack, that you arrive at the office every morning at eight o'clock sharp. I admire people who are punctual." Say that to a worker and notice how rarely he comes in late thereafter. Or perhaps you like a person's politeness or gentle mannerisms. There has to be something to appreciate in every person—let it be known. Don't keep it a secret!

At Mary Kay Cosmetics we believe in putting our beauty consultants and sales directors on a pedestal. Of all people, I most identify with them, because I spent many years as a salesperson. My attitude of appreciation for them permeates the company. When our salespeople visit the home office, for example, we go out of our way to give them the red carpet treatment. Every person in the company treats them royally.

As you probably have heard, based on sales volume we provide pink Cadillacs for our sales directors; to my knowledge we were the first company to award such a fine automobile to so many people. We chose Cadillacs because they have always epitomized excellence. When a Mary Kay consultant drives a pink Cadillac, it really is a "trophy on wheels," and she is recognized as a person who has done an outstanding job. It signifies that she is very important in our organization. And, of course, once she achieves this important status, she doesn't ever want to relinquish the privilege.

We go first class across the board, and although it's expensive, it's worth it, because our people are made to feel important. For example, each year we take our top sales directors and their spouses on deluxe trips, to

Hong Kong, Bangkok, London, Paris, Geneva and Athens to mention a few. We spare no expense, and although it costs a lot extra per person to fly the Concorde, cruise on the Love Boat, or book suites at the elegant Georges V in Paris, it is our way of telling them how important they are to our company. Even in cities that are used to pomp and ceremony, we attract considerable attention. People in the streets stop to watch our beautiful women being escorted from the hotel to limousines, wondering who they were. Those women felt like royalty, and to us they are!

From the beginning we have always believed in going first class with our people. If something is too expensive, we'd rather forget it than economize. For instance, we might settle for one elegant banquet a year instead of two moderate ones. Why do we do it this way? Well, think of the feeling of importance you get from dining at a first rate restaurant. Everything is perfectly done—the cordial greeting of the maitre d', the exquisitely prepared food, everything—and it gives you a sense of satisfaction not experienced in a less elegant establishment.

Just as a fine restaurant extends itself to make its customers feel special, we do everything we can to make our people feel the same way. And if they don't, we're not doing our job. I think it's essential that every manager remember that invisible sign:

MAKE ME FEEL IMPORTANT!

Jessie's Glove

Rick Phillips
International Sales and Management Trainer

I do a lot of management training each year for Circle K Corporation, a national chain of convenience stores.

Among the topics we address in our seminars is the retention of quality employees, a real challenge to managers when considering the available pay scale in the service industry.

During these discussions, I ask the participants, "What has caused you to stay long enough to become a manager?" Some time back a new manager took the question and responded slowly, her voice almost breaking; she said, "It was a $19 baseball glove."

Cynthia told the group that she originally took the Circle K clerk job as an interim position while she looked for better employment. On her second or third day behind the counter, she received a phone call from her 9-year-old son, Jessie. She explained that as a single mother, money was very tight and she had to tell Jessie that her first check would have to be used for bills and that perhaps she could buy his Little League glove with her second or third check.

When Cynthia arrived for work the next morning, Patricia, the store manager, asked her to come to the small room in back of the store that served as an office. Cynthia thought perhaps she had done something wrong or left some part of her job incomplete from the day before. She was concerned and confused.

Cynthia then told us that Patricia handed her a box and said, "I overheard you talking to your son yesterday and I know that it is hard to explain things to kids. This is a baseball glove for Jessie because he may not understand how important he is even though you have to pay bills before you can buy gloves. You know we can't pay good people like you as much as we would like to. But we do care and I want you to know you are important to us."

The story of the thoughtfulness, empathy and love of a convenience store manager demonstrated vividly that people remember more about how an employer cares than about how the employer pays. An important lesson for the price of a Little League baseball glove.

CARING AND THE BOTTOM LINE

Christina Campbell

CEO and President, Christina Campbell and Company
General Partner, Supercuts-Franchise

We launched 1996 as the year of service and caring—not in the traditional business sense—but service beyond self-concern. This focus was a direct result of a conversation I had with an employee at our annual employee Christmas party in Dallas. The party had a country western theme, great music, great food and, of course, great people. After dancing to "We Are Family," our theme song, I went to sit down.

At that moment, Kendall Scott Eastep—we all call him "Scottie"—came up to me. He has been a hairstylist since 1991 and is now confined to a wheelchair as a result of AIDS. He had a big smile on his face and thanked me for the party. He said he almost didn't come because his wheelchair was so old, embarrassing and cumbersome. When he told his physical therapist, she found him a state of the art wheelchair that truly matched Scottie's dapper outfit.

Scottie said he was doing well and planned to be at our Christmas party next year—"I wouldn't miss it for the world." Then he said, "You know, Christina, during the past year I have had to be in and out of the hospital and I am so grateful to the Supercuts family at Oaklawn for their care and support of me. I have had those days when my heart and mind were strong but my body just couldn't support me standing on my feet."

Then tears started in his eyes as he said, "This last time I came out of the hospital—when I arrived home—there were my friends from the salon cleaning my house and preparing for my homecoming! It really made a difference. They were doing this on their own time and just for me." He added, "They know how fastidious I am about having my home looking the way I like it." He took my hand and thanked me for "caring" and said he had better get back to the party—he didn't want to miss a moment of fun.

I wiped a tear from my eye, started to smile and said to myself, "Thanks, Scottie, I don't want to miss a minute myself."

Just a few days ago I received a report of our stores cuts per day growth for 1995, and Scottie's store was in first place! Why am I not surprised!

The Power of Four Letter Words!

Anita Roddick

Founder and Chief Executive, The Body Shop International PLC

Using feminine principles in business is wonderful—leading a company with gut feelings, instinct, intuition, passion. Very strong female ethics revolve around the concept of caring and sharing, and I still believe that women can change the marketplace.

I have long been associated with the four letter words that make market speculators shudder for fear my expletives might lower the share price. So why is it so hard to make the headlines with those four letter words that are used just as often, if not more, in my company: love, give, care, feel, hope, fair, soul and true—all to be found in work, my all-time favorite four letter word?

I have always believed that you can bring your heart to work. Most of us spend most of our time at work. It is the place where we have our greatest daily contact with others, where we expend creative energy and where we form relationships. To fail to understand the role that work plays in the development of people would be wrong. For me, the workplace is much less a factory for the production of goods and much more an incubator for the human spirit.

The workplace is where the compulsive search for connection, common purpose and a sense of friendship and neighborhood can find a special place. It is where a continuous sense of spiritual education can take place, and where self-esteem gives us the ability to express ourselves and to contribute selflessly to a greater good.

Management from the Heart

I wonder if anyone really knows how to "manage" the human spirit. I know I don't. But if leaders would just learn to manage from the heart, great things in business can and will happen.

The people I work with are mostly young and mostly females whose ethics are about "care." They are in search of something more than a kind of nine-to-five death. They want to find deep meaning in what they do. In them, I look for that secret ingredient called "enthusiasm." Enthusiasm created from the heart guides your whole system so that everything seems possible. It increases self-esteem in the workplace of its own free will. But enthusiasm cannot be managed; it cannot be taught. It's simply habit-forming and contagious and is caught from the people you work with.

It's All to Do with Communication

Communication is the single most important tool leaders possess. Competence has to be blended with compassion if any person is to be an effective leader of others. It doesn't matter how enthusiastic you are or how passionately you care. If you can't communicate that, you might as well not be there.

Real communication has nothing to do with hierarchy or organizational charts. It is not about how quickly you can send messages across the globe via computer networks. It's not about facts and figures buried among glossy PR-speak. It's about heart-to-heart, open dialogue. Creating dialogue, in whatever way, is the key.

I believe in getting out of my chair and moving around the workplace. I don't wait for people to come and see me. I go and talk to staff, without appointments. It's more insightful taking them by surprise and talking about their work on their patch. Also, when I see an interesting gathering of people, I will often gatecrash their meeting. The communication is spontaneous and in this way I find out more about what is happening in the company, and how people are reacting, than by sitting in my office with the door closed. It works both ways: staff abandon the telephone or the e-mail and come over to see me for a face-to-face chat (and a hug!).

But as the company grows, it's becoming harder to see everyone and share news in an informal way. My solution to this is to have my own newsletter in which I talk personally to staff across the world. I share stories of my travels, let staff know what's getting my creative juices flowing, tell them where I see us going, and—this is the important bit—I ask them for their feedback, their ideas and their hopes.

Developing Tactics for Empowerment

In one edition, we inserted a fax sheet for staff to return to me with their thoughts and feelings (a simple tactic that was almost overlooked because it was so simple). Boy, did we ever get a huge response.

Giving staff the opportunity to tell the CEO what they are feeling about the company is empowering and is a big boost to self-esteem. Empowerment means that each staff member is responsible for creating the company's culture. Empowerment, however, doesn't appear overnight. It takes time to gain and develop trust and respect.

It also comes in many guises: from writing on sheets hung on the walls of lavatories (honest, the staff speak out, the directors respond), to talking about values in two hour meetings with a board of directors and a cross section of staff, to conducting a full social audit of all stakeholders.

The directors may not want to hear everything that's being said, but knowing that they listen is important for encouraging staff to be true to themselves. Whatever the tactic employed, it is vital that everyone, no matter what their position, is given the opportunity to talk straight to the person at the top of the company and have their views heard and responded to in some way. Being heard is often a reward in itself.

Successful Strategies for Self-Development

I have a board above my office door that reads, "Department of the Future." In the future, I don't see how business can operate in isolation of the community. One of the most important jobs I have is to develop more opportunities for our staff to spend company time in the service of the local community, to be able to measure their greatness by those experiences and to find the heroes in themselves by caring for others.

All staff at The Body Shop are allowed paid time off, half a day per month, to take part in a community project of their choice. Whether caring for locally disadvantaged people, cleaning up the local environment or working with sick animals, staff can feel connected and uplifted. It is another of those not so secret ingredients that help our staff raise their sense of self.

Let me share another example with you. In 1990, shocked by the news coverage of the legacies of Nicolae Ceausescu's 26 years of dictatorship in Romania, I went out myself to see how we could help. I was horrified by what I saw. The horror filled my thoughts for weeks. But within just six weeks, we'd set up the Romanian Relief Drive. Staff clamored to be among the volunteers to go out there and help refurbish the orphanages, hold babies with AIDS and give them something many had never had before—love and care.

Now called the Eastern Europe Relief Drive, the program is still run, on next to nothing, by a handful of young staff members. Their commitment to helping the children in Romania and Albania can be humbling to us all. Their desire to help out has been shared by over 450 members of our staff from around the world who have been out to work as volunteers. The staff come back changed people. Their values suddenly take a leap into a previously unknown source of power for them. They start dreaming of noble purposes.

Politics of Consciousness

For too long, business has been teaching that politics and commerce are two different arenas. I disagree. Political awareness and activism must be incorporated into business. In a global world, there are no value-free or politically disentangled actions. Few motivating forces are more potent than giving your staff an opportunity to exercise and express their idealism to influence change—locally, nationally and globally.

Campaigning is not only about changing the world, but changing how individuals work together. Giving people a sense of their own power is as much a part of the goal as resolving the issues. It provides a new forum for staff education. They can get into issues and into areas where they might not normally ever venture. Campaigns are a fabulous way of integrating the behavior of staff at work with the values they hold dear as individual citizens in the larger world. Business leaders need to realize that this is the way forward in the workplace: the personal becomes the political, which becomes the global.

Helping Women Find a Voice

It is perhaps ironic that the platform I have chosen to shout out for is women's rights in the cosmetics industry. It is an industry still run by men, who create false needs by preying on women's insecurity. For 20 years, I have been asking the same old questions. Why does the cosmetics industry only concern itself with what you see? Why doesn't it celebrate how you feel about yourself, what you care about, what you do, where your sense of passion and relationship is? Is it really only skin deep?

The outward appearance doesn't say anything about the soul or character, what women are feeling and thinking, what they care about, and what they feel strongly about. As the majority of my work force are women, it is vital for me to understand what makes women tick at work and what raises their self-esteem.

Although women make up two thirds of my company's total work force in the United Kingdom, the ratio of female senior managers to male is, very disappointingly, less than a third. I get so frustrated, therefore, when I see how women are often too willing to give away power. Part of the reason for that is a lack of confidence in themselves, where self-esteem obviously plays a role. Women *must* be willing to be powerful. They must cherish the prospect of leadership. If they don't, they are not helping themselves or other women.

With this in mind, we've initiated a program within the company for women in management. In our first course this year, we brought over a lecturer from Stanford University whose intensive course focused on personal development, leadership styles and management techniques. Those who attended wanted to build on the experience and create a women's network, as a forum for sharing. This is music to my ears.

But what about all the other hundreds of women at the head office? How do they feel? To find out, we did a spot survey of women from the different areas of the company. It was a very heartening and reassuring exercise. We asked, "How does your self-esteem get boosted at work?" They were asked to list just one or two examples, but many a long list came back! Here's what matters to them at work:

"When my daughter's friends are envious of her because her mum works at The Body Shop!"—Head of Department

"Freedom of choice—we can wear whatever we like to work."—Administrator

"Feeling that vision and ideas are not underrated or ignored—everyone can have a voice."—Director

"When directors bother to say hello."—Trainer

"Being told that I inject my personal values in everything I do at work."—Product Manager

"Explaining how this company works and talking about our values and visions."—Franchise Coordinator

"The more varied my work, the better I feel at knowing I have managed to do it all."—Administrator, Supply

"Knowing that the company is involved with human rights campaigns, charity work, fair trade, animal protection and doing its best to protect the environment."—Head of Department, R&D

"A combination of believing in the products and an empathy for the company policy of social responsibility. The ability to change things."—Studio Manager

"Working with people who are not afraid to laugh at themselves."—Tour Leader

"Being given the time and respect to fulfill my voluntary role of departmental environmental advisor."—Researcher

"The trust that the company places in me to accomplish my vision within an accountable and safe structure."—Project Leader

"The number of people who genuinely contact me for my advice or my perspective."—HR Manager

"Knowing that people are listening to me, taking in what I say and are truly appreciative of the time I have spent with them."—Coordinator, Inductions

And what appeared to be the easiest route to increased self-esteem? The obvious, but often forgotten, "Thank you"!

It's a Crazy, Complicated Journey

There are no rules or formulas for success. You just have to live it and do it. Knowing this gives us enormous freedom to experiment toward what we want. Believe me, it's a crazy, complicated journey. It's trial and error. It's opportunism. It's quite literally, "Let's try lots of this stuff and see how it works." I'm proud to look at my company and see that we're at least on the right track. It's taken years of experimentation, experience, expertise, energy and yes—expletives! But most of all it's taken love.

A Pair of Socks

Trevor B. Kwok

We make a living by what we get, but we make a life by what we give.

Norman MacEswan

I'm a local businessman in my community, and sometimes to relieve stress and to put perspective into my life, I volunteer at a soup kitchen in one of the city's poorer districts.

On one of my shifts I was sweeping up outside when I saw an elderly lady come around the corner. She was wearing an old flower print dress, a faded yellow knit sweater and a pair of tattered black shoes. The night was very cold and I couldn't help but notice she had no socks on.

When I asked where her socks were, she told me she didn't own any. I looked down at this frail woman and I knew she needed so much, but what I could offer her right then was a pair of warm socks. I took off my running shoes and pulled off my new white socks and put them on her, right there in the parking lot. I considered it a very small act of kindness but I will always remember her response. She looked up at me with such love, as a grandmother would look at her grandson, and she said "Thank you. Thank you very much. If there is one thing I love, it's going to bed at night with warm feet. I can't remember the last time I did." I drove home that night with a swelled heart.

The following night I was working another shift at the soup kitchen when two police officers walked in. They wanted to get some information about a woman, whom a neighbor had found dead. They showed me a picture of the woman to whom I had given my socks. I painfully asked, "What happened?"

The police told me she was an elderly widow with no family and few friends. She lived in an old shack of a house with no heat, about two blocks away. A neighbor, who visited her occasionally, found her.

As I poured the officers a cup of coffee, I said "What a sad story." The officer looked up from his coffee and said, "You know, I was there when the coroner picked up the body. It's the strangest thing, but I swear I saw a look of complete contentment on her face. A look of satisfaction, of comfort and peace. I hope I look that way when I go."

I drove home that night thinking about the difficult life that lady must have had, about all the hardship and loneliness she must have endured. Then I remembered the words she said when I put my socks on her feet. "If there is one thing I love, it's going to bed with warm feet." Materially I didn't give this lady very much. But internally, I can't help but think I gave her a little bit of comfort in her last night on Earth.

ALL IN A DAY'S WORK

Naomi Rhode, CSP, CPAE

Professional Speaker
Former President, National Speakers Association
Author, *More Beautiful Than Diamonds: The Gift of Friendship* and
The Gift of Family: A Legacy of Love

If I can ease one life the aching,
Or cool one pain,
Or help one fainting robin
Unto his nest again,
I shall not live in vain.

Emily Dickinson

He was admitted to emergency receiving and placed on the cardiac floor. His hair was long, he was unshaven, dirty, dangerously obese. A black motorcycle jacket had been tossed on the bottom shelf of the stretcher.

An outsider to this sterile world of shining terrazzo floors, efficient uniformed professionals and strict infection control procedures.

Definitely an untouchable!

The nurses at the station looked wide-eyed as this mound of humanity was wheeled by, each glancing nervously at my friend Bonnie, the head nurse. "Let this one not be mine to admit, bathe and tend to ..." was the pleading, unspoken message from their inner concern.

One of the true marks of a leader, a consummate professional, is to do the unthinkable. To touch the untouchable. To tackle the impossible! Yes, it was Bonnie who said, "I want this patient myself." Highly unusual for a head nurse, unconventional! But "the stuff" out of which human spirits thrive, heal and soar.

As she donned her latex gloves and proceeded to bathe this huge, very unclean man, her heart almost broke.

Where was his family? Who was his mother? What was he like as a little boy?

She hummed quietly as she worked. It seemed to ease the fear and embarrassment she knew he must be feeling.

And then on a whim she said, "We don't have time for back rubs much in hospitals these days, but I bet one would really feel good. And it would help you relax your muscles and start to heal. That is what this place is all about ... a place to heal."

The thick, scaly, ruddy skin told a story of an abusive lifestyle. Probably lots of addictive behavior—to food, alcohol and drugs.

As she rubbed those taut muscles she hummed and prayed. Prayed for the soul, of a little boy grown up, rejected by life's rudeness and striving for acceptance in a hard hostile world.

The finale was warmed lotion and baby powder. Almost laughable: such a contrast it seemed to this huge, foreign surface. As he rolled over onto his back, the tears were rolling down his cheek and his chin trembled. With amazingly beautiful brown eyes he smiled and said in a quivering voice, "No one has touched me for years. Thank you, I am healing."

Touching people at tender times!

In a day when we have increasing concern about the appropriateness of touch, the challenge for a hurting world is to still dare to touch the untouchable ... through eye contact, a warm handshake, a concerned voice or the physical reassurance of warmed lotion and baby powder.

Thank you, Bonnie, for being a true professional in a hurting world.

Now it is your turn to touch!

Touching

Sid Friedman

CEO, Corporate Financial Services
Leading Motivational Speaker and Consultant

I have such love for all my employees. Unfortunately, I have to be very careful in today's world, because touching is so entangled with all the sexual harrasment issues. I've never been sued and I've been lucky, but the fact of the matter is, it's very dangerous today because I am a touchy feely guy. I hug all, unless one says, "Keep your hands off of me."

Nothing illegal, nothing immoral, but you will know that I care about you. As I walk down the hall I'm very visible and my people see the effects of touching and love it. They see me do it, they do it and in turn I see them do it. It's just infectious. It is one of the best germs in the hospital.

IT CAN'T HAPPEN HERE?

Jack Canfield

We need 4 hugs a day for survival.
We need 8 hugs a day for maintenance.
We need 12 hugs a day for growth.

Virginia Satir, MSW

We always teach people to hug each other in our workshops and seminars. Most people respond by saying, "You could never hug people where I work." Are you sure?

Here is a letter from a graduate of one of our seminars.

"Dear Jack,

I started out this day in rather a bleak mood. My friend Rosalind stopped over and asked me if I was giving hugs today. I just grumbled something but then I began to think about hugs and everything during the week. I would look at the sheet you gave us on *How to Keep the Seminar Alive* and I would cringe when I got to the part about giving and getting hugs because I couldn't imagine giving hugs to the people at work.

Well, I decided to make it "hugs day" and I started giving hugs to the customers who came to my counter. It was great to see how people just brightened up. An MBA student jumped up on top of the counter and did a dance. Some people actually came back and asked for more. These two Xerox repair guys, who were kind of just walking along not really talking to each other, were so surprised; they just woke up and suddenly were talking and laughing down the hall.

It feels like I hugged everybody in the Wharton Business School, plus whatever was wrong with me this morning, which included some physical pain, is all gone. I'm sorry that this letter is so long but I'm just really excited. The neatest thing was, at one point there were about ten people all hugging each other out in front of my counter. I couldn't believe this was happening.

Love,
Pamela Rogers

PS: On the way home I hugged a policeman on 37th St. He said, "Wow! Policemen never get hugs. Are you sure you don't want to throw something at me?"

4 The IMPORTANCE and POWER of ACKNOWLEDGMENT

The deepest principle in human nature is the craving to be appreciated.

William James

There are two things people want more than sex and money—that's praise and recognition.

Mary Kay Ash

I consider my ability to arouse enthusiasm among the greatest assets I possess. The way to develop the best that is in a man is by appreciation and encouragement.

Charles Schwab

Am I doing something wrong? You don't say "Good dog" to me anymore.

How to Really Motivate an Employee

Brains, like hearts, go where they are appreciated.

Robert McNamara
Former U.S. Secretary of Defense

Glenn Tobe & Associates conducted a survey in which they asked supervisors to rank the importance of ten motivators for their employees. They then asked the employees to rank the same list in order of what they most wanted from their supervisors.

Here is the list of what the employees wanted most and a list of what their supervisors thought they wanted.

Employees	Supervisors
Appreciation	Good wages
Feeling "in" on things	Job security
Understanding attitude	Promotion opportunities
Job security	Good working conditions
Good wages	Interesting work
Interesting work	Loyalty from management
Promotion opportunities	Tactful discipline
Loyalty from management	**Appreciation**
Good working conditions	**Understanding attitude**
Tactful discipline	**Feeling "in" on things**

Is anybody paying attention?

ALL IN THE FAMILY: BUILDING
SELF-ESTEEM AT HOME AND AT WORK

Harvey Mackay

President, Mackay Envelopes Corporation
Author, *How to Swim with the Sharks without Getting Eaten Alive*
and *Sharkproof*

People ask me what the most important preparation is for being a chairman and I tell them being a dad. The issues are the same as raising adolescents; it's growth and development, growth and development.

Dr. Tim Johnson
Chairman, Obstetrics and Gynecology
University of Michigan at Ann Arbor

Healthy families remind each other of their goodness; unhealthy families remind each other of their failings.

Matthew Fox

I t's not your business success that I want to hear more about, Harvey," said a woman friend recently. "It's how you did such a good job with your family. All three of your kids have gone out into the world and found loving partners and careers they care about. And they even get along with their parents! What's your secret?"

It's simple, but not so easy, and it's sometimes just a matter of good luck. The secret is to have a happy marriage.

When the insults—or worse, the lamps and furniture—are flying, a kid's neck pulls in like a turtle's. When you grow up amid distrust and upheaval, your growth is compromised. But given constant loving care in an atmosphere of safety and security, the opposite is true. You have a real shot at being independent and productive.

Actually, I told my friend, my business success and my family success have a lot in common. Most importantly, my goal in both situations has been the same: to create an atmosphere where everyone can function at the highest level both individually and as a part of the whole. That's what happens when responsive leadership creates a supportive environment—the kind of environment that builds self-esteem.

Everybody needs to feel like somebody.

The image we have of ourselves exists largely because of our past experiences. However, those experiences have not made you the way you are; they have made you believe you are the way you are.

Even the smartest, ablest, most talented children or employees won't make much of their resources if they don't believe in themselves. They'll underperform, or they won't perform at all. Good parents and good managers help the people they lead feel worthy and strong.

And how do you do that?

The most obvious way, of course, is to be generous with praise. How many times do we fall into the trap of responding only to the negative and ignoring the positive? My dad taught me the value of praise. When a specific occasion warranted, he'd sit down and write me a letter to tell me how proud he was of me. I followed his example with my own children, because I know what an enduring gift this is. Even today, rereading one of my dad's letters can give me a boost.

At Mackay Envelope Corporation, the company I started thirty some years ago, we're always looking for the chance to tap an employee on the shoulder and say, "Hey, what you just did was great." We do that 52 weeks a year.

But praise alone isn't enough. In fact, blanket praise can seem a little insincere, like those trophies some well meaning people give to the entire team so that no one will feel bad. They don't make anybody feel especially good either. What's really helpful is to identify a kid's or worker's strong points, to identify them and reinforce them so that person knows his or her talent is there as a tool, to be hauled out as needed.

I noticed that two of my kids had terrific hand-eye coordination. I pointed this out to them and gave them tennis lessons to build those skills. My other child wasn't that concentrated, and I knew he wouldn't excel at a team sport, but what he did have was feistiness. So I encouraged him to take karate lessons, to build on that.

At my company, we discovered that one of our salespeople was terrific at cracking accounts. (That's sales speak for opening new accounts. A "holder," in contrast, is someone who shines at servicing them.) We identified his skill, challenged it and built on it. Unique in our sales force, he has no particular territory. He's encouraged to go wherever he sees a potential "crack."

Building self-esteem also means making your kids and your workers feel secure. It means making them comfortable to speak up and speak out without fear of rejection and criticism. This encourages risk taking, and I don't think any of the world's truly original ideas have come to fruition without somebody taking a risk. It also teaches them to be unafraid to ask.

As a parent, you hear so many sentences that begin with "Can I ...?" that sometimes you may be tempted to cut them off in the middle. That's a bad idea. You may still say "no" the same number of times—which is okay, because consistency is important—but your child should feel free to make the request. I notice that my best salespeople are those who aren't afraid to ask for more.

It's also vital to give people a sense of their own strength. This means giving them some control. Another thing my mom and dad did was to make a real point of spending time with each of their children alone. Both Carol and I do the same. Naturally, we learn to know them better. But also I found the kids enjoyed these one-on-one opportunities to hash over their minor complaints about the other members of this family.

At Mackay Envelope, everyone gets a chance at self-assertion. If you think that you've been passed over unfairly or that your duties aren't properly assigned—whatever the reason—you're encouraged to make an end run around your superior and appeal to the next level. Furthermore, there aren't any consequences to this act. In the unlikely event a manager decides to get hostile, the minute we hear about it, that person is history.

Finally, it's important to give everyone a sense of being significant. In a bad environment, everyone feels like a victim. In a good one, people feel as if they have equal worth—perhaps not equal power, but equal worth. A production line worker may not be able to enforce his desires in the same way a senior executive can, but the production line worker has an equal chance to be heard, in the same way that the youngest child gets equal air time at the dinner table.

What this all adds up to is one loud, clear message. You're special, and we care about you. For your child and your employee to succeed individually and the entire family or organization to thrive, each has to care about the other.

> *My parents were constantly affirming me in everything I did. Late at night I'd wake up and hear my mother talking over my bed, saying, "You're going to do great on this test. You can do anything you want."*
>
> Stephen Covey
> Author of *The Seven Habits of Highly Effective People*

Applying the Principles of Family Counseling to Corporate Meetings

Susan E. Davis

President, Capital Missions Company

The companies that are best at creating a good quality of work life will be able to attract and retain the most skilled workers.

Rosabeth Moss Kanter
Editor, *Harvard Business Review*

Virginia Satir, the founder of the family counseling movement, created a model for building healthy families through the use of four-part "family meetings." We use this structure at Capital Missions Company for our weekly staff meetings.

1. Appreciations

We begin with appreciations. Each team member is asked to stop and think about whom they would like to thank for something—support, encouragement, an idea, a personal quality or strength they have demonstrated. Then they are encouraged to share that with the other person. This ensures that we all take time to stop and smell the roses.

2. Concerns and Solutions

Every employee is responsible for raising any concern they might have along with a proposed win-win solution. The suggestions are negotiated, a resolution is reached and buy-in is affirmed. This can sometimes raise tough issues and may require individuals to grow emotionally as well as professionally. Ultimately, however, each employee becomes a part of the solution necessary to move forward.

3. Tactical To-Do's

In this part of the meeting we lay out our to-do lists, coordinate plans, prioritize work loads and seek whatever synergies are needed.

4. Hopes and Dreams

The fourth section is hopes and dreams, in which we pause to bless each employee's hopes and dreams for that week. This level of sharing ensures that the company and its employees are usually dealing with core issues and expressing their underlying emotions. This is contrary to the traditional corporate practice of false politeness and pretending that emotional issues are best left alone.

These meetings are the hardest work that our employees do each week, but we believe they are responsible for CMC's startling productivity. More than any other tool we use, they also increase employee self-esteem. They are a reflection of our underlying commitment to empower and facilitate each employee to take the necessary action to design the job they most want. Usually this is also the job at which they will be most productive.

The Amazing Power of AcknowledgmentSM

Michael J. Wyman
Corporate Consultant
President, Global Acknowledgment Foundation

How do you humiliate and demean someone and then expect him or her to care about product quality?

Tom Peters

By appreciating, we make excellence in others our own property.

Voltaire

One day I was called into a big insurance company by the human resource chief, to help create a new mission statement for the company.

As I was led through the company on the way to the boardroom, I was introduced to quite a few of the people working there. One person in particular stuck out. Besides being the only Puerto Rican, he really saw the value and need for The Power of AcknowledgmentSM being taught to everyone in the company. He realized what was truly needed more than a mission statement was the education of the staff in giving acknowledgment, recognition and appreciation to each other for the contributions they made to the company. He knew this would raise self-esteem, morale, productivity and sales.

He said, "But I'm just one of many vice-presidents, so my word doesn't have much power." Then laughingly he said, "But if I were the president ..."

I looked into his eyes and said, "Don't underestimate your powers and abilities. You have what it takes to be the president because you understand the underlying cause and motivator of people being empowered and appreciated. You would make a great president."

He blushed and said, "Thank you for your acknowledgment. I'll see you in the boardroom."

For the next four hours I challenged all eighteen vice-presidents and the president to create the most empowering mission statement they could imagine. As I was pressed for time, I asked everyone to kindly stay with the program and not joke around or go off purpose. Amazingly enough, the only two people who kept disrespectfully breaking my request were the president and his crony. Each time I asked them to stop

Bob finally gets the recognition he deserves.

they laughed in my face and continued. He said, "Look, I'm the president and I can do whatever I want. I'm paying your fee."

As I became more and more enraged, all I could think of was "If I had the power, I would fire you and your jerky friend and replace you with Jose." Each time I requested them to please be quiet, they both kept glaring at me. At one point I was so angry I actually said to myself, like in the commercial, "It's not nice to fool mother nature." I kept thinking, "What a disempowering pair of jerks they are. They can only be bad for everyone's morale and self-esteem." All I kept imagining was Jose being the new president.

Right after the program was completed, both the human resource guy and Jose came over to apologize for the rudeness of the president and his sidekick. I said, "I think it's time to stop making excuses for them and start realizing how they are hurting everyone's self-esteem by disrespecting everyone's 100% commitment today in creating a new mission statement." I looked at Jose and said, "Jose, if I had my way, you'd be the president."

Jose smiled and said, "Thank you, Michael, but there is no chance of that happening."

Two weeks later I received a phone call from the head of human resources at the insurance company. He said, "Hold onto your seat, Michael. Guess what just happened?"

I asked, "What?"

"Our company was just bought by a big conglomerate, and guess who got fired?"

"Who?"

"The president and his jerky sidekick. And guess who's the new president?"

"Who?"

"Jose! I knew acknowledgment was important, but I never knew how powerful it really was until now."

Jose later told me, "We truly are more magnificent, unlimited and powerful than we or anyone else has ever acknowledged. Just look at the miracle that happened to me!"

The power of acknowledgment is truly amazing.

Let no communication proceed out of your mouth, but that which is good to the use of edifying, that it may minister grace unto the hearers.

The Bible, Ephesians 4:29

Love and the Cabbie

Art Buchwald

Syndicated columnist

I was in New York the other day and rode with a friend in a taxi. When we got out my friend said to the driver, "Thank you for the ride. You did a superb job of driving."

The taxi driver was stunned for a second. Then he said:

"Are you a wise guy or something?"

"No, my dear man, and I'm not putting you on. I admire the way you keep cool in heavy traffic."

"Yeah," the driver said and drove off.

"What was that all about?" I asked.

"I am trying to bring love back to New York," he said. "I believe it's the only thing that can save the city."

"How can one man save New York?"

"It's not one man. I believe I have made the taxi driver's day. Suppose he has 20 fares. He's going to be nice to those twenty fares because someone was nice to him. Those fares in turn will be kinder to their employees or shop-keepers or waiters or even their own families. Eventually the goodwill could spread to at least 1,000 people. Now that isn't bad, is it?"

"But you're depending on that taxi driver to pass your goodwill to others."

"I'm not depending on it," my friend said. "I'm aware that the system isn't foolproof so I might deal with 10 different people today. If, out of 10, I can make three happy, then eventually I can indirectly influence the attitudes of 3,000 more."

"It sounds good on paper," I admitted, "but I'm not sure it works in practice."

"Nothing is lost if it doesn't. It didn't take any of my time to tell that man he was doing a good job. He neither received a larger tip nor a smaller tip. If it fell on deaf ears, so what? Tomorrow there will be another taxi driver whom I can try to make happy."

"You're some kind of a nut," I said.

"That shows you how cynical you have become. I have made a study of this. The thing that seems to be lacking, besides money, of course, for our postal employees, is that no one tells people who work for the post office what a good job they're doing."

"But they're not doing a good job."

"They're not doing a good job because they feel no one cares if they do or not. Why shouldn't someone say a kind word to them?"

We were walking past a structure in the process of being built and passed five workmen eating their lunch. My friend stopped. "That's a magnificent job you men have done. It must be difficult and dangerous work."

The five men eyed my friend suspiciously.

"When will it be finished?"

"June," a man grunted.

"Ah. That really is impressive. You must all be very proud."

We walked away. I said to him, "I haven't seen anyone like you since *The Man of LaMancha*."

"When those men digest my words, they will feel better for it. Somehow the city will benefit from their happiness."

"But you can't do this all alone!" I protested. "You're just one man."

"The most important thing is not to get discouraged. Making people in the city become kind again is not an easy job, but if I can enlist other people in my campaign ..."

"You just winked at a very plain looking woman," I said.

"Yes, I know," he replied. "And if she's a schoolteacher, her class will be in for a fantastic day."

THE LAST SUPPER

Excerpted from Bits & Pieces

The worst prison would be a closed heart.

Pope John Paul II

When Leonardo da Vinci was working on his painting "The Last Supper," he became angry with a certain man. Losing his temper he lashed the other fellow with bitter words and threats. Returning to his canvas he attempted to work on the face of Jesus, but was unable to do so. He was so upset he could not compose himself for the painstaking work. Finally he put down his tools and sought out the man and asked his forgiveness. The man accepted his apology and Leonardo was able to return to his workshop and finish painting the face of Jesus.

The Power of Unkind Words

E. J. Michael

Quoted in *The Oracle Newsletter*

Every word that is not first bathed in thought becomes a stone tossed in our path.

Rudolph Steiner

One day a man came to Mohammed and voiced his sadness and frustration. He was miserable at himself for having argued angrily with a friend. He felt sorrow for his unkind words and asked the Prophet what he should do to make amends.

Mohammed told the man to go around the town placing feathers on the steps of many homes. He instructed the man to leave the feathers there during the night and retrieve them in the morning, then he was to report back to Mohammed.

The next day he came to Mohammed with a look of distress on his face.

"Mohammed," he cried. "I did as you told me, but when I returned this morning to gather the feathers I left last night, I could not find a single one!"

"So it is with your words," explained Mohammed, "for they have flown from you and done their work, never to be recalled again."

It is possible to mend the harm done by our ill advised or negative words by speaking new and better words to replace them; however, it is smarter to be aware that our words do, in fact have much more power than most of us imagine.

Better to stumble with the toe than with the tongue.

Swahili Proverb

ALL YOU NEED TO KNOW

Steve Wilson, MA, CSP

Psychologist, Professional speaker
Author, *The Art of Mixing Work and Play*

Mend your speech a little lest you mar your fortunes.

William Shakespeare

A Curious Lecture

Norman Guitry grabbed our attention with his first sentence, "Everything you need to know about mental health can be summed up in only two words."

He was tall and had a distinguished bearing. White-haired. Gentle. Soft-spoken. Articulate. Caring. A man dedicated to humanitarian service, Norman Guitry taught what is probably the single most important lesson in human relations and mental health. It is elegant in its simplicity and as powerful a truth today as the first time I heard it, in September 1973.

I was teaching a freshman class in mental health and I had invited Norm to present the very first guest lecture. I was delighted to have him come to our class, but had no idea of the profound impact he would have on all of us.

He had accepted the formidable challenge of addressing his talk to an incoming class of mental health technology students. The topic was "The History of the Delivery of Mental Health Services." Norm had founded the local Mental Health Association, and was its first president and executive director. He had been an active and effective advocate of the best interests of the mentally ill and their families for a long, long time. Norm was the Grand Old Man of mental health in our community. No one was better qualified by experience, practice and people-savvy to speak on the subject.

If his first sentence, "Everything you need to know about mental health can be summed up in only two words," grabbed the group's attention (and it did), then his next sentence certainly had them riveted. "Ninety-five percent of the mental health problems we deal with today could be eliminated if everyone would practice this two word prescription, if everyone would live by these two words."

Norm Gives Us the Word(s)

I could tell from his facial expression that he was enjoying giving this a really good buildup. More emphatically than the first time he said, "I honestly believe that 95% of the mental health problems we deal with today could be eliminated if everyone would practice this two word prescription ... if everyone would live by these two words."

He picked up a piece of chalk and spoke the words as he printed them neatly on the chalkboard and drew a box around them.

The two words are ...

DON'T BELITTLE

It took several moments for us to take in what he was saying.

"Don't belittle. Don't put people down. Don't make anyone feel small. Don't be judgmental or critical in ways that diminish another person's sense of themselves. If everyone would live by that principle, you would see most of the problems that we associate with mental health problems disappear. Most of the problems of crime and abuse, academic failures, problems between bosses and workers, broken homes and addictions can be traced to low self-esteem.

"Therefore, lift people up. Respect differences. Value the uniqueness of every human being and teach them to value themselves. You can do it by the consistent practice of this uncomplicated dictum, 'don't belittle.'

"In the years to come, you will learn many theories of personality development and therapeutic techniques, but the best of them will only be embellishments on this fundamental idea. Make this your creed: 'don't belittle.'

"I wish you the best of luck and great success in your noble endeavors in the field of mental health. And remember: you now know the most important principle for mental health, human relations, peace of mind and love in your heart. Remember it. Teach it. Live it. Don't belittle."

The Wranglers vs. the Stranglers

Ted Engstrom

Years ago there was a group of brilliant young men at a midwestern university, who seemed to have amazing, creative literary talent. They were would-be poets, novelists and essayists. They were extraordinary in their ability to put the English language to its best use. These promising young men met regularly to read and critique each other's work. And critique it they did!

These men were merciless with one another. They dissected the smallest literary expression into 100 pieces. They were heartless, tough, even mean in their criticism, but they thought they were bringing out each other's best work. Their sessions became arenas of literary criticism such that the members of this exclusive support group nicknamed themselves "The Stranglers."

Not to be outdone, the university's women of literary talent were determined to start a support group of their own, one comparable to "The Stranglers." They called themselves "The Wranglers." They, too, read their works to one another, but there was one significant difference between the two groups. The criticism of "The Wranglers" was much softer, more positive, more encouraging. In fact sometimes there was almost no criticism at all. Every effort, even the most feeble attempt, was gleaned for some bit to be praised and encouraged.

Twenty years later, the university's alumni office was doing an exhaustive study on the careers of its alumni, when it was noticed that there was a great difference in the literary accomplishments of "The Stranglers" as opposed to "The Wranglers." Of all the bright and talented young men in "The Stranglers," not one had made a significant literary accomplishment of any kind. From "The Wranglers" had come six or more successful writers, some attaining national reputation.

Praising Your Way to Team Success

Ronald E. Guzik

President, Entrepreneurial Visions

46% of those who quit their jobs last year did so because they felt unappreciated.

U.S. Department of Labor

Many managers ignore or underestimate the power of praise.

Roger Flax
President, Motivational Systems

Haven't we heard it all before? Motivate, empower, reward your employees and be gracious to customers and suppliers alike. Be a coach instead of a dictator. Be someone whom others like being around. Terrific. But how do you do that on a day-by-day basis? After all, you can't be giving employees bonuses every day—or surprise parties or trips to the beach. And how many days a year can you give customers or suppliers calendars and ball-point pens?

What you *can* do every day is to show your appreciation through praise. It's the single most forgotten—and least expensive—management tool anyone can command.

Recent U.S. Labor Department statistics indicate that 46% of those who quit their jobs last year did so because they felt u-n-a-p-p-r-e-c-i-a-t-e-d. And in every study I've seen about what people want from their jobs, recognition and appreciation rank high. Moreover, customers will cling like ivy to a source of products or services where they are made to feel good just by showing up.

All employees want to be recognized for work that they believe they did well—or at least tried to do well. Recognition promotes satisfaction and high self-esteem among your people, whether they number just one or 1000.

Some large companies understand the value of praise and are familiar with the organizational development maxim that goes, "What gets rewarded gets done and gets done right." It's time that all small businesses, too, understood the truth of this bit of popular wisdom.

Our word "boss" has too often been synonymous with someone who criticizes or pressures. That's probably because we've become acculturated to management by focusing on what wasn't done right and by browbeating improvements out of hired hands. Stern looks, verbal warnings and written reprimands have been far more common in the work-place than encouraging smiles, congratulations or written commenda-tions. This is changing, but in many quarters we still have far to go.

No doubt everyone reading this has at one time or another been an employee or a subordinate in some organization. And surely each reader can remember someone's saying a simple, "Thank you for a great job!" Didn't that compliment really make your day? It made you feel appreci-ated, increased your self-confidence and gave you a positive attitude about your job. I'm sure everyone, however, can also recall many more times when you put extra effort into a project—and no one seemed to no-tice. If there was a "thank you," it was a perfunctory one.

The same is true for being somebody else's customer. Haven't we all responded positively to smiling clerks or friendly bellhops? And haven't we wondered why we bothered to come and spend hard earned money in places where the wait staff scowled or counter clerks acted as if our arrival was an annoying distraction from something else they had been doing?

The Power of Praise

Successful managers have become so in part because they learned the power of acknowledging others' accomplishments. That's one of the rea-sons their people may consider them "charismatic" leaders. It feels good just to be around them, because you know a compliment isn't far off.

Every compliment the employee receives is also like a little launch-ing pad—sending him or her up higher in attitude and performance. Every sincere "thank you for coming and please come back" that a cus-tomer receives makes him or her just that much more loyal to you as a vendor. And people who supply you with what you need—computer re-pairs, marketing research or just paper items for your facility's rest rooms—will *all* be timelier and more thorough if they know you're giving them part of their quota of warm feedback.

To praise others, however, you first need to be able to recognize yourself, treat *yourself* to little rewards, know how to pat yourself on the back when you deserve it. In other words, you must feel good about yourself and take pride in your own accomplishments. Someone who is always down on himself is not very likely to recognize or praise his employees.

Next, cultivate the habit of *looking for what people do right* (instead of looking exclusively for what might be done poorly). The emergence of this habit in you, the boss, will in itself have a great impact on morale in your shop, office or plant.

Be especially watchful for the kind of behavior that is so predictable it can almost go unnoticed, such as the employee who is *always* on time; someone whose work is so routinely complete and error free you are tempted to take it for granted; the supplier who never lets you down and will even make extra deliveries in an emergency; the customer who keeps relying on your services year in and year out.

After that, prompt yourself to speak up when you see something—a report, a process, a sales record—that looks good.

In my own work, I usually do most of my praising one-to-one, that is, out of the hearing of other people. But if done sensitively, there's really nothing wrong with praising someone in front of others. Just be sure you spread the praise around from day to day so that everyone gets some.

Be Natural but Creative

It's very important, however, that your praise be *natural,* not forced or exaggerated. True praise is not flattery. It's simply telling people that you appreciate them for the job they did (but don't try to motivate them by using more praise than their efforts are really worth. It doesn't take very much intuition for people to recognize overblown or phony praise for what it is).

"Nice" and "good," however, are two of the most overused words used in acknowledgment. They are bland and have little impact. Expand your praise vocabulary by using adjectives such as "terrific," "great," "wonderful," "thorough," "complete," "fine," "superb," "imaginative," "creative," "conscientious" and similar words.

"John, that was really a superb presentation of our materials. I'm sure you'll be a great hit on the road."

"Paula, thanks for bringing over those reports from your market research instead of putting them in the mail. Because of you and your group going the extra mile for us, we're going to make that deadline. We really appreciate what you've done."

"You know, Larry, you've been our accountant for years. But let me tell you, without you bearing down on the numbers so carefully, we would never have been able to budget this project as tightly as we did. Your work was a very significant part of our success on this one."

"Mary Jane, it's been two years now since you came to work for us, and I don't believe you've been more than 5 minutes late *ever* and 99% of the time, you're right on the dot. That's a wonderful record and a great example to everyone."

Acknowledgment works best when you do it just to brighten someone's day and give praise where praise is due. Don't be calculating about praising, figuring on a certain increase in production because you're using the technique. Good things will happen on their own. You don't have to quantify everything. Finally, here's a summary of praising tips from *The One Minute Manager* by Ken Blanchard and Spencer Johnson:

- "Tell people up front that you are going to let them know how they are doing.
- Praise people immediately.
- Tell people what they did right—be specific.
- Tell people how good you feel about what they did right, and how it helps the organization and the other people who work there.
- Stop for a moment of silence to let them "feel" how good you feel.
- Encourage them to do more of the same.
- Shake hands or touch people in a way that makes it clear that you support their success."

Like most habits, praising others will take effort to acquire and to perfect. So practice, practice, practice! Your staff, your suppliers and your customers will all love you for it.

Wise sayings often fall on barren ground, but a kind word is never thrown away.

Sir Arthur Helps

The Power of a Blue Ribbon

Helice Bridges

President, Helice Bridges Communications
Chairperson, Difference Makers International
Author, *Shaking Hands with Destiny* and *Up Is Better* (both forthcoming)

Words have great power and should be used carefully. Aloha, for example, should not be seen as just a frivolous tourist greeting. Alo means the bosom or center of the universe, and ha, *the breath of God, so to say this word is to appreciate another person's divinity.*

Nana Veary
Hawaiian Kupuna

Denise, senior vice-president of sales and marketing for a large California-based company, fumed as she took a seat next to me. She was in an unusual huff. I had grown to love this woman, with her spontaneous wit and willingness to see the best in everyone. It was unlike her to be angry.

"I'm so livid," Denise puffed. "The security guard over by the door is the rudest man I have ever met. He asked to see my lunch ticket before I could enter the room. Being a guest of the keynote speaker, I did not realize I needed a lunch ticket to get into the room. I pointed to my building industry badge demonstrating that I was entitled to enter all the convention activities, but he told me that was not good enough. He actually shouted at me, 'No ticket, lady, no food.' Being cool, I asked him politely where I should go to get a luncheon ticket, but he wouldn't answer. He even put his arm out to hold me back from getting into the room.

"I demanded his name and badge number and told him that I was going to report his rudeness to his supervisor.

"He said, 'Tough, I'm not going to tell you anything!'

"I wrote down his badge number and told him I was going to report him. Then I stormed past him and went in. I can't believe how angry I am. I can usually get along with most anyone and try to be a loving person, but this guy is something else. This anger is such a shock to me. I know, Helice, you always teach us to see the good in others, but this has got to be the exception!"

Those seated at our table agreed that this 250-pound security guard was Mr. Gestapo.

"Good that you told him how you felt," I responded. "I imagine that before this afternoon is over you will honor him and tell him what he has done to make a difference."

"I was afraid that you would say that." Denise grimaced.

The keynote speaker, John Martin, a leader in the building industry, committed to making a difference, concluded his speech with my "Who You Are Makes a Difference" story from *Chicken Soup for the Soul*. "The boy, touching the blue ribbon his father had just given him, sobbed and sobbed and then said, 'I was planning to commit suicide tomorrow, dad, because I didn't think you loved me. And now I don't have to.'

"Those of us in the building industry, personally and professionally," John continued, "don't always show enough compassion and empathy for people. It is time for reinventing the future, recognizing the value in others, becoming compassionate communicators and making a difference in the lives of everyone. It is important for all of us to let our colleagues, friends and family members know how much they make a difference to us. I would like to invite my business partner up to the stage and acknowledge him for the difference he has made in my life."

When John completed the Blue Ribbon Ceremony, the two men hugged. Then he acknowledged me as the author of the story and invited me to come forward and lead the audience of over 250 building industry leaders in the "Who I Am Makes a Difference" Blue Ribbon Ceremony.[1]

Within a few minutes, I shared with the audience how to acknowledge the person seated next to them. As they turned to one another with the Blue Ribbons, I watched their faces lighten up as tears, handshakes and hugs spontaneously filled the room. Men slapped each other on the back saying, "I never thought I could do this acknowledgment thing." "I can't believe so-and-so actually acknowledged me. I didn't think I made that kind of difference to him." "This acknowledgment ceremony is really powerful. We ought to do this everywhere!"

I was pleasantly surprised to see that someone was even acknowledging the security guard. His face went soft like a puppy dog as the Blue Ribbon was placed above his heart.

Curious to meet this man, I walked up to him smiling and said, "Hi, I'm glad to see that you received a Blue Ribbon. You truly are a man who does his job with gusto. It must be a very difficult job."

"You're right about that, lady. This place is chaos," said the security guard in frustration. "I don't usually work here, but even I can see there needs to be a better system. All they said to me is be sure nobody gets in without a ticket.

"Whether I like it or not, I have to take on extra jobs right now," he continued. "Last month my wife was killed by a drunken driver. I'm a single parent now and it's really a tough time for me and my boy. During the day, I'm an appraiser and at night I am a security guard for the Mighty Ducks. I hardly have time to be with my son. Your story moved me so deeply and is a reminder that I need to let my son know that I love him and how much he means to me.

"By the way," he said enthusiastically, "I got one of these Blue Ribbons at a fancy event about eight years ago. It really made a difference to me. I still have that ribbon on my mirror. I look at it every day and it reminds me that I am somebody. Would you mind autographing my copy of *Chicken Soup for the Soul*?"

My heart melted as I listened to this giant man reveal his deepest feelings. "I'd be honored to autograph a book for you," I said tenderly. I looked up at his kind face and wrote in the book, "Dear Larry, you're a kind and loving father. Thank you for the difference you make."

Tears filled his eyes as I showed him what I had written. As if we had known one another for a lifetime, we gave each other a warm and lasting hug.

As I walked away, I made eye contact with Denise as she was headed directly toward Larry with a Blue Ribbon in her hand.

Denise was now back to her usual loving self. Without hesitation, she went directly over to Larry. I watched her speaking to him and then placing a second Blue Ribbon above the one he had just gotten from someone else.

Later, Denise and I walked out of the convention hall arm in arm. "I can't believe what just happened," she reflected. "I was so wrong about this man. I told him how much I appreciated the difficult job he had. Then he told me that his wife had just been killed. He was sorry for being so rude to me.

"I was shocked and moved to tears. All I could think to do was to ask him for a hug. And that's just what we did.

"When you told me earlier that I would acknowledge Mr. Gestapo with a Blue Ribbon before the day was out, I couldn't even imagine that happening. I think I'm beginning to understand," Denise said introspectively. "From now on I will think twice before making snap decisions about anyone. Instead, I will always remember that everybody makes a difference."

Let everything you do be done as if it makes a difference.

William James

The Power of a Note

Fred Bauer

I can live for two months on a good compliment.

Mark Twain

On my first job as sports editor for the Montpelier (Ohio) *Leader Enterprise*, I didn't get a lot of fan mail, so I was intrigued by a letter plopped on my desk one morning. The envelope bore the logo of the closest big city paper, the *Toledo Blade*.

When I opened it, I read: "Sweet piece of writing on the Tigers. Keep up the good work." It was signed by Don Wolfe, the sports editor. Because I was a teenager (being paid the grand total of 15¢ a column inch), his words couldn't have been more exhilarating. I kept the letter in my desk drawer until it got rag-eared. Whenever I doubted I had the right stuff to be a writer, I would reread Don's note and walk on air again.

Later, when I got to know him, I learned that Don made a habit of jotting a quick, encouraging word to people in all walks of life. "When I make others feel good about themselves," he told me, "I feel good too."

Not surprisingly, he had a body of friends as big as nearby Lake Erie. When he died last year at 75, the paper was inundated with calls and letters from people who had been recipients of his spirit-lifting words. Mr. Toledo Blade, as he came to be known, had indeed made them feel good about themselves.

Over the years, I've tried to emulate Don and other friends who care enough to write uplifting comments, because I think they are on to something important. In a world too often cold and unresponsive, such notes are springs of warmth and reassurance. We all need a boost from time to time, and a few lines of praise have been known to turn around a day, even a life.

Why, then, are upbeat note writers in such short supply? My guess is that many who shy away from the practice are too self-conscious. They're afraid they'll be misunderstood, sound corny or fawning. Also, writing takes time; it's far easier to pick up the phone.

The drawback with phone calls, of course, is that they don't last. A note attaches more importance to our well-wishing. It is a matter of record, and our words can be read more than once, savored and treasured.

Even though note writing may take longer, some pretty busy people do it, including George Bush. Some say he owes much of his success in politics to his ever-ready pen. How? Throughout his career he had followed up virtually every contact with a cordial response—a compliment, a line of praise or a nod of thanks. His notes go not only to friends and associates, but to casual acquaintances and total strangers—like the surprised person who got a warm, calligraphic back pat for lending Bush an umbrella.

Even members of the news media, not normally any president's favorite pen pals, have received solicitous notes from the former Commander-in-Chief. And so have members of their families. One summer day, when Bush invited some of the press corps to Kennebunkport for a barbecue, the young daughter of Jack Gallivan, a director of ABC's "Primetime Live," went swimming in the Bush's pool and lost her tooth. Noticing Katie Gallivan crying, Bush asked her what had happened. When he heard, he knew from his own children what that meant: no proof under the pillow for the Tooth Fairy! He called an aide to bring him a Presidential note card bearing an etching of his Kennebunkport house. Bush made a small X on the card and wrote:

Dear Tooth Fairy—

Katie's tooth came out where the X is. It really did—I promise ...

George Bush

It fulfilled the best prerequisites for inspirational note writing: it was short on verbiage and long on empathy. And most important, it dried Katie's tears.

Another gifted presidential note writer was Abraham Lincoln. One of his most famous personal letters was a tender condolence to Mrs. Lydia Bixby of Boston, who had lost two sons in battle. "I feel how weak and fruitless must be any words of mine which should attempt to beguile you from the grief of a loss so overwhelming," he wrote. "I pray that our Heavenly Father may assuage the anguish of your bereavement, and leave you only the cherished memory of the loved and lost, and the solemn pride that must be yours to have laid so costly a sacrifice upon the altar of freedom."

Lincoln's wartime letter of loss brings to mind a more recent conflict and some letters of gain. When a New Jersey newspaper urged its subscribers to write to service men and women in Operation Desert Storm, schoolteacher Connie Stanzione accepted the challenge with patriotic fervor. In all, she sent 50 or so letters to anonymous troops.

"I told them how proud I was of them and how much I appreciated their sacrifices for the cause of freedom," she recalls. One who wrote back was 30-year-old Army sergeant Kerry Walters, who thanked Connie for her thoughtfulness. She answered him, and so it went. Gradually, as they exchanged letters about themselves, they became friends.

After they traded photographs, romance blossomed. Their letters were no longer signed "your friend," but "with love" and "fondly." After a $129 phone call, Kerry sent a letter that concluded: "I pray that I've touched your heart like you have touched mine and that you would like to build a family together. Constance, will you marry me?" Connie immediately accepted. Fittingly, their wedding ceremony included an inspirational message about love from one of the most famous letter writers of all time—St. Paul. His first letter to a small, embattled band of Christians in Corinth so challenged and inspired them that it has been treasured and preserved for 2000 years. I Corinthians 13 tells us that love never ends. And that is exactly the power in words of praise.

Even top corporate managers, who have mostly affected styles of leadership that can be characterized only as tough, cold and aloof, have begun to learn the lesson, and earn the benefits, of writing notes that lift people up. Former Ford chairman Donald Petersen, who is largely credited for turning the company around in the 1980s, made it a practice to jot positive messages to associates every day. "I'd just scribble them on a memo pad or the corner of a letter and pass them along," he says. "The most important ten minutes of your day are those you spend doing something to boost the people who work for you."

"Too often," he observed, "people we genuinely like have no idea how we feel about them. Too often we think *I haven't said anything critical; why do I have to say something positive?* We forget that human beings need positive reinforcement—in fact, we thrive on it!"

What does it take to write letters that lift spirits and warm hearts? Only unselfish eyes and a willingness to express our appreciation. The most successful practitioners include what I call the four "S's" of note writing:

1. They are *sincere*. No one wants their sails filled with smoke.
2. They are usually *short*. If you can't speak your piece in three sentences, you're probably straining.
3. They are *specific*. Complimenting a business colleague by telling him "good speech" is one thing; "great story about Warren Buffet's investment strategy" is another.
4. They are *spontaneous*. This gives them the freshness and enthusiasm that will linger in the reader's mind long afterward.

It is difficult to be spontaneous when you have to hunt for letter writing materials, so I keep paper, envelopes and stamps close at hand, even when I travel. Fancy stationery isn't necessary; it's the thought that counts.

So, who around you deserves a note of thanks or approval? A neighbor, your librarian, a relative, your mayor, your mate, a teacher, your doctor? You don't need to be poetic. If you need a reason, look for a milestone, the anniversary of a special event you shared or a birthday or holiday. For the last 25 years, I've prepared an annual Christmas letter for long distance friends, and I often add a handwritten word of thanks or congratulations. Acknowledging some success or good fortune that has happened during the year seems particularly appropriate considering the spirit of the season.

Don't be stinting with your praise. Superlatives like "greatest," "smartest," "prettiest"—they make us all feel good. Even if our plaudits run a little ahead of reality, remember that expectations are often the parents of dreams fulfilled.

Today I got a warm, complimentary letter from my old boss and mentor, Norman Vincent Peale. He once told me that the purpose of writing inspirational notes (he is the best three sentence letter writer I have ever known) is simply "to build others up because there are too many people in the demolition business today."

His little note to me was full of uplifting phrases, and it sent me to my typewriter to compose a few overdue letters of my own. I don't know if they will make anybody else's day, but they made mine. As my friend Don Wolfe said, making others feel good about themselves makes me feel good too.

The good man does not grieve that other people do not recognize his merits. His only anxiety is lest he should fail to recognize theirs.

Confucius

Once employees see that what they do makes a difference to the organization and is valued, they will perform at higher levels.

Rita Numerof
President, Numerof & Associates

THREE SIMPLE POINTS

Source Unknown

The group will not prosper if the leader grabs the lion's share of the credit for the good work that has been done.

Lao-tzu

It's football season again and any football enthusiast will most certainly remember the name of the late Bear Bryant, the famous coach for Alabama. When anyone thinks of Bear Bryant, good thoughts come to mind. Everyone not only loved him, they respected him. Bryant knew how to draw the very best out of his players.

Many of the pro ball players quickly point to him as the person who made the greatest difference in their lives. Bear Bryant had a simple philosophy which he used to inspire his players. It is a philosophy any manager would be wise to try.

You don't have to write this down because once you hear it, you will remember it. It's three simple points:

1. If something goes wrong, it is my fault.
2. If something turns out all right, we did it.
3. If something turns out great, you did it.

A philosophy like that is bound to draw the best out of a person. It builds self-esteem and makes any person want to do their best.

We must understand that if people do something wrong, they know it before you do, so there is no point in bringing it to their attention or reminding them of it. However, when people do something right, they want to be recognized and get that pat on the back. Recognition causes them to go on and do greater things. Brandeis once said, "There is a spark of idealism within every individual which can be fanned into flame and bring forth extraordinary results."

Bear Bryant's three simple rules of leadership will work for anyone. They are so simple, yet so effective. Try them!

I'll tell you what makes a great manager: A great manager has a knack for making ballplayers think they are better than they think they are. He forces you to have a good opinion of yourself. He lets you know he believes in you. He makes you get more out of yourself. And once you learn how good you really are, you never settle for playing anything less than your very best.

Reggie Jackson

Rub Somebody the Right Way

Bob Nelson

Vice-President, Blanchard Training and Development, Inc.
Author, *1001 Ways to Reward Employees*

The best thing you can say to workers is "You are valuable, you are my most important assets."

Phyllis Eisen
Senior Policy Director
National Association of Manufacturers

It's funny how we frequently refer to others that "rub us the wrong way" in our lives. People whose personalities, mannerisms or attitudes about life don't agree with our own and who as a result we choose not to associate with. I think it's time we started calling attention to others who "rub us the right way." People who are positive and energetic about life, who are fun to be with and work with and whose energy is contagious. Better yet, I think every one of us should strive to be such a person.

A good place to start is by appreciating others. Everyone likes to be appreciated. Yet how many people take the time to appreciate others? In today's business environment what used to be common courtesies have been overcome by speed and technology. People tend to be too busy and too removed to thank others for their help. Technology has replaced personal interaction with one's manager with constant interfacing with one's terminal. John Naisbitt predicted this would happen a decade ago in his book *Megatrends*. He said the more our work environments become highly technical, the greater the employee need would become to be more personal and human. He called the phenomenon high-tech/high-touch. And all this is happening at a time when employees are looking to find greater meaning in their lives—and especially in their jobs.

How many managers, however, consider "appreciating others" to be a major function of their job today? It should be. At a time when employees are being asked to do more than ever before, to make suggestions for continuous improvement, to handle complex problems quickly and to act independently in the best interests of the company, the resources and support for helping them are at an all-time low. Budgets are tight; salaries are frozen.

Often when I speak with managers I ask for a show of hands of those who have unmotivated employees. Typically one third to one half of the group raise their hands. I then say that an unmotivated employee reflects more on them than on their employees. All employees want to be magnificent. All employees start new jobs excited about doing their best. Yet somehow for many employees the excitement of the job wears off. I believe this is due to how they are treated by their managers more than to anything else.

The irony of the situation is that what motivates people the most takes so relatively little to do—just a little time and thoughtfulness for starters. In a recent research study of 1500 employees conducted by Dr. Gerald Graham, "Personal congratulations by one's manager for doing a good job" was ranked first out of 65 potential workplace incentives he evaluated. And 58% of the employees in the study said they seldom if ever received such a thank you from their manager. Second was a personal note for good performance written by one's manager; 76% reported seldom if ever receiving a personal note of thanks from their manager.

Practice ASAP Praisings

The best place to start appreciating others is with simple praisings or, as management guru Ken Blanchard says, "catching people doing something right." In the workplace, praise is priceless, yet it costs nothing. Although giving praise effectively may seem like common sense, a lot of people have never learned how to do it. I suggest an acronym, ASAP-cubed, to remember the essential elements of a good praising. That is, praise should be done as soon, as sincere, as specific, as personal, as positive, and as proactive as possible.

As soon. Timing is very important when praising. To be the most effective, the thank you should come as soon as possible after the achievement or desired activity has occurred. If you wait too long to thank a person, over time the gesture loses its significance. Implicitly, employees figure that other things were more important to you than taking a few minutes with them.

As sincere. Words alone can fall flat if you are not sincere about why you are praising. You need to praise because you are truly appreciative and excited about the other person's success, otherwise it may come across as a manipulative tactic—something you are doing only when you want an employee to work late, for example.

As specific. Avoid generalities in favor of details of the achievement. Specifics give credibility to your praising and also serve a practical purpose of stating exactly what was good about the behavior or achievement. Praisings that are too broad tend to seem insincere. Instead say, "Thanks for staying late to finish those calculations I needed. It was critical for my meeting this morning." This specifically says what and why an employee's effort was of value.

As personal. A key to conveying your message is praising in person, face-to-face. This shows that the activity is important enough to you to put aside everything else you have to do and just focus on the other person. Since we all have limited time, the things you do personally indicate that they have a higher value to you.

As positive. Too many managers undercut praise with a concluding note of criticism. When you say something like "You did a great job on this report, but there were quite a few typos," the "but" becomes a verbal erasure of all that came before. Save the corrective feedback for the next similar assignment.

As proactive. Praise progress toward desired goals or else you will tend to be reactive—typically about mistakes—in your interactions with others.

Getting Started with Employee Praisings

Probably the biggest obstacle to praise in the workplace is time—especially on the part of managers. Managers are often too busy focusing on what's urgent—such as dealing with daily crises in their jobs—and as a result they don't have any time left to focus on what's important—the people they manage.

The situation is made worse by the false perception on the part of many managers that they are in fact providing employees with plenty of praise and recognition. According to Aubrey Daniels, a leading authority on the topic of performance management, "those managers who feel they do it [positive reinforcement] the most, in my experience, actually do it the least." That is, managers may have learned somewhere that they need to be positive reinforcers of their employees and feel they are doing so, but on a day-to-day basis they often are doing very little to catch their employees doing something right. Worse yet, often the positive reinforcement they are doing is incorrect, for example, providing individual feedback that is nonspecific or insincere, praising some employees while overlooking others that have contributed equally to a given success or having their facts wrong about a specific performance they want to acknowledge.

How can managers start praising their employees more? Like any behavioral change you have to find a way to make it a habit—a natural part of your daily routine. For example, I've been successful at getting analytical, task-oriented managers to start praising employees more by getting them to think of their people as things to do. I have such managers list the names of each person who reports to them on their weekly "to do" list and cross each person off the list once they have given him or her a praising based on that person's performance. For some managers, such a specific technique helps take the activity from being a general, intangible activity to a specific, finite action item—thus much easier to complete.

In another example, Hyler Bracey, president of The Atlanta Consulting Group, knew he wanted to praise employees more, but found his good intentions did not often translate to daily behavior. To correct this situation, he started putting five coins in his jacket pocket each morning and transferring a coin to another pocket each time during the day that he gave positive feedback to an employee. Within a few weeks the new habit took hold and praising employees became second nature to him. Says Bracey: "Praising employees truly works. There is so much more energy and enthusiasm in a workplace where giving praise has become ingrained in the manager."

For managers who for some reason cannot bring themselves to personally praise employees, try to find out what recognition activities they are willing to do. For example, sometimes such managers are less intimidated by writing personal notes to high performing employees, thanking them for doing an outstanding job—which is also a top motivator as reported by employees. Or you may get a manager to sanction a department celebration, even if they don't personally attend the celebration.

You can also provide structure or systems in your work environment that will encourage praisings to take place. For example, at my company, Blanchard Training and Development, we always save some time at the end of every company meeting to ask if anyone has any praisings they'd like to share. People always do.

The power of positive reinforcement can only occur as managers find time to put the principle into practice on a daily basis with each of their employees.

Additional Guidelines for Increasing
Employee Recognition

People often ask me what is most important in getting started with recognition activities where they work. Here are some guidelines that I have found useful in working with individuals and companies to initiate increased employee recognition.

Start in Your Immediate Sphere of Influence. Motivation is a very personal topic, and to be successful with it, you need to operate at a very immediate, personal, one-on-one level. One of the great things about this topic is you don't need anyone's permission to start using the principles involved. You can immediately use positive recognition, praise and encouragement toward performance goals with those individuals with whom you work. Simple praisings, gestures of thanks and public acknowledgments of achievement are the high leverage actions to get employees motivated in your workplace.

Involve Those Individuals You Are Trying to Motivate. Bring up the topic of recognition and ask the question, "Does anyone think we need to do more recognition around here?" Since I've never heard of any employee saying "I just get too much recognition where I work," this is almost a rhetorical question. Take the initial interest employees express in having more recognition and ask if anyone in the group would be willing to help come up with a program for the group. Some of the best recognition programs are driven by volunteers! After initially helping them establish goals, have them develop the criteria and mechanics for the program. From the outset, it can be their program, not management's—and thus be more likely to succeed. Remember, the best management is what you do with people, not what you do to them. Make employees partners in their own success.

Ask Employees What Motivates Them. Whether you have them jot down items that they find motivating on their first day of work, or complete a simple recognition survey of items they find motivating, start with employee preferences for recognition. What motivates us differs from person to person and for the same person over time. Make time to spend with employees, finding out where they want to go with their careers, their personal hobbies and their family situations. All of this information is fodder for motivation. By helping them to reach their goals, you can unleash an excitement and commitment in them to want to do their absolute best to help you and the organization succeed.

Focus on What You Can Do, Not What You Can't Do. In almost every work environment, constraints can keep you from implementing recognition activities. For example, many organizations are unionized, which restricts some recognition practices; public organizations must be careful how they use public funds for recognition activities; nonprofits and smaller companies may not have any financial resources to devote to recognition programs; and larger companies may feel hypocritical conducting motivational activities during or after times of layoffs and downsizing.

Instead of dwelling on what you can't do, focus on the hundreds of things you can do. For example, simply providing information can be very rewarding. In the recent National Study of the Changing Workforce by the Families and Work Institute, "open communication" was ranked as the most important reason employees gave for taking their current jobs.

Everyone wants to know what's going on—especially as it affects them—and just giving them this information is motivating.

Don't Expect to Do Recognition Perfectly. I find some managers attempt recognition activities, then abandon their efforts because they didn't feel they were initially successful. Remember, any new behavior or change will be awkward at first. There is no perfectly right way of doing recognition. Instead, try things, learn from them and seek to improve. Have fun in the process and you will seldom go wrong!

Simple Gestures Count the Most

Recognition does not have to be anything fancy; in fact, the simpler and more direct, the better. The more I work with recognition and rewards, the more I continue to be intrigued with the simple, sincere ways employees use to appreciate each other with a minimum of cost, paperwork and administration.

At Tektronix, Inc., the company instituted a simple way for managers and employees alike to focus on recognizing others for doing something right. Dubbed the "You Done Good Award," this simple certificate was printed in pads and could be given to anybody in the company from anybody else in the company. On it, individuals stated what was done, who did it and when and then gave the certificate to the person. The idea has caught on and is now a part of life at Tektronix. Says one employee: "Even though people say nice things to you, it means something more when people take the time to write their name on a piece of paper and say it."

Another simple yet effective approach is to put notes on business cards. John Plunkett, Director of Employment and Training for Cobb Electric Membership Corporation in Marietta, Georgia, says "People love to collect others' business cards. Simply carry a supply of your cards with you and as you 'catch people doing something right,' immediately write 'Thanks,' 'Good job,' 'Keep it up,' and what they specifically did in two to three words. Put the person's name on the card and sign it."

You can also use technology to leave messages on voice-mail or computer e-mail if it is available to you. These simple gestures indicate that you are not too busy to miss the fact that an employee has done something special. Following are other simple, yet powerful, recognition items that have been done with little if any expense.

The Spirit of Fred Award. At Walt Disney World in Orlando, Florida, one of their 180 recognition programs is called The Spirit of Fred Award, named for an employee named Fred. When Fred first went from an hourly to a salaried position, five people taught him the values necessary for success at

Disney. This help inspired the award, in which the name Fred became an acronym for Friendly, Resourceful, Enthusiastic and Dependable. First given as a lark, the award has come to be highly coveted in the organization. Fred makes each award—a certificate mounted on a plaque, which he then varnishes—as well as The Lifetime Fred Award—a bronze statuette of Mickey Mouse given to recipients of multiple Spirit of Fred Awards.

Thanks a Bunch. At Maritz Performance Improvement Company in Fenton, Missouri, there is a Thanks a Bunch program in which a bouquet of flowers is given to an employee in appreciation for special favors or jobs well done. That employee then passes the flowers on to someone else who has been helpful with the intent of seeing how many people can be given the bouquet throughout the day. A written thank you card goes with the flowers. At certain intervals the cards are entered into a drawing for awards such as binoculars or jackets with the company logo. The program is used during especially heavy work loads or stressful times.

World of Thanks. At AT&T Universal Card Services in Jacksonville, Florida, the World of Thanks award is one of more than 40 recognition and reward programs. It's a pad of colored paper shaped like a globe with "Thank You" written all over it in different languages. Anyone in the company can write a message of thanks to someone else and send it to that person. The program is extremely popular—in four years they have used over 130,000 such notes.

Appreciation Days. ARA Services, headquartered in Philadelphia, Pennsylvania, organizes a day of appreciation for worthy employees. They send out a proclamation announcing Bob Jones Day, for example, with the reason for the honor. The honoree enjoys all sorts of frills, such as computer banners and a free lunch.

The Wingspread Award. The Office of Personnel Management in Washington, DC, uses a "pass around" award that was first given to the division's "special performer." Later that person passed the award to another person who, he believed, truly deserved it. The award came to take on great value and prestige because it came from one's peers. A recipient can keep the award indefinitely, or until that person discovers another special performer. When the award is to be passed on, a ceremony and lunch are planned.

The Golden Banana Award. A Hewlett-Packard Company engineer burst into his manager's office in Palo Alto, California to announce he'd just found the solution to a problem the group had been struggling with for many weeks. His manager quickly groped around his desk for some item to acknowledge the accomplishment and ended up handing the employee a banana from his lunch with the words, "Well done. Congratulations!" The employee was initially puzzled, but over time the Golden Banana Award became one of the most prestigious honors bestowed on an inventive employee.

As Ron Zemke, Senior Editor of *Training* magazine says, "Recognition is something a manager should be doing all the time—it's a running dialogue with people." Adds Larry Colin, president of Colin Service Systems, "We realized that our largest asset was our work force and that our growth would come from asset appreciation." The act of delivering simple, direct praise for a job well done is so easy to do, yet so many managers do not do it. Make the extra effort to appreciate employees, and they'll reciprocate in a thousand ways.

... and I won this one for winning so many awards!

FEEL LIKE THE JOB'S TOO BIG?

Listen to Mother Theresa:

> *I never look at the masses as my responsibility. I look at the individual. I can love only one person at a time. I can feed only one person at a time. Just one, one, one ... So you begin—I begin. I picked up one person— maybe if I didn't pick up that one person I wouldn't have picked up 42,000. The whole work is only a drop in the ocean. But if I didn't put the drop in, the ocean would be one drop less. Same thing for you, same thing in your family, same thing in the church where you go. Just begin ... one, one, one.*

5 CEOs on Self-Esteem

I think if organizations are doing their job, then they create self-esteem in the workplace. The way a company works is because of the people. I think the attitude in the workplace completely dictates the quality of the product.

Nick Graham
Chairman and CEO, Joe Boxer, Inc.

Outstanding leaders go out of their way to boost the self-esteem of their personnel. If people believe in themselves, it's amazing what they can accomplish.

Sam Walton
Founder, Walmart

To be a leader means willingness to risk—and a willingness to love. Has the leader given you something from the heart?

Hubert H. Humphrey

A company cannot distribute self-confidence. What it can do, what we must do is to give each of our people the opportunity to dream, risk, and win, and hence earn self-confidence.

Jack Welch
Chairman and CEO, General Electric

I am a firm believer in the importance of self-esteem in the workplace. After close to forty years at Xerox, I have seen individual success and self-esteem lead to group success and self-esteem, and vice versa. Life requires an environment that allows people to feel good about themselves, but we forget that we have to pass this along to others.

Bob Adams
President, Xerox Technology Ventures

The understanding of the importance of self-esteem is particularly critical for Americans in today's world. Self-esteem is at the heart of competitiveness, and America's competitiveness is at the heart of its political and economic destiny.

Dick Elkus
Vice Chairman, Tencor

Very few companies actually care one wit about understanding the relationship between active involved employees and the overall health and profitability of their firm. Developing the company environmentally, getting the workforce organized and aggressive on campaigns of both environmental and social concerns must be a priority. By building employee self-esteem we will build a powerful workforce.

Kristine McDivitt
Former CEO, Patagonia, Inc.

The real essence of leadership is to care about your people, to help them get as much as they can out of the business environment, and to have as much fun as they can. Anybody who can do that—and really mean it—is a leader.

Robert Townsend
Former CEO, Avis Rent-A-Car

Self-esteem allows you the confidence to excel against seemingly impossible odds.

Steve Lundquist
Olympic gold-medalist swimmer
CEO, Visionary Style, Inc.

More and more service companies are awakening to the fact that their internal employee constituency is one of their most important target markets. The better employees feel about themselves and their company—the better they feel about the customer.

Michael W. Gunn
Senior Vice-President Marketing
American Airlines

A good heart and a good mind—these are what you need to be a good chief.

Louis Farmer
Onandaga Elder

At the heart of any good business is a chief executive officer with one.

Malcolm Forbes

One of the great adages and guides to working in a corporation with its lay-ers of management and never ending rules creation is best articulated by John Gardiner (the founder of the Common Cause movement) in his book, Self Renewal—Don't Let Form Triumph Over Spirit! *I suggest that you don't let form triumph over spirit in your life. I found this commit-ment to spirit and creativity and form useful in my 30 year career at IBM. IBM was the "form" and I looked forward each day to not letting that "form" get in the way of new ideas, creativity and risk-taking. It's easy to do things "by the book." It's harder to think "out of the box" and burst bureaucratic old ways. The last act of a dying organization is a new and better rule book.*

- *Fight for what you believe, even in the face of adversity.*
- *Don't let form triumph over spirit.*
- *Find the inner strength you need to maintain your self-esteem, even when your idea appears to be unpopular.*

Sam Albert
President, Sam Albert Associates

The King's Great Gift

Anonymous

The only gift is a portion of thyself.

Ralph Waldo Emerson

There once was a wise and beloved king who cared greatly for his people and wanted only what was the best for them. The people knew the king took a personal interest in their affairs and tried to understand how his decisions affected their lives. Periodically, he would disguise himself and wander through the streets, trying to see life from their perspective.

One day he disguised himself as a poor villager and went to visit the public baths. Many people were there enjoying the fellowship and relaxation. The water for the baths was heated by a furnace in the cellar, where one man was responsible for maintaining the comfort level of the water. The king made his way to the basement to visit with the man who tirelessly tended the fire.

The two men shared a meal together, and the king befriended this lonely man. Day after day, week in and week out, the king went to visit the firetender. The man in the cellar soon became close to his strange visitor because he came down to the basement where he was. No one else ever had showed that much caring or concern.

One day the king revealed his true identity to his friend. It was a risky move, for he feared that the man might ask him for special favors or a gift. Instead, the king's new friend looked into his eyes and said, "You left your comfortable palace to sit with me in this hot and dingy cellar. You ate my meager food and genuinely showed you cared about what happens to me. On other people you might bestow rich gifts, but to me you have given the greatest gift of all. You gave me the gift of yourself."

You give but little when you give of your possessions. It is when you give of yourself that you truly give.

Kahlil Gibran

LILLIAN VERNON ON SELF-ESTEEM

Lillian Vernon
Founder and CEO, Lillian Vernon, Inc.

Anyone can count the number of seeds in an apple,
But only God can count the number of apples in a seed.

Robert H. Schuller

I have always been a staunch believer that the development of self-esteem must begin very early in life. At a young age, children must begin to develop confidence in themselves.

The development of self-esteem must be based on a sound foundation. It is important for parents to encourage the process by delegating some type of responsibility to children in the home. Giving them tasks such as making their beds every morning or helping in the yard will give them a sense of accomplishment, self-assurance and independence.

One of the greatest gifts a parent can give a child to help develop self-esteem is to teach the child how to think, rather than what to think.

Skills can be learned, but the seeds of confidence have to be planted at a young age, and then nurtured throughout the formative years. Building self-esteem is often an evolutionary, not a revolutionary process.

Children should always be given positive feedback and reinforcement when they do something well. Children thrive and excel when praised.

Use criticism constructively, not destructively. Let them know you don't always expect perfection, but you do expect them to do their very best. Be sure to point out their strengths and capabilities. Compliments and communication are essential for the development of self-esteem.

Since children learn by example, keep your fears and insecurities to yourself. Don't convey them to your children. Influence them positively, not negatively. Instill them with caution and prudence but never fear.

As an adult, never let others determine or diminish your self-esteem. Confidence must come from within. You must believe it to feel it and exude it. Don't dwell on your mistakes or setbacks, instead learn and grow from them and move on. Don't allow mistakes to defeat or discourage you and don't take criticism personally.

It is necessary to work hard on self-esteem—it's something you can't buy at a store! Self-esteem is respecting who you are, not what you are.

Reinforcing the self-esteem of my staff is a vital part of my management philosophy. I write personal notes of praise and acknowledgment to them for jobs well done.

I am proud of the fact that, over the years, I have been instrumental in helping to develop a strong sense of self-esteem among members of my staff. Conveying a simple message, such as, "I know you can do this well," or "I have confidence in your ability," has gone a long way in making a difference in the attitudes of my employees, and has proven invaluable in developing a strong feeling of personal self-esteem in the workplace.

We all have strengths and weaknesses. I emphasize my staff's strengths by letting them know they are all important, all unique and that everyone has something positive to contribute. I believe that self-esteem enhances self-motivation. If you believe you can succeed, then most likely you will.

To maintain self-esteem, set realistic goals. Expecting too much of yourself can be counterproductive and cause stress. Be flexible, change your goals if needed. Give it your best try—if it doesn't happen, try a different strategy: rethink your goal and start anew.

Working with others as a team player can do wonders for stimulating creative thoughts and motivation and is another way to strengthen self-esteem. Try to surround yourself with people who are supportive—avoid those who constantly attempt to discourage you from reaching your full potential.

Be assertive but not overly aggressive. Your demeanor is important in projecting high self-esteem. Always act in a professional manner. You become what you project. Project assurance and you'll become assured. Project confidence and you'll gain confidence. Project self-worth and your self-esteem will rise.

If on occasion you feel less confident, keep in mind it is only temporary. You can always rebound and regain your self-assurance.

The only thing we leave behind that's of worth is that which we generate in moments of peace and personal security. Free from the demon of fear, we manifest the divine.

Ronald Long
Financier

Self-Esteem in the Nonprofit World

Hunter Lovins
President, Rocky Mountain Institute

The promotion of self-esteem in the workplace isn't in the job description of many managers. But its presence is part of what enables employees to have the self-respect to give their hearts to the purposes of a company.

Most modern management theory is directed toward for-profit corporations. But there are thousands of small nonprofit groups struggling with the same issues, and getting little help from the experts.

Perhaps this is with good reason: anyone who claims to be an expert at the balancing act required to manage nonprofits simply hasn't realized the complexity of the situation. It is a skill one learns by doing, experimenting and erring, first on one side, then the other. For 23 years, I have served as a senior manager of various public interest organizations, the last 16 as the President of Rocky Mountain Institute, a 40-person resource policy center. This experience has taught me great humility about definitive pronouncements, but I offer these thoughts in the hope that my experience may help others embarking on or in the midst of this task.

Most of the people employed by for-profits are in it for the money. They may enjoy their jobs, but rarely see the mission of the company (as opposed to the fact that they have a job) as crucial to their sense of self. In contrast, most employees of nonprofits define themselves, in part, by the nature of the work they do. Because of this, they are frequently willing (indeed, required, if they wish to work for the charity) to accept below-market wages. They do this because they find the work itself to be sufficiently rewarding to make up for the monetary sacrifice. Should they begin to feel, however, that the organization is not taking their feelings seriously, their loyalty might shift dramatically.

Employee concerns tend to take two forms: feelings about the righteousness of their work and perceptions about how they are being treated as individuals. To complicate matters, these feelings are usually expressed together. Employees tend to expect a greater say in how the organization makes its decisions and to assume that management will automatically treat them in a humane, ethical fashion.

Nonprofit managers are used to being held to higher standards than most businesses. Part of what gives them their tax advantages is that they are created to serve the public interest. It is, however, widely assumed that they will do this in more ways than just their primary business. Their employees expect management to care about using resources more efficiently than a conventional business might, even if it costs more. They expect that nonprofits will recycle, not discriminate and not turn elderly workers out, and that management will care about employees' feelings.

Few participants in this equation, whether employee or administrator, question this elevation of standards in the abstract. The rub comes in the application. Nonprofits run the spectrum from small, communally run groups to hospitals and universities that differ little in their management techniques from any large corporation. Each group finds a management style that fits its preferences, but the tensions remain. From student demonstrations participated in by many faculty and even administrators, to members demanding greater social responsibility, to the note I recently got from a staff member calling for a meeting of all interested staff to evaluate the Institute's food buying practices (to see if we can provide healthier, more locally grown food for the staff), managers are frequently bombarded with staff initiatives to participate in decisions that in a traditional setting are reserved for the senior executives alone.

Most newcomers to the world of public interest management react with the understandable temptation to tell the employees to butt out, get their jobs done and leave the driving to us.

It won't work. Nonprofit employees aren't like widget workers, rotely installing this nut on that bolt, who can be replaced by unemployed teenagers or foreign workers.

The success of most nonprofits depends on the full-hearted contribution of its staff to the mission. And while the loyalty of the factory worker can be bought by the almighty dollar, the devotion of nonprofit staff members can only be earned. The mission will count for a lot, but the perception that the boss cares what the employees think, that everyone is working as hard as possible and that they're all in it together is the foundation without which nonprofit managers will find their staff reciting Johnny Paycheck's "Take this job and shove it." Worse, managers who lose their people's loyalty won't just have a resignation. They're likely to have an insurrection, taking up everyone's time fighting over an issue that's usually so silly it would quickly be resolved if the supervisor just spent a small amount of time hearing the person out and giving a rational response.

My company is not an encounter group, a family or a democracy. But its success depends on the willingness of its staff to draw from within themselves to propose approaches that haven't been tried before, and then go on and implement them. Being able to do that takes a greater than normal sense of self-esteem and a willingness to take risks. Developing that sense of self is thus important to our operation. The personal development of our staff is important enough to us that RMI pays for all successfully completed continuing education and routinely grants leave to people who want to pursue personal goals. But I firmly believe that the best way to develop more fully as a person and gain self-esteem is to take on a real challenge and accomplish it. To do this, most people need the help of their colleagues and guidance from their supervisors. So we give that, and we insist on accountability. But we also realize that taking risks means failing some of the time, and so is enhanced by having a safe environment to try mightily and still fall short.

Particularly in the nonprofit world, which seeks after all to change the world, it is through real accomplishments that individuals grow as people. We seek, therefore, to shift as much of the limelight from the founders to the younger staff, to let them be the ones interviewed by the media, make the speeches and be the senior author on the latest book. But this privilege must also be earned. The reputation of RMI is on the line whenever one of our people testifies or consults for a company. Staff members need to perform in a professional manner, and convey accurate, useful information. Learning to do that takes time, teaching and experience.

Managing young people as they learn requires a wry humor to realize that, by eliciting their creative energies to problem-solve their assignments, you will also get solutions to whatever else has caught their fancy. The sort of person who works for the betterment of the world is usually of above average intelligence (and thus gets bored just doing what they were supposed to do), possessed of a greater than normal desire to help (and thus a tendency to be meddlesome) and a well developed habit of thinking for themselves (which they do on your behalf, frequently requiring less management to get their jobs done, and on behalf of whatever possibly half baked notion just came to them, requiring more management to get them back on track).

The trick is to find a balance. You don't indulge staff members when the proposal is silly, but you do listen long enough to determine when they've just come up with a great plan, and hope you have the wisdom to know the difference. There is also a great difference between someone constructively seeking to improve the situation and someone acting out aggressions or needing recognition in a way that wastes everyone's time. Most nonprofits have accepted donations from people who believe in the stated mission, not necessarily the satisfaction of one staffer's idiosyncratic values. It is the job of the executive and senior staff to hold the organization on course. It means being willing to take the heat for drawing the line, and having enough personal self-esteem to tell people when the decision has been made and is no longer open for discussion.

Management means having a strong sense of where the organization should be going, which priorities really matter and which can bend to allow for an experiment. Sometimes it means calming the more traditional members of the staff while the whole group tries some off-the-wall idea, because a gut hunch says it'll pay off. For example, when our food purchaser came to me upset that the other staffers were questioning her frugal food purchasing practices, we agreed that her budget would be baseline, but that the staffers who want whatever they define as "more wholesome" food can add to that food budget whatever they can save the Institute in some other way.

The challenge is not just to give people a task and see that it is done in a timely, competent fashion, but to inspire the staff so that they will want to give your outfit's mission—*and their outfit's mission*—their best. The problems facing most nonprofits are unlikely to be solved unless the staff goes well beyond the call of duty and creates innovative approaches to problems for which there are too little money and too few resources to cope in any rational fashion.

And the truth is that fewer and fewer widget manufacturers are left. Most companies today are more like nonprofits than factories, and most employees are more like public interest folk than they are like assembly line workers. As more of us realize that our standard of living is imperiled by irresponsible treatment of the environment and wasteful practices, the lessons learned from managing the nonprofit sector that the experts have long ignored are more likely to be crucial to the success of conventional corporations than the other way around. And perhaps the first lesson is that people count, and it is only by building them up that you build your bottom line.

A New Paradigm

Michael Ray and Alan Rinzler

Coauthors, *The New Paradigm in Business*

In Brazil, Ricardo Semler runs Semco, an equipment manufacturing company, in a way that illustrates a new paradigm in business. Virtually everyone sets their own hours. There is no dress code. Some people with particularly valuable skills make higher salaries than their bosses without having to be in the management track. There is no hierarchy to speak of, other than titles of counselors, partners and associates who do the research, design, sales and manufacturing work.

Employees also make many of the important corporate decisions. For instance, workers, not real estate agents, found three prospective factory sites for one division of Semco. Then everyone from that division got into buses to visit the sites. The employees voted for one building that management didn't really want because it was across the street from a plant with one of the worst labor records in Brazil. But after the plant was purchased, the workers' creativity flourished as they designed the factory for a flexible manufacturing system and had one of Brazil's top artists paint the factory inside and out, including the machinery. As Semler says, "That plant really belongs to its employees. I feel like a guest every time I walk in." But he doesn't mind because the productivity per employee jumped from $14,200 to $37,500 four years after moving into the new site.

At Semco, employees are treated like adults rather than adolescents. More than 150 of the management people set their own salaries. Semco encourages employees to rotate jobs every three to five years. When supervisory people are hired, they are interviewed and evaluated by their future subordinates. There is an openness of information that includes providing classes so that each worker can learn how to understand financial data. Then monthly balance sheets, profit and loss analyses and cash flow statements are provided to each division. This information offers a context for creativity for everyone.

Semco's combination of democracy, profit sharing administered by the employees and open information has created one of Brazil's fastest growing companies. It was voted the best company in which to work, and it has a profit margin of 10%.

REWARDS BEYOND THE BOTTOM LINE

Gil Amelio

Chairman and Chief Executive Officer, Apple Computer, Inc.
Former Chairman, President and Chief Executive Officer,
National Semiconductor Corporation

In my experience in leading corporate transformation, raising the level of individual performance is a critical element of the change process. And it is important to encourage increased performance at all levels of the organization from the executive suite right down to the factory floor.

I also believe strongly that employee centered programs, such as our surveys of employee recommendations for change at National Semiconductor, must be driven by employees themselves in order to be believable and valuable. The input must come from employees, and even the team that evaluates and reports the findings must be made up entirely of grass roots workers—"no managers welcome."

Part of this process at National provides an excellent example of raising the self-esteem of one such worker. The resulting change in the level of her participation and contribution is truly amazing.

The employee selected to join the assessment group at the very first National Semiconductor survey conducted in this style was a woman we'll call Alice—an hourly, nearly minimum wage production worker from a plant in Arlington, Texas. Despite her limited formal education, her never having traveled far from her Texas birthplace and her narrow view of the world and society, the assignment would require Alice to travel to California, interact with people of diverse backgrounds and spend her days cooped up in meetings in corporate conference rooms. Suddenly, she was thrust onto a whole new stage where the pace, content and action would be foreign to her experience.

Alice walked in shyly for the first day's session, unsure of what she might possibly be able to contribute to such a process. By the end of the day, as a result of the atmosphere of acceptance and mutual respect, a change was already becoming evident in the way she felt about herself. She spoke up with observations representing the viewpoint that she and her co-workers held, and she could see that the group welcomed her input. Her confidence grew.

Other participants in the assessment team noticed that Alice's dress, posture and voice seemed to match the growing confidence, which continued to improve over the two weeks of the assessment team meetings.

At the final session, Alice was one of the people who volunteered to stand in front of the group and present some findings and recommendations to her CEO and his top managers, including her own boss's boss. Everyone remembers that day as a watershed for Alice: it was clear to all that she had been a valuable contributor to the group. Back in Texas she would have some unbelievable stories to tell.

The company staged a reception and going away dinner for the survey team and the executives, and Alice—who had never before spoken with any company official above the level of her immediate supervisor— sought me out as the CEO. She told me how the experience had raised her to new heights. She had even surprised herself, she said, by how much she could contribute. Ideas were drawn from deep inside her in a way she had never before been challenged to do. She had tapped deeply rooted capabilities, competencies, knowledge and experience.

I saw Alice again on a tour of the Arlington facility about a year later and was fascinated and rewarded to see that the changes had stuck. Alice had become a much more involved and valuable contributor to our organization.

Based on the recommendations of that original survey group, by the way, National instituted programs that would make the company more responsive to employees' needs—among them an ombudsman program and changes in some of the physical work conditions. The company also agreed to provide better information on the principles behind how compensation is determined, to give workers a much better sense that there is a basis of logic and equity at the root of the system.

Even at the corporate level, there were real changes in the level of effort and problem solving, and thus in profitability.

But it's important to recognize that the "Alices" in our company grow significantly from these experiences. An opportunity like this fundamentally changes the lives of every person involved. We've even seen people going back to school, reshaping their basic attitudes and taking an active part in community activities.

There are rewards beyond the bottom line when you raise people's self-esteem or, more correctly, give them the opportunity to raise it themselves.

CULTIVATING SELF-ESTEEM

Horst M. Rechelbacher
CEO, Aveda Corporation

The old Lakota was wise. He knew that man's heart away from nature becomes hard.

Standing Bear
Lakota Sioux

To wrap our hearts around earth and hold it Holy becomes a simple act of self-esteem.

Terma
The Box—A Gift of Remembrance

In a highly competitive marketplace, a company's survival and prosperity depend on the personal creativity, ingenuity and motivation of its employees. To feel truly successful, people need a higher ideal—an inspiring vision that transcends the motive for pure profit, especially since profit is often gained at the expense of the environment and of the rights of others.

Since our inception more than two decades ago, Aveda Corporation has worked to expand the boundaries of beauty, health and business by implementing innovative policies throughout the company—from our sourcing and procurement of quality ingredients, our research and development of superior products made from renewable plant resources, to our manufacturing, marketing and sales of products and systems that benefit people and the environment.

We've created a company with a conscience. We believe in giving back to the earth what we take from it by building a respectful partnership with our environment and making eco-conscious decisions that will ultimately protect and preserve all of us *and* the planet. Our aim is to foster a deep understanding and belief in protecting the complex, biological network that sustains all life on earth—the interdependent relationship between plants, animals, minerals, humans and the environment.

Our employees are motivated by these environmental and humanitarian concerns. Likewise, we take similar measures with employees—our key resources—by providing them with educational and self-development opportunities that reinforce a healthy respect for each other.

A business is a community, with a life and culture all its own. Aveda operates much like an indigenous tribal community whose culture, knowledge, environment and spirit of cooperation and commitment are shared among all members of the community. Like indigenous peoples, we aim to live in harmony with long term goals of what's best for our people and the environment, for many generations to come.

To survive and prosper, a business needs to be responsible and responsive to its own people, its common mission, its valuable resources and its impact on the world outside its own environment. By doing so, we can help build self-esteem and self-respect, not only among ourselves, but around the globe. It's a matter of developing pride, a spirit of cooperation and a mission of self-preservation.

Our training, corporate facilities and company resources and services are all dedicated to instill and reinforce a high regard for nature as well as an appreciation for our own bodies, minds and spirits—which comprise the "human ecosystem."

Our corporate facilities are designed to enhance the work environment and are surrounded by 65 acres of scenic woodlands and protected marshlands. Natural landscaping and wildlife create a picturesque setting. We also operate a day care facility and an organic foods restaurant—amenities that cater to employee health and convenience. It's our way of creating an appealing, integrated, healthy environment where our employees can flourish.

The concept of self-directed teams has also been integral to cultivating self-esteem and dignity. As in nature, projects and activities are performed by an intricate network of interdependent teams, each dedicated to the same ideals and empowered with the expertise and knowledge to accomplish different tasks on their own. Organized to encourage communication, interaction and cooperation, teams work together as partners to achieve a common goal. Sharing information and ideas, we support one other for the common good.

Because our company is organized by teams, instead of formally structured by department, encouraging teamwork is essential to the company's growth and success. We've devoted numerous hours and resources to providing each employee with special training sessions to develop more effective techniques for interpersonal communication among team members and teams. Our goal is to enhance respect and compassion for the individual and encourage participation and leadership, empowering each team member to implement new ideas. The aim is to share information and ideas freely, provide positive and well intentioned responses to reinforce each others' ideas and performance, and, in this way, generate and nurture the creativity, ingenuity and innovation of each individual.

Employees learn active listening skills—to hear others' ideas without criticizing or judging the individual. We accept and appreciate differences of opinion and a diversity of skills. Acknowledging the value of each person's contributions is vital to ensuring an open environment that encourages individual thought and initiative but discourages competition and rivalry among individuals and teams. Rather than singling out individuals, we prefer to honor and recognize all groups for their contributions.

Significant to this effort is our policy of sponsoring a series of team-oriented and self-development programs to teach employees the basics of biology, ecology, plant aroma studies, indigenous wisdom and self-health. Employees, spa and salon professionals, customers and other members of Aveda's worldwide network team learn how to enhance their lives—with helpful knowledge and techniques to restore personal well-being through intelligent ideas.

This information helps people attain a more balanced, healthy lifestyle. For example, our new Business of Being seminar is a five day spa retreat that incorporates strategies for individual growth. Participants learn methods for business and personal fulfillment: they study the dynamics of team building and personal development, and learn demonstrated techniques for stress management, personal wellness, goal setting, time management, problem solving, leadership, finance and marketing principles. They learn how to harmonize personal and professional life and how to rest, relax and rejuvenate body and mind in order to realize their full potential in life. Critical to the students' learning process is experiencing the actual spa treatments while participating in the seminar.

This healthy approach to living a balanced life is also reinforced by the establishment of the Aveda Holistic Lifestyle Center at our headquarters. A primary resource for all employees, the Center provides a series of educational programs and fitness services to help people attain a sense of physical and mental well-being. Based on the principle that the body is an ecosystem and performs best when in balance, this program provides individuals with the knowledge and means to develop physically, emotionally and spiritually. The Center offers classes and training on a wide variety of topics for self-improvement, including initial health assessments, personal fitness training, exercise programs, health and nutrition classes, massage therapy, dance workshops and a lifestyle resource library. The Center integrates ancient health and philosophical principles and practices from Indian and Asian cultures with contemporary body conditioning techniques and principles of nutrition. As a result, this total approach to personal development enables employees to reduce stress, increase pride and confidence in their physical and mental abilities, and ultimately feel great about themselves and Aveda.

In addition, we hold morning information sessions. Designed to encourage teamwork and voluntarism, and to inspire new ideas, these gatherings are held to share information with employees and promote open discussion. People learn the latest company news and attend presentations on a variety of thought-provoking topics by noted authors, scientists and environmentalists. We also make it a point to host company celebrations during the year to thank employees for their work and express appreciation.

Throughout our history, Aveda's mission and philosophy have helped to encourage respect, understanding and a sense of compassion for each other as well as for the planet. Clearly, our concern for our fellow beings translates into a broader appreciation of the world around us. As with any successful community, people and corporations thrive when self-respect and self-esteem prevail.

MANAGING TO LAUGH

John Imlay, Jr.
Former Chairman, Dunn & Bradstreet Software
Author, *Jungle Rules*

*I prefer things that are spontaneous ... I think it's important for there to
be an element of humor, laughter. It adds to the company. It's one more
thing that makes you want to get up in the morning and go to work.*

Joel Slutzky
Chairman, Odetics, Inc.

The other day I came into our office here (in London) and my car was
missing and sputtering. I pulled into the carpark, forgetting how big our
company had gotten. I was fuming and fussing the way you do when
your car is broken down. So I picked up the phone and called old Harry
down in administration. I said, "Harry, my car is broken. I need to borrow
the estate wagon."

He said, "John, I'm now a senior vice-president. I don't handle that
anymore."

"But what do I do?" I asked.

He said, "Dial 3198." So dutifully, I dial 3198.

A very enthusiastic young voice answers, "Motor Pool."

"Motor Pool?" I said. "What have you got down there?"

He says, "We've got lorries for going back and forth to the factory.
We've got estate wagons to pick up folks at the airport. We've got
Oldsmobiles and Pontiacs for the vice-presidents. We've got a big, old
Cadillac for our big, old president. And we've got a Mercedes for Fatty,
our chairman."

I said, "Do you know who this is!"

He said, "No."

I said, "This is John Imlay—your chairman."

Long pause.

Finally he said, "Do you know who this is?"

I said, "No."

He said, "So long, Fatty."

Editors' Note: Enjoying yourself may be the best thing you can do for
your health, suggests a new study conducted by Arthur A. Stone, PhD at
the State University of New York, Stony Brook. In his research, Dr. Stone

found that pleasant experiences appear to increase immune function for three days (the day you have fun and two days thereafter). Like many other studies, these findings also showed that negative events can inhibit your immune system; however, this research demonstrated that the decreased immunity lasted only for the day that the stress occurred. As a result, enjoyable experiences may have a greater influence on immune function than undesirable events, and people may be able to balance the negative effects of stress with more positive activities, says Dr. Stone. This supports a previous study he conducted in which an increase in unpleasant events and a decrease in enjoyable experiences seemed related to catching a cold.

MEDITATION IN THE WORKPLACE

Robert Roth

Corporate Trainer
Author, *Transcendental Meditation*

I think it would be great some time if a whole company stopped for 15 minutes each day and meditated.

John Bradshaw

In 1983, R.W. "Buck" Montgomery, Jr., wanted to turn around his Detroit based chemical manufacturing company, the H. A. Montgomery Company.

"The company had been in business for over 40 years," Buck recalls. "It had gotten into a routine, a rut of old time management, and it was difficult to get the people to see new thinking. At the time the U.S. automotive industry was in a great slump, stalled by imports from Japan and Germany.

"We needed a new approach to everything—a new attitude, new thinking and new energy to revitalize the company and get it to take off again."

Buck and his staff attended numerous seminars and courses.

"We would go to weekend or week long seminars, and we'd return with these huge books, and we'd still be plagued with the same problems. We'd forget what we learned, or we didn't have time to restudy what we'd learned, due to the demands of the job, and so we just went back to our old routine.

"I was looking for a tool that my employees could utilize every day, that would allow them to change their thinking, allow them to have more energy, be more creative on their own and use more of their potential on the job. I found Transcendental Meditation to be the tool that would work."

Buck sat down with his senior staff and came up with a plan. First, Transcendental Meditation would be offered at company expense to anyone interested among the managers. They would meditate twice a day for six months. They would be asked, on a monthly basis, to write progress reports, pro or con, on what they thought of the program and how it was affecting them in their daily life—both at the office and at home. Then they would decide if the program would go companywide.

"After six months there was 100% agreement among that management group to offer the program throughout the company," Buck says. "Transcendental Meditation was then introduced into research, manufacturing, sales, marketing and administration."

Buck encouraged his managers and employees to meditate at least once a day—in the morning or in the late afternoon—on company time at the plant.

"Productivity improved dramatically," Buck says. "Absenteeism decreased drastically, as did sick days and injuries. The creativity of our research department went up, sales increased 120% in two years and profitability went up 520%."

In 1987 Buck sold the company and retired. He now spends his time with his family and consults with companies that are looking for new avenues for success. He is often asked to speak on the success of the Transcendental Meditation program at his former company to executives who are interested in repeating that success in their own firms.

"The individual is the most important resource a business has," Buck says. "You've got to improve the capacity and capabilities of the individual. If you take a tired individual, or one who is not motivated or who doesn't feel he has any creativity, no matter what tools you put in his hands, it's a waste of time. First you have to improve the individual, increase his potential; then you can give him other tools to work with. The only program that I know that will do that is Transcendental Meditation. The small amount of money it costs today will be of immeasurable benefit to the company on the profitability line and on a morale line—and everything else you can imagine. This is success."

SOURCE: Reprinted by permission of John Grimes. © John Grimes.

Managing from Within

John Goodman

Managing Partner, Sage Company

What makes one company more successful than another? What is the secret to having happy, fulfilled, productive employees? To find the answers, I believe that the company must let go of control, suspend judgment and tap into the creativity, innovation and intuition of each individual employee.

Many companies have a hard time letting go of the control; the rules learned in management school die hard. It's easier to manage according to a set of one-size-fits-all rules, molding a person to fit a job description rather than allowing that person's unique potential to unfold in the job. Traditional ways of considering employees, by job title or employee ID number, no longer work. It's time to look at employees as individuals and to value them for their unique talents and abilities.

Start with Trust

If employees are to become all that they can be, first you must trust them. When you assume that their best efforts will be made, you have bestowed respect. In turn, the employees develop self-trust. Our company, the Sage Company, is a reflection of the people who work here, who are all trusted to take responsibility for their own actions, education, health and relationships. Management can't control, can't manipulate, can't make happen what we think should happen or what we want to happen. We simply encourage our employees to go within, to trust that they have what they need to fulfill their potential.

In each of us, there is a reservoir of energy, creativity and innovation just waiting to be tapped. It's there and, when it works, it's awe-inspiring. Perhaps you've experienced the process when you've procrastinated over meeting a deadline. You just can't get started, but in the final hour, you feel a surge of creativity. Your direction becomes crystal clear and you see the solution easily. You might even say to yourself, "Wow, where did that come from?" When we allow ourselves to trust the process, we increase our ability to tap into that reservoir at will.

If you are engaged in meaningful work, you are naturally more effective. We keep it very simple: if you want to come and work with us, we will support your being all that you are now and all that you want to become. That's the key. If you love your work, then you are involved in the process rather than continually looking for the outcome. If your goal is to make a million dollars, eventually that million dollars doesn't buy what you thought it would. Rather than focus on a monetary outcome, work at being the best in the process. The inner satisfaction and esteem that result are the highest reward.

Learning to live in the present is a valuable skill. This illustration is a shining example of what can happen when we trust our own intuition and live in the moment. Our office building in Minneapolis is across the street from a house with 15 acres of land attached. One of our goals has been to build 76 units of assisted living apartments for seniors adjacent to our office with an additional facility for helping children. This parcel of land was a perfect location and we'd had our eyes on it for a long time. We had discussed several strategies for getting the property, including sending in a third party to do the negotiations with the owner.

One day, on the spur of the moment, I simply turned left into the driveway. I went to the door and knocked. The owner, Mary, answered. I said, "Mary, I'm your neighbor. My company has been across the street from you for three years. I'd like to come in and talk to you about our vision." She agreed to listen to my story. "Mary," I explained, "I have a vision of doing assisted living apartments in the property next to our office. And across the street (Mary's property), I have a vision of establishing a Wellness Center. In it, we'd be taking care of children from abused families and also children who need mechanical assistance. My real love is children and we would like to do an intergenerational day care."

You know what Mary told me? She said, "I've taken care of 700 abused children in my life. I've had seven children of my own, but I've also taken care of abused children." A business person typically would say, "Let's get someone over there to snatch up the property—get it for $100,000 as it's listed by the tax assessor. Mary isn't a sophisticated negotiator; so we'll be able to meet our objectives easily." However, that goes against all of our principles of fairness and respect. It's very simple. I know what Mary wants. She has seven children. She wants money for her children. She would like to expand her dream. It was my responsibility to behave according to my personal values. If I had exercised the "I win, you lose" mentality, I wouldn't have had this beautiful experience with Mary.

To date, the city fathers have not seen fit to grant our rezoning requests. When they do, I can tell you that this project will be dedicated to Mary. It will be known for her because of her life's work. If she had planned 20 years ago to take care of 700 kids so that someone would come along, give her a large sum of money and dedicate a facility to her, the dream would have been impossible to realize. But if we act each day according to our inner compasses and allow our goodness and intuition to guide us, miracles result. Both Mary and I found the miracle.

The Attitude of Self

Each of us has control only over our own belief system and our own attitude. The old saying is true, "If you always do what you've always done, you'll always get what you've always gotten." We seem to make the same mistakes time and again. Think of the acrobat on the trapeze. He wants to go to the second trapeze, but he can't until he lets go of the first. When he does let go of the first, he's hanging for a split second. That moment in space seems to last forever. Ultimately, the acrobat can't reach the second trapeze until he lets go of the first.

It's that point at which you're hanging in space when learning occurs. You must let go of the old attitudes, the old ways of doing things, no matter how comfortable or familiar. Most of us do what we've always done because of the allure, the seduction of the familiar. We encourage our employees to step out into the darkness or unknowingness. That's when the opportunity for change and learning is greatest. The message is—if you've been doing something your whole life and getting the same results, just try something different.

Three Keys to Self-Responsibility

Learning self-responsibility often requires that we let go of the first trapeze. I firmly believe that all of the answers each of us need are already within us, waiting to be explored. Each person's process is different, but key principles remain the same.

1. *You are who you choose to be.* You've chosen to do what you're doing, interacting with the people you've selected. You are neither victim nor unwitting hero. You have made a full and conscious decision to be the person you are today.
2. *Don't be judgmental.* Making judgments about ourselves or others is a waste of energy. It's subjective and typically based on perception, interpretation or prejudice. It should have, would have, could have— and has no power to affect change. Take responsibility to look for the positives.
3. *Develop a healthy attitude toward change.* If you want your life to be different, you need to visualize it differently. What the mind can conceive, the mind can create.

Putting Principles to Work

How do we visualize our life at Sage? At the heart of our vision is balance—between body, spirit, mind and emotions. We believe that your thoughts affect both your physical body and your emotional body. That connection starts within each person and then reaches outward into the environment and the world.

We are a team committed to one another—encouraging, nurturing and enhancing self-esteem and fostering a sense of belonging and love for ourselves and others. This may seem like a lofty ideal, but it's really just common sense. I have a choice when I go to work every day. I can work in an environment that empowers and nurtures me, working with people who share my vision. Or I can keep my life separate from my work—clinging to the first trapeze. That's not much fun and it certainly doesn't allow much room for growth.

We didn't always operate according to these principles. We didn't wake up one day and say, "Here's our new vision for the company. This is what we want to be." Like most companies, ours is a reflection of the slow process of both individual growth and mutual trust. We've developed our own knowingness along the way. I encourage people to leave and I encourage them to stay; it's their choice. It's up to each person to decide; if they want to stay and work through the tough issues, I'll support them in that. That's one thing that we do; we provide a safe harbor for people to go through life's changes. We don't expect them to be robots.

Self-responsibility means acting according to our own conscience. All persons are given a specific area of responsibility. Ultimately, the freedom to plan and implement programs and to make decisions rests solely with them. If they need resources, they'll get resources. If they have questions, we'll help them find the answers. But the responsibility is theirs alone.

We believe that wellness is a way of life. It's the lifestyle you design in order to achieve your highest potential for well-being physically, emotionally, mentally and spiritually. This includes the dimensions of nutrition, physical awareness, stress reduction and self-responsibility. It's knowing what your real needs are and addressing them daily. It's knowing how to create and cultivate close relationships. It's responding to challenges in life as opportunities. It's creating the life you want rather than just reacting. It's enjoying a basic sense of well-being even through times of adversity. And so our vision of values has manifested itself through our employees.

What we can do as a company is just provide room for people to be all they can be. That's the key. We remove our corporate ego; we manage less and facilitate more. You won't find layers of structure at Sage. If you put levels on top of levels, you are saying to the level below it is not capable—needs watching or needs guidance. It subtly undermines self-esteem rather than instill pride and self-trust. Our people make their jobs their own, without people looking over their shoulders.

This philosophy dictates that each person is vulnerable, revealing the self to co-workers. The reward is that each person is allowed to make decisions more readily and exercise judgment both freely and coopera-tively. As a result, you'll find employees internally motivated. There is built-in accountability and personal responsibility. In short, it makes happy, fulfilled, productive employees. And that, I believe, is what makes a successful company.

I was once asked to sum up what I have learned about relationships in the form of a letter to my son. It illustrates what I believe about per-sonal relationships as well as those we have in our public, working lives. The letter reads,

> *Dear Shane: My task is to communicate to you what works and doesn't work in a relationship. First, let me assure you that you know what's best for you with respect to relationships. Let me tell you what my soul needed to learn:*
>
> *First, you get no more out of a relationship than you are willing to put in; you can't have love and commitment unless you are willing to give it. Second, learn not to sabotage the goodness in your life. If you believe that good things don't last, you'll expect good relationships to end. Third, know yourself and what you need in a relationship. Realize that a positive, healthy relationship can only enhance who you are but can't fill your voids. Work on yourself because as you learn to cherish and love yourself, then and only then will you be able to love and cherish someone else. Fourth, learn from life's experiences. As you relate to people, see how it affects you and others. Know that people are either lovers or teachers and that we can learn from both. It is not the mistakes we make that create change, but rather it is our own ability to learn from our experiences. Fifth, there is no such thing as perfection because life is constantly changing. Realize it's a process: do the best with what you have available. Learn to make decisions that bring joy, love and compassion. Sixth, listen to your heart. The models you see, such as Mom and me, may or may not be how you decide to pat-tern your life. Each of us comes here to learn different lessons; you and your soul know what those will be for you in your lifetime.*
>
> *My learning has been about relationships; I needed relationships that were changing, sometimes very painfully, to help me grow and learn what is important. I have learned that there is a tremendous difference be-tween loving and cherishing someone versus a strong attraction. Loving brings with it a strong sense of support and respect, cooperation rather than competition, and unconditional acceptance.*

I believe that as I change my attitudes about relationships in life, I will attract others who share similar beliefs. Shane, if you trust and believe in yourself, you will know no limitations to your ability to love and be loved. Remember that God helps and guides you and loves you very much.

Dad.

Pride of Ownership

Jack Stack

Chairman and CEO, Springfield Re-Manufacturing Corporation
Author, *The Great Game of Business*

*There is in this world no such force as the force of a man determined to
rise. The human soul cannot be permanently chained.*

W. E. B. DuBois

Where you begin will depend entirely on your circumstances. When I
came to Springfield, there was so little mutual trust and respect that I had
to start at the most basic level—listening. In my first couple of months, I
met with every single one of the hundred or so employees. I brought them
into the conference room in little groups, three, four, five at a time. I asked
them what they wanted, what they felt, where they wanted to go, what
they wanted to do. We talked about life. We talked about dreams. We
talked about winning. I asked them what tools they needed to do their
jobs. People talked very freely, and they had harsh things to say about
management. I asked them just to give us a chance.

Of course, most companies aren't in as bad shape as we were. Yours
may not need the kind of intensive treatment we had to administer to the
Renew Center before we could start teaching people the numbers. But
there is no such thing as a management team with too much credibility or
a work force with too much enthusiasm. The truth is that we still use
many of the techniques we developed back in those days, and we are still
guided by many of the lessons we learned then.

Pride before Ownership

For people to feel like winners, they must have pride in themselves and
what they do. There is no winning without pride, just as there is no ownership without pride. Pride is all about caring. It is the sense of pleasure
or satisfaction you take in what you do or in what you have. If you don't
care, you're not going to do what is necessary to be a winner or an owner.
So pride has to come first. The problem is that a lot of people don't know
how to be proud of something. They were never taught to care as kids. So
how are you going to get them to care about their work or their company? It requires a whole training program. But if people don't feel proud of
the company they work for, they won't ever want to own it, and they
won't ever feel responsible for it.

In the first couple of years after I came to Springfield, I worked very hard to instill a sense of pride in the people who worked at the Renew Center. We used very simple techniques—an open house, for example. We put one on at Melrose Park, and it was a huge success. We held it on a weekend, in the employee parking lots. We brought in tractors, and people invited their moms and dads and kids to come in and see where they worked. We created a lot of goodwill. It was a way of letting people feel important. I decided to do the same thing at the Renew Center. I wanted people to feel proud of their jobs. I wanted them to feel like giants. I wanted a kid to look up to his dad and say, "Wow, you really do this, Daddy? You're a welder? That's really important."

In preparation for the open house, we gave people buckets of paint and allowed them to decorate their machines and their work areas. Some of the guys got their wives, who were generally more artistic, to paint bold statements on the walls. We had American flags, Hell's Angel insignias, everything you can imagine. Some departments put up slogans, like "Machining—We Make It Work." There were signs and symbols everywhere, and none of it was color coordinated. It looked awful, but it was theirs. They were putting their own identities out there for everyone to see. When they brought their families in, they could say, "Here's where I work; this is my environment."

We also hoped the painting would encourage good housekeeping, which is important in a factory for reasons of both safety and efficiency. We figured that people would be more likely to keep the shop clean if it was theirs, if they put their mark on it. We also figured they'd want it to be clean for the open house. But what turned out to be the best thing for housekeeping were the tours we started having a few years later. When outsiders began coming in to tour the facility, people started taking extra care to keep their areas clean. They wanted to be proud of their work areas.

We used every technique we could think of to generate pride. We held fishing and baseball tournaments. A local radio station decided to raise money for charity by sponsoring a frozen carp throwing contest. Contestants would be given frozen fish to throw as far as they could. So we entered, and sure enough someone from our plant won.

We never turned down a chance to compete. We took part in relay races against other companies. We had some major event going on at least once a month. We wanted people to wear our colors all the time, and we changed them frequently. We were real big on hats, caps and jackets. We created events in which they could win these things—housekeeping games, attendance games. We had attendance award dinners. If you had perfect attendance for a certain period of time, we would give you a plaque to take home, and we'd take you and your family out to dinner. I usually took them myself. Let me tell you, I ate out a lot for about two years. Then we had Christmas parties, and we gave out Christmas gifts. We always tried to surprise people. One year we'd give out turkeys, another year cheese balls. It was all part of getting people to feel great about the place they worked.

We still work hard at instilling a sense of pride and ownership, but now we rely more on things like our bonus program, the Employee Stock Ownership Plan, the weekly staff meetings, and the games we play around the numbers. We got to the point where people were ready to learn financials, which allowed us to do much more than we could in the beginning. What changed were the methods, not the goals. You have to start very simply. You can't get much simpler than a paintbrush and a bucket of paint.

SOURCE: Reprinted by permission of John Grimes. © John Grimes.

Getting an "A" or a star is all right, but I'd like some sort of profit sharing plan around here.

Self-Esteem at Rhino Records

Richard Foos

Founder and President, Rhino Records

I have strong feelings about self-esteem being something important and something all too lacking in the workplace and in our society. I think most people in our society believe in motivation by fear. Every experience bears this out, from going to school, where if you're bad you'll get bad grades, all the way up to the most obvious example, the army. And by virtue of this I think most businesses are set up to really demean the individual by a kind of militaristic approach—this is the way you do it, this is what you're going to do, this is how you're going to do it. For this reason inherently it's very difficult in the workplace to help people with self-esteem.

At Rhino we try to enhance self-esteem as much as we can. To begin with we try to have more fun. The product that we're putting out is fun so we try to have fun working and enjoying ourselves. In terms of working together we try to show our responsibility as a business, in the city of Los Angeles, and in our community, to contribute something, to give back something. This, in turn, enhances teamwork and camaraderie and bonding. So it has a positive business effect too.

In terms of social responsibility, we encourage each of our employees to do 60 hours of community service a year. In return, they get the week off between Christmas and New Year's, and then, if they accumulate more than 60 hours per year they get additional time off. We have a volunteer team within the company that administrates the whole program. They really work with people in terms of the community service they're going to do. We also have a community service day, where a group of employees goes somewhere to either put on workshops, visit a community center in South Central Los Angeles, visit a Seniors' Home, or even take a group of kids camping.

I think if you asked people in our company, or anybody who does volunteer work, "Do you get out of it more than what you give?" they would say yes! Any employee who goes out and tutors someone in the inner city who is having problems reading, prepares food for the homeless or visits a nursing home is going to ultimately feel better about themselves because they can help. Does it help their self-esteem? Absolutely.

In addition to community service programs at Rhino, we also have a speakers' series. For example, we've had the Chairman of the Office of Americas come and speak to us about the situation in Central and South America. We had a Rabbi come teach an eight week, nondenominational class on personal growth. We have had speakers on homeless issues, affirmative action—any one of a hundred different topics.

We also have something called a Bucks A Week program, which our Social/Environmental Responsibility team administers. This is a program in which employees donate money to homeless organizations and it's taken out of their paychecks. This team also decides where our corporate nonprofit giving goes every year. They look at things like recycling programs and office environmental programs, too.

We serve a lunch every day, which we subsidize and it's always healthy and includes a vegetarian choice. We have yoga classes on site that are reduced in price, as well as nightly aerobics and exercise classes. We have a gym and a ping pong table. Also, we have a masseuse come to the office once a week, and people sign up on a rotation system, free. I think all these things make it just a more human, fun, enjoyable and interesting place to work. And all these things are not a lot of trouble, and they cost the company relatively very little.

Basically, if somebody tells me that there's a better way to run the company, and I agree that it is a better way, I have to do it, or I won't be satisfied. I guess it's my ambition, but I can only run the company in the best, most responsible way I can or I will feel badly. I would say I have moderate self-esteem, which fluctuates, but acting responsibly and consciously helps to build it.

I attended a Businesses for Social Responsibility meeting, for example, and it was so good to know that a hundred other companies are thinking as we are. A lot of them have similar backgrounds to mine, having been a radical in the 1960s, and then getting into business, and eventually looking around and asking, how can I marry my ethics and politics and social values with a business? I didn't know that before. Most of my friends didn't go into business because, in the 1960s and 1970s, it was considered so capitalistic.

But I love what I do. I love pop culture. So I love the music we put out, the videos we put out. I collect these kinds of things. So I kind of live what I do.

At Rhino, mostly we just believe in the importance of the individual, and we treat our employees with a lot of respect and we think about every action. We try to act consciously and responsibly in everything we do.

I think low self-esteem plays itself out in the workplace and in society through an attitude of machismo: "I don't think much of myself; so I'm going to build myself up and have this false sense of pride." Then you see these huge corporate takeovers, and every time there is one of these takeovers, there's not a lot of thought given to the people. The people get laid off or one company swallows the other company and doesn't need the employees any more.

I would say to other business owners, I would urge you to run your business as responsibly as possible. I guarantee you it won't hurt your profits. Really look at the big picture. Ask, "What am I doing? How is what I am doing affecting my society and my employees?" I hope that businesses will start looking at that more and more. I hope they ask what is the result of running a business by fear, conducting motivation by fear? Over the long run, is that helping or hurting?

One extra large guy, no onions.

On Self-Esteem

L. S. Barksdale

Founder, The Barksdale Foundation for the Furtherance of Human Understanding
Author, *Building Self-Esteem* and *Essays on Self-Esteem*

I began my life on a cattle ranch in the heart of the Colorado Rockies and was graduated from Colorado State University in the depth of the great depression of 1929 with a Bachelor of Science degree in mechanical engineering. To support myself and my family, I did various manual and semiskilled work on new road construction and worked as a general mechanic and high line rigger on three dam construction jobs. I also worked as a brakeman, "chuck tender" and "gandy dancer" on the Colorado River Aqueduct. I really thought I had it made when I finally succeeded in landing my first engineering job with a major oil company in the fall of 1935. I was sadly disillusioned when the company's new chief engineer called me into his office one day early in the recession of 1937. He not only fired me but told me: "Barksdale, you just don't have what it takes to get ahead in the world. You had better get some routine job and be content with it." My already abysmally low self-esteem really hit bottom and I had no place to go but "up."

Feeling very unworthy and "less than," I experienced a desperate and compulsive need to prove my worth through my achievements—not then realizing that my very existence proves my innate worth and importance. With such intense motivation, I opened a successful engineering and development firm. Later I became the co-partner and president of a business that furnished over 80% of the hydraulic control valves used on U.S. aircraft, both military and commercial. I also became the co-partner of the largest costume jewelry manufacturer west of the Mississippi.

Disposing of my interest in these firms, I founded three other highly successful firms, which did a thriving business throughout the free world. I developed a revolutionary valving principle and pioneered extreme pressure fluid controls for both aircraft and industry. Among other accomplishments, I designed and built highly specialized valves for the *Nautilus*, the first atomic powered submarine, after other valve companies had given up.

In spite of my material success and, although the recipient of numerous honors and awards, I found, to my dismay, that my intense feelings of inferiority and unworthiness had in no way diminished. What was wrong? Hadn't I shown both my past critics and myself that I was a success in both engineering and business?

Finally, my continuing deep sense of inferiority and unworthiness caused me to question my values and frantic lifestyle and to embark on an intense search for self-understanding. There followed years of unhappiness, of penetrating self-probing and observation accompanied by agonizing migraine headaches, high blood pressure, ulcers, arthritis and finally, a heart attack.

My desperate and ceaseless search, however, gradually opened insights into the cause of my years of intense hurting and unhappiness. To my amazement, I discovered that I had been attempting to live a normal happy life in a world of impossibly high standards erected by myself and society, in a compulsive effort to prove my worth. In this strange and unreal world anything less than perfection was inadequate and blameworthy, and thus a cause for deep feelings of inferiority, shame and guilt. I strove so hard to meet my unreasonable standards of performance that I achieved a high measure of material success but was continually plagued with accompanying physical ailments. Neither did I achieve the genuine "feel good" I have since found is everyone's birthright. For no matter how hard I tried or how well I did, I never felt I had done "well enough." Thus, I was never able to overcome my extreme sense of inadequacy, inferiority and self-rejection.

I was in a continual state of emotional turmoil and hurting and finally realized that, without a drastic change in my concepts and values, I would never be able to "feel good." This realization sparked a desperate search for the solution to my self-rejection and hurting. The resulting insights made it abundantly clear that all my self-accusation, shame, guilt and remorse—my sense of unworthiness and feeling "less than" every time I made a mistake, my extreme unhappiness—were the products of faulty cultural conditioning.

Once I was able to discover the false concepts of human behavior that perpetuated my unhappiness and hurting and that, I also discovered, were totally invalid, I was able to replace them with concepts in alignment with the realities observable in human behavior. It was then I realized that my very existence proves my worth and importance, and that I could in no way improve my worth by my accomplishments. This realization enabled me to achieve true success—that is, happiness in my personal life.

These insights revolutionized my life and in 1964 motivated me to dispose of my business interests, both at home and abroad, in order to devote the balance of my life to helping people achieve sound self-esteem, which is *genuine love of self*. This is done by enabling them to get rid of their false and destructive concepts and replace them with the observable *realities* of human behavior.

My greatest motivation, however, for contributing my energy and fortune to this endeavor is the clear realization that children yet unborn will suffer as I have suffered, through the destructive lifestyle passed on from generation to generation by parents with low self-esteem. Unless this vicious cycle is broken, we will have more and more battered children, parent-child alienation, suicides, crime in the streets, an ever increasing welfare load, more overflowing prisons and mental health institutions, more and more alcohol and drug abuse centers and an ever more staggering divorce rate—all stemming from a hurting or crippling lack of self-esteem, from the self-rejection resulting from a false sense of inadequacy, inferiority and worthlessness.

To this end I founded the Barksdale Foundation, a nonprofit, self-funding institution *For Furtherance of Human Understanding.* I cite my own personal experience as evidence of the dynamic effectiveness of its Self-Esteem Program. At 68, after many years of both emotional and physical pain, the deaths of both my only son and my cherished wife and other devastating personal problems, I feel better mentally, physically *and emotionally* than I have ever felt in my life.

Eighteen Ways of Perpetuating Low Self-Esteem

Here are 18 ways I have discovered that you can perpetuate low self-esteem.

1. Identifying with your actions rather than with your nonphysical essence—a lack of realization that you are a unique and precious being, however unwise or inadequate your actions.

2. Not being in conscious charge of your own life and not accepting full responsibility for your own growth and total well-being, regardless of handicapping circumstances beyond your control.

3. Not having and actively pursuing a life objective that is meaningful to you; a lack of clear-cut and meaningful goals to guide your decisions and to preclude "coasting," self-indulgence, procrastination and lack of self-discipline.

4. Not recognizing and exercising your inherent authority over your own life and affairs; not doing your own thinking and making your own decisions; requiring the permission, confirmation and agreement of others for what you think, say and do.

5. Being a "professional people pleaser."

6. Working at an occupation that you heartily dislike, especially one that is not meaningful to you.

7. Neglecting or ignoring your own needs in order to "serve" others; not recognizing and accepting your own growth and well-being as your number one responsibility.

8. Not realizing that you are invariably doing the best you can possibly do at the time, regardless of your mistakes, unacceptable behavior or human frailties.

9. Harboring shame, guilt and remorse—and/or self-pity.

10. Indulging in destructive criticism and self-accusation; belittling and condemning yourself for your mistakes and failures.

11. Depending on others for a sense of importance and realness rather than realizing that everyone is of equal worth and importance; not recognizing that we vary only in our individual awareness—in our specific talents and capabilities.

12. Not allowing yourself the right and freedom of full expression; not "doing your own thing"; not developing your innate talents and capabilities.

13. Not following your endeavors through to a logical conclusion, i.e., "giving up" before the job is finished.

14. Comparing yourself and your accomplishments, i.e., your actions, with those of others as a gauge of your individual worth and importance; having a conviction that you must prove your worth through superior performance and achievements.

15. Not speaking up for your own convictions; letting others ignore and belittle you; not realizing that others cannot insult or "put you down" unless you accept their worth and authority over your own.

16. Depending on others for doing things that you are capable of doing for yourself.

17. Not realizing that your very existence proves your innate worth and importance, regardless of how well or how poorly you conform to accepted standards.

18. In short, not thoroughly understanding and being aware of the "Realities of Human Behavior" and acting accordingly—especially continuing to *value judge* yourself for every mistake, shortcoming, defeat and human frailty.

Since you cannot escape the consequences and therefore the responsibility for your actions, you are the final authority for your every thought, word and deed. Therefore, exercise this authority and consciously take full charge of your own life and affairs. It is much better for your self-esteem to make mistakes through unwise decisions than to fail by default.

Why should we praise or condemn—reward or punish—people for saying or doing what their current awareness compels them to? Especially when we know that peoples' awareness is the automatic product of their heritage and total conditioning—that at any given instant it simply is what it is, and therefore is subject to neither credit nor blame.

Praise without blame is like a stick with only one end, for we cannot justify either without, at the same time, validating the other. Neither has any more reality than a coin with only one side. Recognition and appreciation, however, are both valid and constructive actions, and therefore highly desirable.

The act of drinking a cup of coffee is mute evidence that a man is not his actions—that he is merely satisfying his need or desire for a drink of coffee. Is he any more his actions if, in anger, he throws it in another's face? Is this action not also simply a means of satisfying his dominant need, even though it is distorted?

In appraising one's character, it is not the action but the motivation that counts.

Humility and gratitude are natural reactions for aware persons toward their outstanding characteristics and achievements, for they realize that it is only their Awareness that is responsible—and that for their Awareness they can claim no credit.

You can succeed in building sound self-esteem only by having sufficient motivation, maintaining a clear vision of its achievement and persevering with faith in its accomplishment.

May the blessings of sound self-esteem be yours all the days of your life.

A Capitalist Looks at Self-Esteem in the Workplace

George E. McCown

Chairman and CEO, McCown and De Leeuw & Co.

Take away my people, but leave my factories, and soon grass will grow on the factory floor. Take away my factories, but leave my people, and soon we will have a new and better factory.

Andrew Carnegie

Editor's Note: Management innovation and the development of human capital provide many businesses with their most important tools for competitiveness in the 1990s and beyond. This article discusses the challenges, opportunities and results of employee self-esteem and empowerment from the personal perspective of an investor in more than 25 companies that collectively represent more than $4.5 billion in annual sales.

Changing the Way We Look at Business

We are living in a period of sweeping and perhaps unprecedented global change. People want some degree of mastery over their lives, to know they can strive and enjoy the fruits of their labors, a sense of their own value. Quite simply, they deserve the self-esteem that can only come through empowerment.

Individual empowerment is the key, and it must begin in the workplace. As the dominant institution in the world, business must be as effective socially as it is economically. The success, and perhaps even the survival, of any business enterprise will in large part be dependent on its response to this challenge.

Business has always been a means of creating value, but most businesses have concentrated on the value they can create in the marketplace, not in the workplace. Increasingly, we will be unable to accomplish the first without also accomplishing the second. We must change the way we look at business—what its role is and how it is organized to fulfill that role. We must recognize that creating value for employees can be a *means* of creating market value.

The most fundamental strategy for achieving this lies in empowering the work force to nurture individual, and thus organizational, self-esteem. Through empowerment, every employee throughout the organization becomes a *business person* responsible not only for the

SOURCE: Dilbert by Scott Adams. Reprinted by permission of United Feature Syndicate, Inc.

quality of his or her own work and working experience, but for the overall outcome.

Workers to some degree become the leaders; management becomes a coach or facilitator. The business serves its constituencies by allowing the creativity and knowledge of the people who are closest to the action to really guide what happens—to cut through and solve problems and to recognize opportunities on a more or less continuous basis.

The Views of a Capitalist

This is no utopian vision. My views on the importance of employee self-esteem and empowerment are the result of many years' experience as an engineer, manager and investor. After working with venture capital pioneer Georges Doriot as a young man, I spent 18 years at Boise Cascade in a variety of operating management positions. Personal and peer experiences suggested that many operating divisions of large corporations could be more successful if they were more entrepreneurial. I felt, and still feel, that the key is empowering management and employees with the freedom and responsibility of ownership.

In 1984, investment banker David De Leeuw and I founded McCown De Leeuw & Co. (MDC), which we call a "venture banking" firm. MDC acquires relatively mature operating companies if we believe revitalization can lead to improved performance. Our acquisitions share two common, fundamental features. First, we back excellent management teams, and we expect them to take significant ownership positions in their company. Second, because of the size of the companies we target (usually with sales in the range of $50–$300 million), our acquisitions typically involve recapitalization or leveraged debt. Our leveraged acquisitions are very different from the asset stripping that has given leveraged buy-outs a bad name in many circles. We see our acquisitions as the beginning of a long term partnership aimed at value creation through improved performance and future growth. Accordingly, there is often a strong mandate for organizational transformation.

We have seen time and time again that such acquisitions are most successful when they empower management *and* employees, and this belief has become a distinguishing aspect of the way we conduct business. We believe a critical part of our job is to serve as a catalyst for change and to assist with whatever organizational transformation is required.

Ownership Transition:
A Unique Opportunity for Change

A change in ownership provides a unique opportunity to revitalize a corporate culture. It creates a period of flux that opens the door to new practices and principles. The first questions management must ask itself are: Do we need a change in culture? Can we create real value from change? Can we accomplish it alone? I have found the answers to those questions—even for truly excellent companies—are often "yes, yes and we don't know."

Some common issues can undermine an organization's vitality, and they often provide a roadmap for change. First, of course, is the implicit and natural fear of change itself. One technique that we have used at MDC and with other managers is to ask the question: "What would you do if you weren't afraid?" In other words, if you knew that the outcome would be okay, what would you do? This suggests the second roadblock—language. We have to find the language and the ways to discuss spirituality and personal values within the discourse of business. The third issue is commitment. I have been told that Total Quality Management programs have failed around 80% of the time because people took it as a "project," which smacks of "we're doing this because somebody else wants us to" rather than as a fundamental culture change. Finally, a company's reward system often is where the rubber hits the road when it comes to an employee's perception of corporate culture.

Common Qualities of an Empowered Organization

There is no universal blueprint for transforming an organization. In fact, each organization is most successful when it creates and reinforces its own individual personality. But I have noticed three common qualities in successfully empowered organizations, and they are really the answer to the question: "If we could forge any corporate community we wanted, what would we base it on?" These qualities are integrity, intention and information.

Integrity is absolutely crucial, and it must exist at both the individual and the organizational level. Obviously, there must be the personal integrity of an individual within the organization's accepted value system.

But the organization *itself* must possess an integrity that allows each person to line up personal objectives with the objectives of the company.

Dynamic organizations also are infused with the *intention* that this is going to work, that we are going to find a solution because we are going to stay in dialogue and we're going to keep working these issues and find solutions as we progress.

Finally, everyone in the organization should have access to *information* from which they can learn, not just the data they need to perform a given task. The goal is an organization in the continuous process of learning how to do things better, where learning is valued and access to information is expected by everyone as a fundamental right.

The Business Results of Employee Empowerment

We can all agree that these qualities I've mentioned previously are desirable in almost any organization. Nevertheless, at the end of the day, management must still be able to justify the considerable effort required to transform an organization as a sound business decision. While the simple fact that a better place to work has been created may in itself be an acceptable justification, more tangible and quantifiable results suggest that empowerment is not just an enlightened approach to employee relations. Time and time again I've seen the concrete evidence that an empowered work force results in a more dynamic and ultimately more successful business.

Certainly, there may be tertiary benefits like a decline in turnover and absenteeism, decreased training costs and an increased internal promotion rate, indicating both the skills and desire to improve. There are also intermediate benefits like increased productivity, reduced manufacturing cost, better turnaround time and improved margins. But eventually, it gets to the bottom line—sales and revenue growth, increased earnings and better market share. I don't have to go any further than the companies we've invested in to find examples of success. While all of these are tremendous companies, two in particular come to mind based on their efforts in organizational transformation: Vans Inc. and BMC West.

Vans Inc., one of the few remaining domestic sneaker manufacturers, has built its business around a flexible production system and extremely short delivery lead times to customers.

To help bring this about, people from virtually every department go through organizational training in areas like consciousness raising and integrity building, as well as on Total Quality cycle time reduction. Consultants work one on one with people to get them to better understand their own behavior patterns and the impact of their behavior on others, and then work in groups for team building.

Now Vans has started a program called Make And Ship Today (MAST) at its new manufacturing facility, aimed at decreasing manufacturing cycle time from 19 days to 24 hours. This will dramatically decrease their finished goods inventory, already the lowest in the industry, and should significantly decrease total manufacturing costs. More than 150 employees were involved in the cross-functional task teams that created the plans and implementation strategies for MAST. This resulted in a much better program, due to the extent and diversity of the input, and created much more "buy-in" among the company's employees.

Vans achieved real success. Just three and a half years after we acquired the company, they were able to complete a successful initial public offering and a large private placement. From 1989 to 1992, yearly revenues nearly doubled from approximately $51 million to more than $91 million. Due to its efficient manufacturing and low inventory, Vans has the highest profitability and gross margins of any publicly traded footwear manufacturer.

BMC West, formerly a division of Boise Cascade Corporation, is the leading building materials distributor that serves professional contractors in the western United States, with operating units in eight states. The company has more than 53 profit centers, each of which tailors its products and services to the specific needs of its local market.

Following acquisition by management and MDC in 1987, BMC West realized that they had to get everyone involved in taking responsibility for the company's success. But they also realized that management must first demonstrate its intentions; so they started by putting 75 managers through a three day consciousness raising, team building program.

Through continuous attention to employee empowerment and Total Quality Management, the company has gone from a hierarchical to a decentralized organization. Recognizing the ability and integrity of the people in the field, top management is now evaluated by their *response* to field staff. Thus everyone in the organization works for the customer, with the people closest to the customer driving the process. Locational managers have a high degree of autonomy, and all systems are based on performance rather than seniority.

BMC West's annual sales are approaching an estimated $750 million, up from around $145 million in 1987 when the company was acquired. The company has more than tripled in size, acquiring 40 additional locations and selling or consolidating seven. BMC West completed a successful IPO less than four years after its formation as an independent company, followed by an additional offering the next year.

A New Paradigm for Business in the 1990s

These are just two examples of businesses that are rising to the challenge of increased responsibility toward employees as a fundamental means of creating value in the marketplace. Many more like them are recognizing that employee empowerment and self-esteem are critical elements of the most viable new paradigm for creating value in the 1990s and beyond.

In this new paradigm value is created through the development and empowerment of human capital. This will come through an investment in management innovation.

The Cultural Impact of Employee Empowerment

One of the wonderful things about employee empowerment is that it has a life of its own, because it's about human nature—the way people really want to be and the contribution they want to make. It's not about the quality of work life in terms of "this is a nice place to work;" it's about the quality of the *experience* of working, which is central to people. When that experience is good—when it's exciting and creative and challenging—then it has vast societal implications.

If you're happy in your work, you tend to be happier with your family at home. You tend to treat people better. Most importantly, you tend to have fewer problems yourself. All that is basically part of the fabric of society. So what you get from employee empowerment is a *society* that is empowered. Only through an empowered society, composed of healthy individuals, can we ever begin to confront the myriad problems such as war, crime and drugs which we are already beginning to regard as endemic and intractable. Business must, and I believe will, rise to this challenge.

Senior Management Must Provide the Impetus

Regardless of the level to which these roadblocks exist in any organization, absolute support by senior management is a prerequisite for the success of any organizational transformation. Senior management must thoroughly understand the *business objectives* that underlie the shift away from what the organization has become to what it must become. They must understand the culture they are trying to create, and they must be absolutely enrolled in that vision. Finally, they must clearly *communicate* and *demonstrate* their intentions through their actions and behavior.

There is no longer any question in my mind that the Chief Executive Officer must drive the process. Why do I stress the CEO when what we're talking about is a less hierarchical organization? Because that emphasis doesn't mean there is no leader. Every organization needs a leader regardless of how decisions will ultimately be made. The leader may simply be a coach or the person who makes sure the environment is correct. But without the leader's enrollment, understanding and active support, nothing will happen.

Once senior management has made the decision to transform the organization for better performance, it really becomes a top down process: needs assessment; establishing bottom line business objectives; establishing principles, values and ethics; educating management by layers; offering ongoing support to management; establishing compensation systems; instituting employee programs like group work and team building exercises. It is important to realize that these are not programs designed to achieve specific business objectives. Rather, they are the fundamental elements of a program to instill and nurture a *culture* of empowerment—such that employees take the initiative and every person takes personal responsibility for performance—which makes a myriad of specific programs, like Total Quality Management, re-engineering cycle time reduction or cross-functional problem solving groups, successful.

6 Further Insights

Accepting responsibility for ourselves and our actions and being accountable for ourselves and others is intrinsically linked with our feelings of self-esteem. Self-esteem has everything to do with how well all human beings live and work. We are painfully aware that low self-esteem is closely related to substance abuse and the toll it takes on a person's life and livelihood. And it is heartening to know that all of you are looking at ways employers can confront and solve this problem in the workplace. Whatever you do to create a more positive environment for your employees will benefit not just them and your businesses but all of us that need a better understanding of how to nurture self-esteem.

Barbara Bush
From a letter to the California conference
on Self-Esteem in the Workplace

Self-Esteem in the Workplace

Emmett E. Miller, MD

President, Source Cassette Learning Systems, Inc.
Leader in the field of Mind/Body Medicine and Psychoneuroimmunology
Corporate consultant in the field of stress management

The California Task Force on Self-Esteem and Personal and Social Responsibility, on which I had the privilege of serving, defined *healthy* self-esteem as:

> *Appreciating my own worth and importance, and having the character to be accountable for myself, and to act responsibly.*

As a specialist in psychophysiological medicine, it has been clear to me for decades that many diseases are triggered or exacerbated by frustration and anger on one hand and fear, anxiety and helplessness on the other. These diseases range from relatively mild ones such as heartburn, overeating, smoking and overuse of alcohol, to much more serious ones including cardiovascular disease, chronic immune system imbalances and even cancer.

In today's world, people spend more waking hours at work than in any other single place. Further, since family, possessions and social status are usually dependent on succeeding at work, the workplace proves to be a most important source of these inner imbalances. As the pace of social change and the degree of economic instability increases, so too do the doubts, fear, frustrations and concerns related to the workplace.

For a few superstars, every project turns out to be even more successful than the previous one, but such individuals are few. The pyramid gets smaller and smaller toward the top, and most workers, of necessity, plateau in one or more of the following: income, authority or acceleration in their progress up the ladder. (I am reminded of the man who thought he could jump off the Empire State Building and survive unscathed. As he hurtled past each floor, people inside could hear him saying, "So far, so good; so far, so good.")

If no attempt is made to transform the origin of esteem building from external to internal, it is a formula for failure all around. Physical diseases increase health care costs, missed days of work and missed deadlines. Alcohol and drug usage impair performance and hurt morale. Mental frustration and anxiety impair creativity and when the job-related stress leaks over into the family, the resulting domestic disharmony worsens the situation.

The "Stress Carrier"

In my practice, many people have come to me with these kinds of illnesses when, due to their unhealthy image of themselves, they begin to self-destruct. Just as often, l have found that it is the co-workers of such people who seek treatment.

When individuals with low self-esteem reach the point where they are no longer receiving the needed ego strokes, certain defenses are employed. These are often a combination of denial (which allows them to numb themselves to their own tension) and protection (in which they convince themselves that they cannot "soar like an eagle," because they are "working with turkeys"). They then become negative, critical, vindictive, territorial, uncaring and unwilling to share. These negative attitudes and behaviors have a powerful impact on the lives and performance of co-workers. As inner tensions build, co-workers develop bleeding ulcers, high blood pressure, panic attacks and migraines. "Stress carriers," like the infamous "Typhoid Mary," cause others to suffer while experiencing no symptoms themselves. When the stress carrier is also a superior, employees are afraid to report the behavior; everyone knows that "whistle blowers" quickly become expendable.

Organizational Effects

Abraham Lincoln pointed out, "A house divided against itself cannot stand." The same is true of the workplace. Every work group is really a team. It is the same team spirit that is the all-important ingredient that brings about victory in sports. Jealousy, competition, mutual disrespect and vindictiveness destroy this spirit. Sexual and racial slurs and other such behaviors devastate performance. The result is a company that performs much like a car driving with the emergency brake on. Turning around this kind of situation is a consultant's nightmare.

High-Tech/High-Touch

The term "high-tech/high-touch" coined by John Naisbitt hints at the importance of attending to the "soft" human issues. With our inexorable development into an information processing society, we relate more and more to our machines as sources and recipients of information.

The cliché "nerd" who is a whiz on the computer but totally lacking in social skills is actually a threat to workplace harmony. I had one patient who developed stress symptoms as a result of dealing with a superior who, though he worked in the same room as those he supervised, insisted that all requests and comments, no matter how simple, be directed to him through e-mail. The possible gains in clarity were more than offset by the devastating effect of the near total cessation of face-to-face communication. If people are unfamiliar with acknowledging, appreciating, supporting and honoring others in face-to-face conversation, it is even more rare when all message transmissions have been reduced to ASCII text.

Is Self-Esteem an Issue in the Workplace?

We tend to think about the importance of self-esteem in the lives of *children*. Certainly, it is easiest to awaken or destroy self-esteem in the young and vulnerable, and their unguarded natures show so vividly its presence or absence.

We cannot take comfort in the belief that adults with low self-esteem can be found primarily on skid row, in battering relationships or among the ranks of those addicted to alcohol or some other drug. Business persons who believe that "you're only as good as your last victory" and parents whose self-worth varies with the scholastic or athletic performance of their children are, in fact, lacking healthy self-esteem. Similarly, executives who are so dependent on constant attention from other people that they are panic-stricken at the thought of spending a weekend completely alone, although externally they may show abundant signs of success, do not have high self-esteem.

Just as public opinion polls show that 75 to 80% of people believe themselves to be "above average in intelligence," many people think it is *other* people who have self-esteem problems.

Abandonment, the Deepest Cut to Self-Esteem

For the developing infant, the continued presence and availability of the parent is taken as an affirmation of self-worth. Children whose disinterested parents seldom respond to their tears with warmth or nurturance feel unimportant and unworthy of esteem.

A similar kind of abandonment and betrayal often occurs in the workplace. I can recall some of my first experiences of consulting for corporations. On finding they had published a list of corporate values, mission and vision, I proceeded to base my work on these assumptions. They included respect for the individual, openness and honesty, openness to suggestion, showing appreciation and so on. I was quickly informed by workers that these were simply notions that had been developed by PR consultants, primarily to enhance the corporate image and boost recruitment. In truth, day-to-day functioning had no relationship to these principles, and there was no commitment to them. To recruit a new worker by using such PR is outright betrayal and disrespect.

Assuring someone that they are doing a good job, then suddenly laying them off, is a similar betrayal. Not following through with promises, scapegoating and manipulation through spying and secrecy are also ways of telling people they are not worthy of respect, and they injure their self-esteem.

If individuals possess or receive a great deal of healthy self-esteem, they will be self-starters, motivated to work diligently, and will enjoy the *journey* as well as the *destination*. Elaborate workplace support is not necessary for the maintenance of employees' self-esteem. Of course, if employees *receive* respect and support, they will enjoy the work even more. If there is disrespect and no appreciation, they will find the workplace unpleasant, and will soon seek a more congruent work situation.

> *It is only with the heart that one can see rightly; what is essential is invisible to the eye.*
>
> Antoine De Saint-Exupéry

You Can't Cut Your Way
to Prosperity

Joel Brockner

Professor of Management, Columbia University
Author, *Self-Esteem at Work: Research, Theory and Practice*

*I'll tell you what self-esteem means to me ... of the top 25 people in my
office, 22 have been with me for more than 20 years.*

Sidney Friedman
Chairman and CEO, Corporate Financial Services
Motivational Speaker and Consultant

One of the things that we are finding in our research is that how well
people react to a change situation depends on how much of the change is
experienced by them as a threat to their sense of self. Their sense of self
can be taken to mean either (1) their sense of self-esteem, how much they
like themselves, (2) their sense of self-identity, how they define themselves or (3) more general feelings of control that they might have. These
are to me the three major psychological issues that determine how well
people adapt to change situations. Managers who don't pay attention to
the self issues will often find that the change process is not going very
well.

To me, all three of the above are managing people issues and a
major subset of the managing people issues involves dealing with people's egos and senses of who they are—both esteem and identity kinds of
issues.

A major aspect of that has to do with the management of self-esteem,
the management of self-identity, giving people more of a sense of control
in the workplace.

One of the things we find in a downsizing situation for the people
who remain behind—the layoff survivors if you will—is that they are
very resistant to what they've seen happen. "Resistance" is a critical term.
The way it shows up in the workplace is that productivity and morale really suffer and, on closer analysis, we find that they are suffering because
the survivors feel as though their whole sense of self and in particular
their feeling of control have been taken away from them. The advice we
often give managers in a downsizing situation is to try to find some way
to enable people to regain their sense of control as an antidote or as a way
to offset the stress that they are experiencing from the downsizing event
in the first place.

tree

tree after
downsizing

tree after
reorganization

It's a very mixed result. Some organizations have profited from that advice but on the average they have not. An interesting study, done a number of years ago at the University of Colorado, found that most organizations, when downsizing, find that the productivity gains they were hoping for were not realized, which in turn causes them to downsize again. You can see lots of examples of this in corporate America. In the old days I used to ask people in companies I was working with, "Is this the first time you have downsized?" Now I ask them, "Is this the first time you have downsized this year?"—because the repeat business, so to speak, is growing. So it becomes a vicious cycle. Often the layoff process is mismanaged, survivors are less productive, morale plummets, prompting the perceived need for further downsizing. Without careful intervention, which often means paying attention to the survivors' self-esteem and identity feelings of control, the process could go on indefinitely or until the company disappears.

The same study found that the employees' theft rate in the organization went up when their paychecks went down. It is almost as if people were saying, "Well, if I'm not going to get it at the office, I'll take it from the office." That was one way of interpreting that finding. Not surprising. People feel as though they are being treated unfairly, and they feel as though they are going to even the score by taking things from the organization that don't belong to them.

I have a very good friend who had his own jewelry business, and it had been failing for a couple of years. He was very stressed, as you can imagine. Ultimately, he did go out of business but it was a long decline that ultimately met with absolute failure. At the same time things were going downhill in the business, he took it upon himself to start doing volunteer work in the community trying to help adults learn how to read. At first it struck me as very surprising and perplexing. After all, you would think he would be so burned out by what was going on in the workplace that he wouldn't have any kind of emotional energy to invest elsewhere. Then, when I thought about Steele's work on self-affirmation and reaffirmation kinds of prophecies, it occurred to me that it would be precisely because he was feeling so stressed in the workplace that he would try to undertake something outside of the workplace to reaffirm his self-integrity.

That's an example of an individual trying to do something outside the workplace that would compensate for the threat to self he was feeling in the workplace.

Today there is more receptivity to the idea of selfhood and the things that drive that. The increased interest in spirituality is one example. Once we recognize that self is the key and that how people think about themselves and feel about themselves determines their reaction to the changing organizational landscape, then we will all know it's changing. Then the sky is the limit. Then we are limited only by our own identity or control. That's why you want to shine the spotlight on that core sense of self as something that needs to be attended to and nurtured.

Self-Esteem: A Formula for 21st Century Living and Working

John Vasconcellos

California Assemblyperson, Former Chairperson, Ways and Means Committee
Creator, California State Task Force on Self-Esteem and Personal and Social
Responsibility
Coauthor, *Toward a State of Esteem* and *The Social Importance of Self-Esteem*

$\mathcal{S}$elf-esteem is every human's birthright, the key to personal responsibility, the most promising "social vaccine" to address our critical social problems and the formula for healthy, prosperous workplaces in the 21st century.

We are all therefore responsible to enlist ourselves in a crusade to move self-esteem onto our national agenda, and to commit ourselves to leading model lives that serve to enhance the self-esteem of every person we encounter in every aspect of our lives.

That's especially true in these times of profound change, chaos and challenge. They require us to wonder who we are, how we are going to lead our lives, rebuild our communities and prepare ourselves for the 21st century. We will find that self-esteem fits the prescription for a smart politics for the 21st century and fills the prescription for healing a troubled America.

We must begin by owning up to today's reality. Ours is a troubled nation: verging on fiscal bankruptcy, socially divided and disintegrating, economically besieged and politically cynical and self-destructive. In addition, our government is broken. Each major party has a singular and insufficient solution: Republicans find hope only in our private sector, Democrats only in our public one.

I come to these sad conclusions not by abstract analysis, but rather by personal painful experience, which both embodies the conditions of our culture and lives and especially equips me to carry this self-esteem standard. After succeeding throughout my early life, I came apart (much as our nation recently has) the year I was first elected to the legislature. I began searching for myself, striving to become a person of ever more integrity, vision and passion with the courage to act in politics and government.

Along my way, I have asked for and received much help. I began my therapeutic odyssey with Jesuit psychologist Leo Rock (a protégé of Carl Rogers) who held me and assured me through the darkest times that it was okay to be who I was. I most recently concluded it with Jesuit graduate Lou Pambianco, who fuses bioenergetics and gestalt as a management consultant in Silicon Valley and who inspired my enlightenment.

Along my route, I was privileged to study in person with many modern masters of human development, including "searching for myself" with Rollo May; becoming a "transparent self" with Sidney Jourard; "becoming a person" with Carl Rogers; becoming a "self-actualizing person" with Abraham Maslow; "reinhabiting my body" with Stanley Keleman; and developing "self-esteem" and "family" with Virginia Satir. That personal odyssey prepared me to see and to say who and where we are today.

We are living in the midst of seven profound revolutions: technology, gender equity, racial diversity, self-esteem, ending the Cold War, the emerging global economy and interactive communications. Each alone profoundly alters the course of history; all cumulatively amount to a force equivalent to the tectonic shifting that leads to earthquakes and disintegration.

How can we find and help an emerging order amidst our chaos? How do we proceed to bring ourselves back together?

Alvin and Heidi Toffler trace our political paralysis to both parties arguing an obsolete economic paradigm—manufacturing products—while we have fast-forwarded ourselves into an information and services economy. No wonder they are obsolete and cannot solve problems.

Both parties likewise argue an obsolete psychological paradigm—evil human nature—as many of us fast-forward ourselves into a faithful, self-esteeming culture. Irrelevant and paralyzed, they cannot solve our problems. An obsolete paradigm is incapable of solving problems in our new era; more likely, it is the cause of problems.

We are searching for the American dream through a rear view mirror. Common sense instructs us to look ahead (beyond our old assumptions, beyond left and right) and to go out front.

These two shifting paradigms profoundly alter and make unworkable traditional political philosophies, educational pedagogies, parenting, healing and management practices.

Both the Republicans' laissez faire and the Democrats' command and control no longer fit who we are and our new ways of being. Only collaboration fits and works.

Both the Democrats' "We'll take care of you socially" and the Republicans' "We know what's best for you personally" (both based on the assumption that we humans do not know what is good for us and cannot take care of ourselves) no longer fit who we are and our ways of doing. Only autonomy and self-determination fit and help to solve our problems.

Ironically, the shifts in both paradigms (economic and psychological) lead in the same direction: the empowerment of the individual human being as we become fully functioning persons. This accounts for our high level of dissatisfaction today; we have outgrown our institutions and their ways. Our movement toward individual empowerment implies trust in our inherent human capacity for self-governance. That leads us to entire new theories and practices of individuality, self-determination and self-realization, rooted in self-esteem.

That occasions our facing the ultimate American paradox: a political system designed on a faithful vision of our human nature and a belief in our innate capacity to become self-governing and to exercise self-determination responsibly—and a traditional culture designed on a cynical vision of our human nature and a belief that we haven't the innate capacity to know what is good for us or to take care of ourselves.

At the heart of our lives and all of our choices is our underlying vision of ourselves. Our major conflict today is based on these two contrary visions of our human nature: the traditional "we humans are evil monsters needing to be tamed" and that of Carl Rogers' "we humans are innately inclined toward becoming constructive, life-affirming, responsible and trustworthy."

These contrary visions lead to two contrasting ways of facilitating human development in all arenas of our lives—in relationships, parenting, teaching, health care, management and politics.

Let's begin with self-esteem.

I come to this self-esteem movement via the convergence of my personal and professional paths. My professional need came from becoming chair of the Assembly Ways & Means Committee in 1980 and having to find ways to balance our state budget.

My personal need was rooted in having been the first child of a school principal in a traditional religious family. Until age 33, I was the highest achieving, best behaved Catholic boy in California, yet I was without self-esteem. Then I cracked, went into therapy, discovered it was okay to be who I am, and have since been on the path of recovery.

I happened across articles that suggested a pattern—that self-esteem might be the antidote to educational failure, violence and teen pregnancy. I called my friend Jack Canfield, who agreed to work with me to design legislation to create the California Task Force to Promote Self-Esteem and Personal and Social Responsibility.

My newfound intuitive strategic capacities led me to enlist the Assembly's two leading Republicans as coauthors. I split membership appointments among the Governor and both houses and parties of the Legislature. I went to the Republican Governor George Deukmejian, and reframed the issues in economic terms he could understand and relate to. He recognized the promise of the Task Force and signed the bill.

That bill unleashed a huge wave of enthusiasm, receiving more applicants to be on a task force than ever before in state history and attracting persons of faith and passion to involve themselves and improve our society.

The dedicated group labored for three years, and on January 23, 1990, produced its report, *Toward a State of Esteem*. It made front pages nationwide, spawned self-esteem task forces in Maryland, Louisiana, Illinois, Michigan, Hawaii and in 50 of California's 58 counties. Sixty thousand copies of the report were distributed to people who requested it.

The Task Force succeeded in legitimizing self-esteem, moving it from the private therapeutic encounter into the mainstream of American life and culture. In 1995, a Gallup poll found that 75% of the parents of America's school children want their children's self-esteem addressed and improved in our schools.

The Task Force analyzed the role of self-esteem in six problem areas afflicting our nation, with recommendations for addressing each area. It addressed the family ("the crucible of self-esteem"), school, community, workplace and places of failure and recovery.

Educational failure results from insufficiently knowing and valuing myself so as to maintain my innate desire to learn and grow.

Crime and violence result from a negative sense of my self and body, that allows me to damage another.

Drug abuse results from disowning portions of myself, distancing me from my natural energy and leading me to seek a chemical to alleviate my depression or constrain my mania.

Chronic welfare dependency results from my incapacity to know my inherent value; therefore I don't act to realize my innate capacity to become self-sufficient.

Child abuse results from lacking an appreciation of myself and my process, therefore distrusting the goodness of kids.

Teen pregnancy results from a young man who must conquer to prove himself worthwhile and a young woman who must accede to prove herself desirable.

Shame and guilt lead to fear and dutiful behavior, whereas love and acceptance lead to self-esteem and responsible behavior.

Healthy individuality (rather than unhealthy individualism) leads us back into healthy communities, each nurturing and encouraging the other.

Persons who value themselves appreciate their own uniqueness, experience a sense of belonging and believe in their competence. That equips us to lead lives of integrity, vision, courage, community, productivity and satisfaction, in every aspect of our lives, from the most intimate to the most global. That must include our work and workplaces. The 20th century global technological economy requires persons who are healthy, responsible individuals, comfortable within themselves and with diversity, and able to work in harmony.

In California, in the year 2010, three fourths of our retirees will be white, two thirds of our workforce persons of color. The rest of America is not far behind. We must learn to live with diversity.

New management theories speak of individuality, responsibility, initiative, creativity, collaboration, team building and becoming mutually inspiring partners.

Human beings always bring their totality—intellect, emotions, spirit and body—wherever they go, including to their workplaces. We must get ourselves together if we are going to grow into 21st century workers. We deserve healthy workplaces that value individuality and nurture our self-esteem. Self-esteem inspires us to make our workplace better.

In my workplace, attending to the recovery and growth of my self-esteem empowered me to become the person and politician, legislator and leader I am today. Every day I attend to my further recovery, preparing myself for tomorrow.

I am asked how I keep my integrity and sanity, my faith and hope, in the intense, contentious world of politics. It is a combination (changing as needed) of good friends, good staff and good therapists. At the heart of it all is a healthy sense of my self and my self-esteem.

In our age of revolution and chaos, we are designing virtual corporations and reinventing government. We keep up only if we are constantly renewing and reinventing ourselves. We are the bottom line: it is up to each of us to come to know who we are, to value ourselves, to trust ourselves, to lead lives of integrity, boldness, community, productivity and love.

Alex Haley told of finding the village of his *Roots* (whence his seven times removed grandfather had been kidnapped into slavery) and where he found this custom. When a child was born, the father entered the jungle for two days, his mission to choose the child's name. On his return, villagers gathered to celebrate, mother handed the infant to the father, who brought the infant's ear to his mouth, and whispered into it (for the first time spoken) the child's name. "The child ought always be the first person to know who he or she is."

In this "brave new world," our challenge is realizing the promise of our multicultural democracy with gender equity in the emerging global economy and in the age of technology. Self-esteem is central to our capacity to meet our challenge. My father taught me, "I can't give what I haven't got." Virginia Satir reminded me, "What I teach is how I model."

We must commit ourselves, enlist friends and allies, to mutually encouraging and inspiring loving relationships. In such a time we crave leaders and heroes and heroines. Each of us must become a true leader: a person who inspires and enables other persons to recognize and realize their innate capacities to become their own leaders.

My first heroes were Robert Kennedy (the first politician to talk of "the politics of love") and Sidney Jourard (the first psychologist to talk of being open and of "the Transparent Self"). I find I have only one live hero today—my friend, my chosen "granddaughter," Megan Saunders, who will turn six next March.

Last March (a week shy of her fifth birthday), I needed surgery to remove my gall bladder. Her dad took me to the hospital and brought a get well card from Megan. If you would spell out the words, she could already write her own letters, and thus on the outside of the card, she had written, "Grandpa John, I love you—Megan." Then (an independent young woman), she had said, "Mom, I want to write my own inside also."

Her mother said, "Tell me what you want to say and I'll spell it for you."

Megan looked at her mother and said, "Mom, how do you spell … how do you spell *I hope your dreams come true*?"

It is our responsibility to dream and to lead lives that translate our dreams into reality. They will come true only insofar as we grow willing to take responsibility for attending to developing our self-esteem and leading lives of integrity.

In 1994, as I completed a conversation about self-esteem with the College of the Desert leadership group, President David George asked, "What would you have us do?"

I thought a moment and said, "I'd have you lead heroic lives."

He said, "Heroic?"

I repeated, "Heroic!"

He pledged, "I'm ready; count me in!"

I hope your dreams come true. I encourage you, I dare you, to become the first person to know who you are. Trust yourself, open yourself deeply, become yourself, unleash your capacities and lead a heroic life. That's what self-esteem leads us to. That's how we will create a healthy, human, and hopeful future.

Let's begin right now!

Self-esteem is at the core of a healthy nation.

Jack Kemp
From a letter to Partnerships For Change

Spirituality in the Workplace

Martin Rutte

President, Livelihood, Inc. a management consulting firm
Corporate speaker, consultant and trainer
Author, *Being in Business: The Renaissance of Spirit at Work* (forthcoming)
Coauthor, *Chicken Soup for the Soul at Work* (forthcoming)

True Self-Esteem is the product of Self Realization. It is the birthright of every human being ... each of us is a spark of the divine being in whom we live and move and have our nature. Only when the God within is realized can we as human beings advance to our highest spiritual purpose ...

As our self-esteem changes and grows, so does the self-esteem of those around us. We see ourselves in them and they in us. We demonstrate harmlessness, we share, we teach, we cooperate instead of compete, we help others to see and to know that there is purpose and meaning in their lives. What greater gift can there be to aid in raising self-esteem than knowing you are truly a child of God. A soul in physical form. A divine spark whose growth and splendor has no limit ...

David A. Zimmerman
Design Executive, General Motors

The nature and meaning of work is undergoing a profound evolution. Two forces are helping to catalyze the momentum of this evolution: fear as a motivator and the emergence of a more personal and widespread spirituality.

The fear is of losing our job and of having to do more with less. The emergence of spirituality points to the desire that there be more to work than just survival. It's the yearning for work to be a place in which we both experience and express our deep soul and spirit.

Fear in the Workplace

Several factors are causing an increase in fear in the workplace.

The first is massive corporate downsizing. The benefit of downsizing is that it increases profits. Moreover, it cuts the fat and the excess while streamlining the organization. But downsizing also has a downside. It drives people into high levels of anxiety about their job security. It causes pain and suffering. In addition to the pain felt by those people who have been let go, those who are left are asked to increase production with less resources, in the same amount of time and for the same pay. They feel stressed and bone tired. They are anxious about the future of their jobs. They resent that they have to produce more with less. Most painful of all, they don't see any light at the end of the tunnel.

Downsizing works in the short term; in the long term, what you give up is loyalty, engagement, creativity and the full expression of spirit.

A second factor is that work is moving offshore. Years ago, it was just manufacturing work. Now it's also service jobs. India and Israel, for example, are becoming key sites for the development of computer software. We thought that there were certain types of work that would always remain in the developed world—that these were, "Our Jobs," like service or new technology development. It's just no longer so.

And what about *successful* companies laying people off? That's never happened before. The understanding used to be that when a company was in fiscal trouble it would lay people off. And if the company was successful, it would hire people. But with re-engineering and new advanced technology equating to a need for fewer people, successful companies can and are downsizing.

When you put all these factors together, what you are doing is taking the work contract—the implicit agreement that I would come to work for you for life, the belief in security of employment—and smashing it. People have genuinely gotten the message, "You don't have a secure job anymore." And that causes insecurity, it causes anxiety and it causes fear.

It also leads to a sense of "dis-spiritedness" in individuals and in the overall workplace. The spirit has been shut down. It can't express itself fully. There is a sense of disengagement. It may not be quantifiable, but people can feel the lack of spirit in a workplace. They do know when it's diminished.

I don't mean to paint a completely bleak landscape. We can look at these very same factors from another more useful perspective—the spiritual. The security we thought we got from the corporation was a myth. Real security comes from a connection to that which is truly secure—the spirit. We are in the process of moving from dependent "children" at work, with the parental company looking after us, to really coming into our full, responsible selfhood. From this new reality we will begin exploring and expressing more of our true spiritual selves.

The Inner Longing

In addition to fear, there is a compelling inner longing for spiritual fulfillment. Several factors are present in society reflecting the emerging desire for personal and collective spirituality.

The baby boom generation is now entering its fifties. It's entering midlife and looking at the issues that are characteristic for any person of this age: "What is my legacy?" "What are the long term values that I want to leave behind?" "What other arenas of life do I want to invest my energies into now that I've reached the peak of my career?" "What is really important to me as I begin to see my parents, aunts and uncles die?"

These kinds of thoughts are usual for people in midlife. What is unusual, however, is that the baby boom generation is so large as a demographic group. When it begins to think about these issues, then society follows. As the spiritual emerges for baby boomers, it leverages into society as a whole.

Concern and involvement with the bioenvironment also reflects an emerging sense of the spiritual. The environment both supports life and gives us an awareness and consciousness of the whole. It reveals to us how the whole is interconnected and interdependent. And when you think about it, that's a very spiritual metaphor.

> When the concept of human spirit is understood as the mode of consciousness in which the individual feels connected to the Cosmos as a whole, it becomes clear that ecological awareness is spiritual in its deepest sense.
>
> Fritjof Capra

Yet another factor is the maturing of the scientific paradigm. We thought we could solve all the world's problems with science. We thought we could eventually understand everything through science. But the more we know, the more we find out we don't know. Science had been divorcing itself from the spiritual for several hundred years, culminating in the 17th century. From then on, both science and religion would have their own spheres of influence and contribution. But science without spirituality is like a wave without the ocean. A growing number of scientists realize this and are moving more into spiritual exploration as evidenced by who's who in theology and science. The emergence of spirituality on these three fronts is indicative of the more general and overall emergence of spirituality in our time for both individuals and society. Popular culture reflects this in the growing number of books, movies and TV programs about spirituality. And spirituality in the workplace is a part of this overall phenomenon.

What Is Spirituality?

I've found that when people ask me the question, "What is spirituality?" what they're really concerned with is that I will have "the answer" or I will have a dogmatic response. They're afraid that I've already got spirituality nailed down and that they will disagree with my definition, which will then cause separation. They're afraid I (or anyone else speaking about spirituality) will shove a particular point of view about spirituality down their throats. This kind of approach offers the listener no opportunity to search for individual truth.

It's *not* about spirituality as "the answer." It's about spirituality as "the question." A question allows you to look more deeply. It allows you to search for what's true for you, and in so doing, deepen your own experience. But ultimately, what moving from answer to question does is make it safe and permissible to explore this "territory" in a way that is useful.

What is spirituality for you? Where is spirit or spirituality shut down in your workplace? Where is it flourishing? Explore this kind of question, at work, for yourself, your relationships, your division and your company. And in this questioning, in this delving into, notice the deepening of your own experience of spirituality at work.

Remember, work is an act of creation.

Spirituality in the Workplace

What would a more spiritual workplace mean for people? It would mean that work would move from merely being a place to get enough money to survive, from just earning our daily bread, to being a place of "livelihood." By "livelihood" I mean a place where we both survive and are fully alive. We are alive in that our Spirit fully expresses itself. And through our contribution we allow other peoples' spirits to be nourished and to flourish. Livelihood has, at its core, three meanings for work: survival, enlivening of the individual Self and enlivening of the collective Self.

What are the benefits of more spirituality in the workplace? One of the primary benefits is that people are more in touch with the Source of creativity. As businesspeople, we realize the value of creativity and innovation. Creativity is a cornerstone of business. It allows us to come out with new products and services that really are of service. It allows us to do more with less. In essence, it's more efficient contribution.

When we are more in touch with the Source of creativity there is also revitalization, renewal and resilience.

"Human capital" has to be treated differently from "financial capital." As we move more into a service and technological economy, we want to continually expand innovation and creativity. But you can't demand that of people. You have to create an atmosphere in which creativity and innovation flourish; and that is accomplished through the bountiful expression of spirit.

Another benefit is increased authenticity and genuineness in communication. A lot of the work I do as a consultant is to create a "safe space" in which people feel permission to talk about what their truth is without fear of retribution. Businesses aren't used to doing this as a matter of normal everyday practice. However, when the truth is allowed to be spoken, old problems clear up, new possibilities open up and people feel more aligned. They work together in a trusting team.

Increased ethical and moral behavior is yet another benefit. But who cares if a company is ethical or moral? Isn't business just a place where you see how much you can get ahead? An important value of ethical and moral behavior in a business is trust. We trust people who operate in an ethical framework. Employees trust employers. Employers trust employees. And customers who trust a company remain customers longer.

Spirituality in the workplace also promotes the expression of talent, brilliance and genius: talent in the sense of our Divine gifts; brilliance in terms of our intellect and the intensity of the light we have to shine; and genius, not as a scarce commodity, but as something that everyone has. Our true job is to connect with that genius.

> It's not genius as a rare commodity but genius as the underlying base of us all.
>
> Copthorne Macdonald

Spirituality in the workplace also leads to an increased sense of self-fulfillment, contentment and a deep sense of belonging.

Opening up the Workplace to Spirituality

In most businesses today spirit and spirituality aren't talked about. The first thing we must do is to make it safe and permissible to talk about it, if people choose. It should be as normal and as natural as the other conversations we have at work: about profitability, about new products, about research, about accounting, about career, about personal issues and so on. Our first step then is to open it up.

We do this simply by beginning. Talk to those you trust, talk to others in business, talk to your colleagues, but do begin to talk about Spirit. There may be an initial fear, but after a while the momentum will be unstoppable.

If we assume that it is safe and permissible to talk about spirituality in your workplace, what does that mean for you? I suggest you begin by looking for the opportunities and possibilities to experience and to express spirituality within yourself, your relationships, your department, your company and your industry. Look in each of these arenas for ways to express spirit and ways to remove the blocks where spirit and spirituality are closed off. And then just start.

Managing in the New Spiritual Workplace

We are now in the transition period between the old definition of work as "survival" and the new definition of work as "livelihood." New management techniques and new organizational structures will be needed to handle this emerging context.

Management in the survival mode has been based on command and control. In this mode, the way you get people to produce is by telling them what to do and making sure it gets done. But in a spiritual workplace, productivity is achieved through nurturing the expression of the self and the spirit.

Our job, as managers, is to facilitate the discovery of spirit, to esteem it, to celebrate it and to hold others accountable for their expression of it.

One way to do this is to work with your employees and make it clear to them that part of their job is a responsibility for the clarity and the expression of spirit, namely, their own life's purpose, vision and gifts.

> *Take your passion and make it happen.*
> Song lyric from the movie *Flashdance*

A senior vice-president of a large utility told me that the role of companies in the future will be to help employees discover their life purposes and to make sure that their work is consistent with and demanding of that purpose. "Imagine what would happen," he said, "if you had a company in which all the people were doing their life's work. You would have more loyalty, more resilience, more creativity, more innovation and a deeper sense of self-reliance, self-renewal and self-generation."

Another new function will be helping people unleash and express their full, creative spirit. One of the ways to do this is to reconnect people with their artistry, whether that's music, painting, dancing, poetry, cooking or whatever. Poet David Whyte, who wrote *The Heart Aroused*, goes into companies and reads poetry. Boeing Aircraft is one of his clients. The managers he works with begin to realize other aspects of themselves. Poetry helps them delve more deeply into their creative selves, it rounds them out and it helps contribute to new insights, both personal and corporate. (A great way for you and your employees to reconnect with your creative selves is to read and do the exercises in *The Artists Way*, by Julia Cameron.)

An Invitation

The next phase of the evolution of work has begun. Spirituality is now being openly recognized as an integral part of work. If this is something that speaks to you, that you want more of in your workplace, step into the arena. You may be challenged, you may be criticized. It doesn't matter. What is important is what is true for you. I invite you to jump in.

Work is an Act of Creation.

Self-esteem is enhanced when we walk the mystical path with practical feet.

Angeles Arrien, PhD
Cultural Anthropologist
Author, *The Four-Fold Way*

Self-Esteem and The Impact of Change

Ichak Adizes, PhD

Founder and President of the Adizes® Institute, Inc.
Author, *Mastering Change, Corporate Lifecycles,* and *How to Solve the Mismanagement Crisis*

Many factors deplete Esteem. One of the critical ones is change.

When things change there is a new order. The question is, is it for better or for worse? Was the change a constructive or a destructive one?

Change is constructive when it advances us to our goals. But in order to advance to the goal, energy has to be freed from operational purposes, which means that the system needs to be integrated—it needs to have its Esteem. Thus, whether change is constructive or destructive depends among other factors on the degree of mutual trust and respect and on the degree to which holistic (inter- and intra-) personal, family-wide, organizational, social and (yes) environmental Esteem are prevalent in that society.

Entities with higher Esteem can handle threats from a changing environment more easily that those with lower Esteem. They have more energy to reposition themselves in the new environment. They will be the ones recognized as the fittest to survive. When a threatening change occurs, those with lower Esteem will disintegrate. Internal fighting will increase, accelerating the demise of that entity.

The nature of change is such that it happens by itself (if for no other reason than the passage of time). Entropy happens by itself; things will fall apart if one does nothing. Leave your new car unattended for a while. You will not be able to start it later. The summer home that you did not visit for a few months is unlivable until cleaned. There is nothing that one needs to do to cause entropy. The nature of the universe is such that entropy happens when no one takes action to counter it.

For healing and integration to occur, one has to take initiative, because they do not happen by themselves. It is also a never-ending task because change is never ending. We have to make the effort, allocate the energy and invest the time (that is take the time) to build Esteem. With higher Esteem, less energy will be necessary for operational purposes and thus more energy will be available for application purposes.

The task of building Esteem is getting both harder and more critical for survival of people, families, organizations and civilizations. Change is *accelerating.* The higher the rate of change, the faster the systems might fall apart. The more cases of depression, suicide, divorce and crime, the faster people, families and communities fall apart. There are two obvious choices. One is to slow down change; some religious and political leaders are *de facto* recommending it. The second choice is to increase and speed up the process of healing by building and nourishing Esteem.

We know from history that over time, change cannot be slowed down. We face the choice of building Esteem or destroying ourselves. While building Esteem does not happen by itself, losing Esteem happens when we do nothing. The choice is OURS.

Self-Esteem and Women

Mary Kay Ash

Founder, Mary Kay Cosmetics

My purpose in life is to help women know how great they really can be and how great they are. I feel like God planted the seeds of greatness into every single one of us but it is up to you and me to reach down within ourselves and bring those seeds into fruition.

The feminist movement started with women cutting their hair short, burning their bras and putting on trousers. Doing things, even lowering their voices, to be like men because men were the only people who were successful. In my opinion, you can be feminine and successful at the same time. You don't have to sacrifice your femininity. I feel God gave me this business because I believe in femininity.

Listen, Mom, I'm not your little girl anymore.

SOURCE: Drawing by Bruce Eric Kaplan; © 1996 The New Yorker Magazine, Inc.

Spirituality–the Heart and Soul of Every Successful Business

Terry Cole-Whittaker

Founder and Chairman of the Board, Adventures in Enlightenment
Author, *What You Think of Me Is None of My Business, How to Have More in a Have Not World, The Inner Path From Where You Are to Where You Want To Be,* and *Love and Power in a World Without Limits*

What Is Possible?

Imagine what a dynamic team you can have in your business or organization when whole people show up and work together for the greater good of all. Is this possible? If so, what if anything can you and I do to facilitate the workplace being a place where wholeness, genius, cocreativity, teamwork and fulfillment are the norm?

There are two basic parts to every person: one is the spiritual or masculine and the other is the soul or the feminine. Each part has specific abilities and needs and functions in a particular way. Spirituality is universal intelligence, unattached, expansive, the sky, loving, space and impersonal. Soul is mind, personal, focused, artistic, the law, nature, the soil, earth, individuality and creativity. You could call these two aspects, love and the law. Yet, we cannot separate these two aspects as we cannot separate the fragrance from the rose. We have a right brain and a left brain. We have a right side and a left side and an inside and an outside to our bodies, and, if you separate them, you no longer have life in the body. When the parts are working for the good of the all, we have synergy. Trouble in the marketplace occurs when one or both aspects of the self are ignored, made wrong or not utilized. Success, happiness and fulfillment are the natural result of harmony and harmony means making beautiful music together. Spirit/Soul are partners and inseparable lovers who live together as one in the same body.

How can we facilitate whole people participating wholly, so that work becomes a holy or sacred experience? Let us look to success in the past for a glimpse of what is possible in the present.

Many, many hundreds of years ago in India, there was a virtuous king named Ramachandra and his chaste wife, Sita—the ideal couple. He was a loyal and devoted husband and he was as a father to his subjects and looked out for their well-being and prosperity as he protected them. He was honest, hard-working, truthful, humble, God-minded and self-realized. She was chaste, loving, empowering and practiced the 64 arts and sciences of feminine creativity. Together they were the example of balance and the ideal human existence.

Under their rule, the land produced an overabundance of grains, fruits, vegetables, seeds and nuts. The cows produced an abundance of milk. Everyone was engaged in their purposeful work and they all lived together in harmony, love and prosperity. Why? King Ramachandra loved God and service to God was first and always in his mind and activities. He lived by high spiritual ideals, values and practices and by his example and leadership everyone was respected, protected and empowered. Prosperity is the natural byproduct of persons and society living in tune with the laws of God and nature.

We do not have King Ramachandra ruling at this time, so it is up to you and me to discover and apply the principles of natural good fortune, success and prosperity and be an example of what is possible. To solve a problem, overcome an obstacle or achieve an objective, it is important to take a few moments to have an overview of the situation and decide where we want to go and what we need to do to get there.

The challenge of business is: How can we provide an environment in which people can best utilize their talents, skills and genius to achieve our mission of serving the greater good of everyone through the offering of our goods and services? How can we do this so that everyone wins or has their spiritual and material needs met?

The problem is: the human tendency to cheat, to make mistakes, to make decisions based on their unreliable senses, to be in a continual state of anxiety and limitation and to be greedy. All this is the result of forgetting one's true nature and therefore being covered by ignorance and not applying the principles of success and good fortune.

The results are: poor communications, underutilized spiritual and human resources, environmental disasters, abuse of women and children, and poverty.

The solution is: self-realization and a personal commitment to excellence! Self-realization solves all the problems of human existence and guarantees a successful and opulent life. Excellence is one's commitment to give the best of what is available in service to God and all living entities.

How Does Self-Realization Solve the Challenge of Business?

As a researcher and student of the principles of successful living for over 35 years, I have found by studying religion, psychology, philosophy, science and common sense, there are 21 principles common to success, prosperity, well-being and good fortune that when applied bring forth the fulfillment of a person's heart's desires in any and every area where applied.

The fundamental shift that needs to take place is a change of heart within the individual and in business. This change of heart needs to take place within the heart of the visionary leader/example. Because spirit is intelligent, it is important to use the intelligence, intelligently. The leader is the spiritual spark that ignites the others. This leader/boss has the vision inside and is turned on. A turned on leader is contagious and lights the dormant flame in others by mere presence. A great mission catches people who naturally find fulfillment doing work that nourishes their souls. We follow the example the leaders set by the example of their work, their commitment, their attitudes, their words and their actions. *Self-realization is the realization that each and every living entity is an eternal spiritual being and as such they are drawing from the one infinite Supreme Being.* Self-realization occurs when people remember who they are, the purpose for human life and what they are to do to fulfill their potential and to be perfected souls. Persons who are accessing all their personal parts and qualities we call geniuses.

Where Do We Get Our Information as to What Works?

The opportunity available to us is to discover how to access what is within us—our genius—and bring our wholeness to the workplace. Self-realization involves receiving nourishment, answers and guidance from within, intuition, common sense, body response and wisdom.

We have three ways to test whether or not our own inner guidance is correct. One is from the scriptures, ancient wisdom passed down generation upon generation about who we are, our purpose and how to succeed as human beings. The Old Testament gives us the Ten Commandments; Jesus gives us "The Sermon on the Mount," the Beatitudes and his two commandments—"To love the Lord thy God with all thy heart, soul and mind and love thy neighbor as thyself." Eastern religions give us the Vedas, including *The Bhagavad Gita,* which means the song of God. The second way to test ourselves is by example and instruction from the guru, teacher or living example of success. If you want to become a good carpenter offer your services to a master carpenter and follow his or her example. Associate with the people who are the best examples of what you choose to be. And the third way is the feedback from the group, the team and the customer or client. In essence, we have four sources of guidance and information to help us meet our challenges: our inner true self, the scriptures, the teacher by example and the feedback of the group.

What Is Success?

Some say that success is measured by how much money you have or can borrow, when actually success means that you have found out who you are and you are rendering devotional service at the best of your ability and resources. There was an Emperor of India in the 3rd century B.C.E. His name was Ashoka. While emperor, he became a Buddhist monk. This commitment to his spiritual self transformed his whole way of governing, which produced a total of 60 years of peace, prosperity, nonviolence, family happiness and environmental health. Opulence naturally follows integrity, excellence, devotional service and commitment to the higher qualities of existence.

What Does It Take in Business to Be Successful?

People thrive in an atmosphere of high thoughts, beneficial attitudes and constructive actions. An elevated business has an elevated mission and a highly principled person at the helm as the example.

Having a Strong Sense of Mission and Purpose

Personal fulfillment, enthusiasm, genius and productivity above and beyond the call of duty occurs when one is motivated by a spiritual mission or an all consuming purpose greater than oneself. For some, this purpose is God and for others, it may be humanity, the environment or some idea whose fulfillment would be a contribution. What is the spiritual or higher purpose and mission of your business or organization?

There are many people who are volunteers in our society who are never paid money and who put in 48 hour weeks and do their work with excellence. Why? They are inspired, believe in the mission of the organization, know they are making a difference and get to do things they couldn't do at a regular job. They know they are there by choice, they are appreciated and they are getting soul satisfaction.

Any business that has a purpose greater than its own survival is vital and alive and attracts exceptional people as part of its team. What purpose or mission attracts you? What work, if you could do anything at all, would capture your heart and soul? These are important questions because where, how and with whom you spend your time empowers or disempowers you.

If you want to attract great people, have a great vision.

How Do We Solve the Problems of Business, Overcome Obstacles and Prosper?

There is always an answer and a solution. We can solve every problem we have on earth if we live in harmony with God's laws, the laws of mother nature and use our God-given creative abilities intelligently. You are connected with universal intelligence.

Here is the crux of this essay: It is up to each person to take a stand to honor your true self, who is forever sourced by the Most High Supreme God. The big challenge is for you as the individual person to activate your power of choice and honor your true self, ideals and spiritual values. This is called *integrity and commitment.*

Center your mind on God and ask how you can serve, and ask for what you need to fulfill your purpose and do your work, this day, instead of honoring the multitude of fears generated by your ever-changing mind. Steady your mind on that which is good, beautiful, honorable and worthwhile. Focus your mind and activities on assisting your co-workers, family and clients to flourish and succeed. This is the Golden Rule, the secret of enduring success in business, relationship, government, child raising, ecological balance and one's eternal life. Follow the spiritual teachings of your religion for they are there to help you get beyond materialism and animal behavior and into the higher qualities and blessings. Work is a perfect place to practice what you preach. And remember to be forgiving of others and gentle on yourself. We are all in process. By agreeing and assisting one another to flourish, we can succeed.

What Will Build Strength, Teamwork, Quality and Wealth?

Develop agreements and ground rules for your company that take into consideration the spiritual values of all the employees and the needs of the business in fulfilling its purpose and mission.

First decide the kind of person you want to be, the kind of business you want and then find the priorities, values and principles that will help you and your business to become that ideal. Look to your religious teachings for guidance and help. You are not alone and it is honorable that you are willing to develop yourself by pursuing the real purpose of life—self-realization and devotional service.

Spiritual values and ideals give us a space in which we grow. Each of us is a divine seed and when nurtured and empowered, we grow into our true selves. Ground rules or agreements help us to remember who we are, our purpose and our methods for developing our potential as we serve one another, the earth and our clients and customers. Some examples of agreements are: Keep your agreements and, if not possible, be responsible. Speak with good intent. Be kind. The customer is always right. Do your work with excellence, and soon. A major part of the human experience is to be balanced both in one's individuality and in one's partnerships. Agreements build teamwork and a great team will naturally produce beneficial results for everyone. Put God first and do your best to put into practice spiritual principles which include how to treat others and how best to do your work, whatever it may be.

The Secret Key in Bringing Spirituality into the Workplace

Do your work for the sake of the work itself. Do your work as if you were in God's temple serving your Beloved. Every job is just as important as another, and the difference is one's attitude. Fulfillment, pleasure and bliss can be obtained by doing any job, from digging ditches to being King or Queen as a service. No job is too humble or too grand, for the payment is in the amount of pleasure you are experiencing moment to moment. If you are working for something else, there is no amount of money that can make up for what you are not getting naturally. Spirituality brings the bliss and the pleasure to what was before a mundane experience. Enjoy!

Afterthoughts

Jack Canfield
and Jacqueline Miller

It has been said that we all teach what we need to learn. And if that is true, then based on the hundreds of self-esteem seminars and speeches we have collectively given, we have a vast amount to learn about self-esteem and the spirit at work.

> *All good things ... come by grace and grace comes by art and art does not come easy.*
>
> Norman Maclean
> *A River Runs Through It*

We believe that this book is a good thing, and, as the above quote suggests, it did not come easy. In the writing of this book, we got to look at many of our own issues around self-esteem in the workplace. First, in processing the issues that emerged in our relationship with each other as the compilers and editors of this book, we were afforded the opportunity to examine many of our own fears and dysfunctional relationship patterns. Working in the same office day after day—many of them 16 hour days—reading, writing and editing stories and pieces about self-esteem, spirit and soul, put us face to face with our own "holes in the soul" as Chérie Carter-Scott call them. This was an eye opening and growth producing process that neither of us had anticipated, and we're not sure we always welcomed. Nevertheless, it provided us both with deep and profound lessons for which we both will always be grateful.

Those who build the house are built by it.

Maori Elder

We spent many hours experiencing the concepts of the book. Interestingly enough, we found ourselves resisting doing some of the very things we were writing about—respecting each other's unique working styles, honoring each other's world views, telling our emotional truths and taking the time to really listen to each other's pain and listening for the deeper needs that were being expressed in the moment. Several times we found ourselves mouthing the very words that we have heard so many times from managers in the corporations that we work with—"We don't have time for this; we have a deadline to meet." "I can't believe anyone really thinks like that."

Fortunately, we would begin to edit the next piece in the book and it would be as if God had placed a mirror into our hands and was speaking the very words we needed to hear to remind us of what was really most important—the quality of our divinely inspired relationship, our caring and our love for each other, as well as the integrity that comes from being forced to live our own message. At times it felt like an emotional roller coaster ride, but each time we stopped, told the truth, listened from the heart and honored each other's needs, we emerged a little more whole, a little more connected and a little more aligned with the message of the book and with our life purposes.

Work is a passage of self-discovery. It is not the pots we are forming, but ourselves.

M. C. Richards
Potter

In his book *Artful Work,* Dick Richards sums up our feelings in a chapter he entitled "Creating Me." He writes:

This work has created me, the me I am today in contrast to the me I was before I began. When I began this writing I was annoyed with all of us, myself included, for our seeming inability or unwillingness to create lasting change in our organizations and to seek joy in our work. As my writing proceeded, I became more compassionate toward all of us, myself included, as well as more forgiving and understanding. It is a difficult thing we are attempting to do—reinvent ourselves.

We are indeed reinventing ourselves every day. That is what these times seem to demand of us if we are to survive as individuals, companies, nations and, yes, even as a species. And, no, it is not easy. It takes a commitment to ourselves, our families, our organizations, our communities, our ideals, our values and our visions of the future.

As we were talking in the final days of completing this book, we realized that even if this book were never published, it would have been worth all of the effort we expended—and the effort was considerable—because of what we had learned and how we had grown. The ego constantly wants to create things, have success and thereby prove that it is worthy. The soul wants to have experiences that allow it to grow and expand in consciousness. Perhaps we shall have accomplished both here, but it is the latter that will remain most valuable in our hearts and minds.

The second reason that writing this book was so valuable is that we have each come to see that we have a long way to go in making our own organizations more self-esteeming environments in which to work. Every time we read through a list of six pillars, eight keys or ten building blocks to self-esteem in the workplace, we had to admit we weren't doing all of them as well as we would like to be. With each new article we found ourselves making long lists of things to do to make our own workplaces more humane, balanced, healthy, relaxing, fun and affirming places to be. We also found ourselves falling back into the old trap of thinking "as soon as the book is done."

Well, before the book was done, we found ourselves giving more recognition and praise, instituting staff lunches with healthy organic food paid for by us and prepared by Chef Rosalie Miller, providing free massages to a frazzled staff of typists and office support, and taking more time to listen to people's frustrations and suggestions for better systems and saner schedules. We saw that perhaps some of our overcommitments in the name of "making a difference" were our own self-esteem and codependency issues of needing to be of service in order to "justify" our existence. We have both made plans for more days off, vacations and fun times for ourselves and our staffs. We have committed to saying "no" more often and to taking better care of ourselves.

Some other things on our organizational to-do lists—all a result of creating this book—are:

1. Institute regular staff play days with each day being the responsibility of a different person to set up.
2. Set aside a sum of money from the proceeds of this book to be given to charity and allow the staff to decide where it will go.

3. Provide bonus money for time spent by the staff for participating in community service projects.

4. Have the staff mutually decide on personal growth stretches—spending a complete day in silence, learning a new physical skill like juggling or completing a public speaking class—and providing bonus money for their successful completion.

5. Offer both yoga classes and instruction in meditation to the staff on site.

6. Provide more on site training in communication skills, conflict resolution and problem solving.

7. Take time at the end of each staff meeting for appreciations and recognition.

8. Take the staff to a ropes course.

9. Solicit more feedback on a regular basis about what is working and what is not working in the organization.

10. Hire two of the consultants whose articles appear in this book to consult with us on a regular basis. Even though we are considered experts in this field, we see the need for a new set of eyes who can see things that we habitually overlook and lead us in directions we might not otherwise consider.

A Final Note

Now that you are almost finished with this book, let us make a few final suggestions.

1. Please take time to read the resources section and continue your reading in this field. There is so much to know and do to truly create transformational work environments.

2. Write or call all of the consultants, trainers and training organizations that are listed in the resources section. Consider taking their seminars, listening to their tapes and hiring them to work with your company or organization.

3. Reread this book several times. As we learned from our own experience of compiling this book—often rereading and reworking many of the pieces in this book ten or more times—each reading revealed something new to us. Some of the articles only made sense on the third reading and then—pow!—we would be struck by a profound insight. Give yourself the gift of these deeper insights.

4. Please feel free to duplicate the things that touch you the most and share them with your colleagues, employees and supervisors. We

wrote this book because we wanted to make a difference in the workplace. We hope you will share the stories and the ideas presented here with the widest audience possible.

5. Make a list of 10 or 20 things that you want to begin to implement in your life, your office, your plant, your school or wherever else you may work, and begin to implement those things today. Start today with one small thing and keep building.

6. Finally, please send us your stories, poems, articles, techniques and reports about building self-esteem, expressing caring, releasing spirit and awakening the soul in the workplace. These can be things you have written, clipped out of a company newsletter or read in another book. We welcome you in joining us as we all work together to create more "Heart at Work!"

MORE HEART AT WORK?

Share your heart with the rest of the world...

If you have a story, poem, article or other piece—either your own or someone else's—that you feel belongs in a future volume of *Heart at Work,* we invite you to please send it to us.

If you have favorite stories, strategies, newspaper articles, comments, compliments or concerns you feel belong on our *Heart at Work* **website** and in our *Heart at Work* **newsletter**, please send them to us.

Jack Canfield & Jacqueline Miller
Self-Esteem Seminars—
   Heart at Work
c/o Partnerships for Change
PO Box 471647
San Francisco, CA 94147
Phone: 1-800-2-ESTEEM
Fax: 415-863-0543
E-mail: hello@heartatwork.com

Jacqueline Miller & Jack Canfield
Partnerships for Change
PO Box 471647
San Francisco, CA 94147
Phone: 415-922-1851
Fax: 415-863-0543
E-mail: pfc@thecity.sfsu.edu
Website:
   http://www.partnerships.org

We will make sure that you and the author are credited for your contributions. Thank you.

Again, we will make sure that you get credit for your contributions

And visit our website for new and updated stories not found in the hard copy of *Heart at Work* ... the beat goes on!

http://www.heartatwork.org
http://www.heartatwork.com

You can also contact us at the above address and numbers for consulting and speaking engagements, information about our newsletters, other books, audiotapes, workshops and training programs.

RESOURCES

BOOKS

For Yourself

Building Self-Esteem by L.S. Barksdale. Idyllwild, CA: The Barksdale Foundation, 1972.

Chicken Soup for the Soul: 101 Stories to Open the Heart and Rekindle the Spirit by Jack Canfield and Mark Victor Hansen. Deerfield Beach, FL: Health Communications, 1993.

A 2nd Helping of Chicken Soup for the Soul by Jack Canfield and Mark Victor Hansen. Deerfield Beach, FL: Health Communications, 1995.

A 3rd Serving of Chicken Soup for the Soul by Jack Canfield and Mark Victor Hansen. Deerfield Beach, FL: Health Communications, 1996.

The Confidence Factor: How Self-Esteem Can Change Your Life by Judith Briles. New York: Master Media Limited, 1990.

Creating an Imaginative Life by Michael Jones. Berkeley, CA: Conari Press, 1995.

Cut-Through: Achieve Total Security and Maximum Energy by Doc Lew Childre. Boulder Creek, CA: Planetary Publications, 1996.

Developing Self-Esteem; A Positive Guide for Personal Success by Connie Palladino, PhD. Los Altos, CA: Crisp Publications, Inc., 1989.

Essays on Self-Esteem by L.S. Barksdale. Idyllwild, CA: The Barksdale Foundation, 1977.

Freeze Frame by Doc Lew Childre. Boulder Creek, CA: Planetary Publications, 1994.

Getting Past OK: Getting Your Life Into the "Wow" Zone! by Richard Brodie. New York: Warner Books, Inc., 1993.

NLP, The New Technology of Achievement edited by Steve Andreas and Charles Faulkner. New York: Quill William Morrow, 1994.

Revolution from Within: A Book of Self-Esteem by Gloria Steinem. Boston: Little, Brown and Company, 1992.

Self-Esteem: The Power to Be Your Best by Mark Towers. Shawnee Mission, KS: National Press Publications, 1991.

The Six Pillars of Self-Esteem by Nathaniel Branden. New York: Bantam, 1994.

Taking Responsibility: Self-Reliance and the Accountable Life by Nathaniel Branden, PhD. New York: Simon & Schuster, 1996.

Trust: A New Vision of Human Relationships for Business, Education, Family, and Personal Living by Jack Gibb. North Hollywood, CA: Newcastle Publishing, 1991.

The Serenity Principle by Joseph Bailey. San Francisco: Harper & Row, 1990.

You Can Be Happy No Matter What by Richard Carlson. San Raphael, CA: New World Library, 1992.

You Can Feel Good Again by Richard Carlson. New York: Penguin, 1993.

You Can Have It All by Mary Kay Ash. Rocklin, CA: Prima Publishing, 1995.

For the Manager, CEO and Leader

1001 Ways to Reward Employees by Bob Nelson. New York: Workman Publishing, 1994.

Business As Unusual: Intuition and Tarot in the Workplace by James Wanless, PhD. Carmel, CA: James Wanless, 1996.

CARE Packages for the Workplace: Dozens of Little Things You Can Do to Regenerate Spirit at Work by Barbara A. Glanz. New York: McGraw-Hill, 1996.

The Creative Communicator: 399 Tools to Communicate Commitment Without Boring People to Death by Barbara A. Glanz. New York: Irwin Professional Publishing, 1993.

Creativity in Business by Michael Ray and Rochelle Myers. Garden City, NY: Doubleday & Company, Inc., 1986.

Driving Fear Out of the Workplace by Kathleen D. Ryan & Daniel K. Oestreich. San Francisco: Jossey-Bass Publishers, 1991.

Empowerment Takes More Than a Minute by Ken Blanchard, John P. Carlos and Alan Randolph. Escondido, CA: Blanchard Training and Development, Inc., 1995.

The End of Bureaucracy and the Rise of the Intelligent Organization by Gifford and Elizabeth Pinchot. San Francisco: Barrett-Koehler Publishers, Inc., 1993.

The Great Game of Business by Jack Stack. New York: Doubleday, 1992.

The Heart Aroused: Poetry and the Preservation of the Soul in Corporate America by David Whyte. New York: Doubleday, 1994.

The Human Element: Productivity, Self-Esteem and the Bottom Line by Will Schutz. San Francisco: Jossey-Bass, 1994.

Human Robots & Holy Mechanics: Reclaiming Our Souls in a Machine World by David T. Kyle. Portland, OR: Swan Raven & Co., 1993.

Managing the Obvious by Charles A. Coonradt. Park City, UT: The Game of Work, Inc., 1994.

Managing to Have Fun: How Fun at Work Can Motivate Your Employees, Inspire Your Coworkers and Boost Your Bottom Line by Matt Weinstein. New York: Simon & Schuster, 1996.

Mary Kay on People Management by Mary Kay Ash. New York: Warner Books, 1984.

The Positive Power of Praising People by Jerry D. Twentier. Nashville, TN: Thomas Nelson Publishers, 1994.

Reawakening the Spirit in Work by Jack Hawley. San Francisco : Barrett-Koehler, 1993; New York: Fireside, 1995.

Recognition Redefined: Building Self-Esteem at Work by Roger L. Hale and Rita F. Maehling. Exeter, NH: Monochrome Press, 1993.

Rediscovering the Soul of Business edited by Bill DeFoore and John Renesch. San Francisco: New Leaders Press, 1995.

Ritual, Power, Healing and Community by Malidoma Patrice Somé. Portland, OR: Swan Raven & Co., 1993.

Second to None: The Productive Power of Putting People First by Charles Garfield. New York: Avon Books, 1992.

Self-Esteem at Work: Research, Theory, and Practice by Joel Brockner. Lexington, MA: Lexington Books, 1988.

Toward a State of Esteem: The Final Report of the California Task Force to Promote Self-Esteem and Personal and Social Responsibility. Copies of this historic document are available for $4 each (plus sales tax for California residents) from the Bureau of Publications, California State Department of Education, PO Box 271, Sacramento, CA 95802-0271.

The Truth Option: A Practical Technology for Human Affairs by Will Schutz. Berkeley, CA: 10 Speed Press, 1984.

When Corporations Rule the World by David C. Korten. West Hartford, CT: Kumarian Press, Inc., San Francisco: Barrett-Koehler Publishers, Inc., 1995.

Work and the Human Spirit by John Scherer with Larry Shook. Spokane, WA: John Scherer and Associates, 1993.

The Worth Ethic: How to Profit from the Changing Values of the New Work Force by Kate Ludeman. New York: E.P. Dutton, 1989.

Audio Tape Programs

How to Build High Self-Esteem: A Practical Process for Your Personal Growth by Jack Canfield. (Six cassettes) Chicago, IL: Nightingale-Conant, 1989. Call 1-800-323-5552 for Nightingale-Conant's catalog.

Self-Esteem and Peak Performance by Jack Canfield. (Six cassettes) Boulder, CO: CareerTrack, 1988. Call 800-334-1018 for CareerTrack's catalog.

Self-Esteem for Women by Julie White. (Six cassettes) Boulder, CO: CareerTrack, 1990. Call 800-334-1018 for CareerTrack's catalog.

Spirituality in the Workplace by Martin Rutte. Livelihood, 64 Camerada Loop, Santa Fe, NM 87505.

Writing Your Own Script (#202), Health and Wellness (#18), Accepting Change and Moving on: A Unique and Powerful Process for Dealing with Grief and Transition (#48), Personal Development & Overcoming Obstacles (#803), Power Vision: Peak Performance (#650), Stress Fitness, Self-Esteem: I Am, I Can (#14, #15), The Power of True Self-Esteem (#37), Finding Inner Direction (#336) by Emmet Miller, MD, Source Cassette, Learning Systems, PO Box W, Stanford, CA 94309. Phone: 1-800-52-tapes; Fax: 415-328-4412 to place orders.

Video Tape Programs

Chicken Soup for the Soul Live by Jack Canfield and Mark Victor Hansen. Boulder, CO: CareerTrack, 1996.

Self-Esteem and Peak Performance: Volumes 1 & 2 by Jack Canfield. Boulder, CO: CareerTrack, 1988.

The Psychology of Self-Esteem by Julie White. Boulder, CO: CareerTrack, 1991.

Call 800-334-1018 for CareerTrack's catalog.

Video-Based Self-Esteem Training Programs

Achieving Professional Excellence: Strategies for Self-Development (developed by Jack Canfield) is currently offered in five cities by The American Management Association, 135 West 50th Street, New York, NY 10020-1201. Phone: 800-262-9699. Call or write for a catalog of course offerings.

GOALS: A Multi-Media Self-Esteem and Motivation Program for Low Income and At-Risk Adults with Jack Canfield. Available from the Foundation for Self-Esteem, 6035 Bristol Parkway, Culver City, CA 90230. Phone: 310-568-1505. Fax: 310-337-1078. The program contains a three-hour video program featuring Jack Canfield, a *Guidebook to Personal Success*, a one-hour audio-cassette *The Ten Steps to Success*, and a *GOALS Facilitator's Manual*.

Increasing Human Effectiveness Program with Bob Moawad. Edge Learning Institute, 2217 N. 30th, Suite 200, Tacoma, WA 98403. Phone: 800-858-1484. Fax: 206-572-2668. Teaches people how to build their self-esteem, empower themselves and reach new heights of effectiveness in every area of their lives.

Investment in Excellence with Lou Tice. Pacific Institute, 1709 Harbor Ave., Seattle, WA 98104. Phone: 206-628-4800.

STAR (Success Through Action and Responsibility) with Jack Canfield. Self-Esteem Seminars/The Canfield Training Group, PO Box 30880, Santa Barbara, CA 93130. Phone: 800-2-ESTEEM or 805-563-2935. Fax: 805-563-2945. A three-day multi-media professional development program for corporations. Originally developed for New England Telephone/NYNEX, the program has since been purchased by numerous corporations including G.E. Capital/Monogram Bank, PEMCO, AT&T, and Capital Bank. The program was also adopted by the American Management Association as a flagship course entitled **Achieving Professional Excellence: Strategies for Self-Development** and is currently taught in five cities. The following consultants are also available to offer **STAR** to your organization.

> **Steve Cashdollar,** Cashdollar, Inc., 4409 Kings Row, Muncie, IN 47304. Phone: 317-286-8122.

> **Kate Driesen,** Kate Driesen & Associates, 12827 Friar St., North Hollywood, CA 91606. Phone: 818-763-6610.

> **Judy Haldeman,** 16530 West Glenn Farms Drive, Wildwood, MO 63011. Phone: 314-458-8299.

> **Ruth Johnston,** Performance Development Group. 2408 Nob Hill Noth, Seattle, WA 98109. Phone: 206-282-6705.

> **Rich Wilcinski,** SMR Associates, 31 Moore Avenue, Westford, MA 01886. Phone: 508-692-3434.

CORPORATE SELF-ESTEEM TRAINING PROGRAMS

The Human Element with Will Schutz and Associates. PO Box 1339, Mill Valley, CA 94942-1339. Phone: 800-INCLUSION. Fax: 415-389-1630.

WSA conducts corporate trainings and seminars and publishes a wide range of training and development materials in the areas of self-esteem, work relations and team building.

Management and Self-Esteem with Patty Howell and Ralph Jones. Howell Jones Trainings, 12045 Passiflora Avenue, Leucadia, CA 92024. Phone: 619-436-3960. Fax: 619-436-3997. This one or two-day workshop is designed to give business leaders, managers and supervisors the skills they need to focus on ways to enhance employees' self-esteem—and thus their achievement.

PACE (Personal And Corporate Effectiveness) Training with Jim Newmann. PO Box 1378, Studio City, CA 91614. Phone: 818-769-5100.

Self-Esteem and Peak Performance with Jack Canfield. Self-Esteem Seminars/The Canfield Group, PO Box 30880, Santa Barbara, CA 93130. Phone: 800-2-ESTEEM or 805-563-2935. Fax: 805-563-2945. This one or two-day seminar is designed to teach people how to build and maintain their own self-esteem in the context of work. It also teaches a "ten steps to success" model that is based on thirty years of research into the disciplines, thinking patterns and behaviors of the world's top peak performers.

The Self-Esteem Seminars, 19 Lorong Rahim Kajai 2, Taiman Tun Dr. Ismail 60000 Koala Lampur, Malaysia.

The Worth Ethic with Kate Ludeman. 4210 Spice Wood Springs Road #205, Austin, TX 78759. Phone: 512-794-9272. FAX: 512-794-9483. Consultant and author of *The Worth Ethic, The Corporate Mystics* and *Earn What You're Worth.*

OTHER GOOD TRAINERS
AND CONSULTANTS

There are literally thousands of wonderful, powerful and effective trainers and consultants in the fields of self-esteem, peak performance, empowerment and respiriting the workplace. It would be impossible to list them all here. We would need a 400-page directory to do that. However, we are listing here the people that we know and have experienced personally and whose work we can stand behind with no reservations. In addition to contacting these consultants and trainers, you may want to put the word out in your local community to find people closer to home.

We recommend that you write, fax or call all of the individuals and organizations listed below and ask them to send you a brochure on their work.

Joe Bailey, Health Realization Consultants (including substance abuse), Minneapolis, MN. Phone: 612-870-1084.

Nathaniel Branden, PhD, PO Box 2609, Beverly Hills, CA 90213. Phone: 310-274-6361. Fax: 310-271-6808. (Self-Esteem and Optimum Achievement)

Helice Bridges, PO Box 2115, Del Mar, CA 92014. Phone: 619-634-1851. (Self-Esteem and Acknowledgment)

Chérie Carter-Scott, PhD, The MMS Institute, 145 Canon Drive, Santa Barbara, CA 93105. Phone: 800-321-6342. Fax: 805-563-1028. (Self-Esteem and Individual and Organizational Transformation)

Robert Gass, 895 Rainlilly Lane, Boulder, CO 80304. Phone: 303-442-7381.

Dr. Prasad Kaipa, 4832 Pinemont Drive, Campbell, CA 95008. Phone: 408-866-8511. (Mithya Institute for Learning—Executive coaching and creativity)

Elisa Lodge, 25585 Flanders Drive, Carmel, CA 93923. Phone: 408-626-2974. (Walk Your Talk—Presentation coach and motivational speaker)

Dr. Hanoch McCarty, PO Box 66, Galt, CA 95632. Phone: 209-745-2212. Fax: 209-745-2252. (Self-Esteem)

Roxanne McDougall, 5708 Lokelani Road, Kapaa, HI 96746. Phone: 808-822-5798. (Self-Esteem Training and Organizational Development)

Emmet Miller, M.D., 770 Menlo Avenue, Suite 200, Menlo Park, CA 94025-4736. (Self-Esteem, Stress Reduction, Optimum Health)

Bob Moawad, Edge Learning Institute, 2217 N. 30th, #200, Tacoma, WA 98403 Phone: 800-858-1484. Fax: 206-572-2668. (Self-Esteem and Optimum Performance)

Robert Reasoner, 234 Montgomery Lane, Port Ludlow, WA 98365. Phone: 360-437-0300. Fax: 360-437-0300. (Self-Esteem)

Martin Rutte, 64 Camerada Loop, Santa Fe, NM 87505. Phone: 505-466-1510. Fax: 505-466-1514. (Spirituality in the Workplace)

Michael Owen Schwager, Media Relations Group, 145 Avenue of the Americas, New York, NY 10013. Phone: 212-366-1312.

Dr. Sandra Seagal, 20304 Croydon Lane, Topanga Canyon, CA 90290. Phone: 310-455-1149. (Human Dynamics International)

Frank Siccone, 2151 Union Street, San Francisco, CA 94123. Phone: 415-922-2244. (Self-Esteem and Responsibility Training)

Team Climate Associates and Hawley Consultants, Jack Hawley, 806 Manhattan Beach Boulevard, Suite 206, Manhattan Beach, CA 90266. Phone/Fax: 310-376-5448. (Spirit in the Workplace—consultants in organizational re-spiriting)

Dr. James Wanless, 25585 Flanders Drive, Carmel, CA 93923. Phone: 408-626-2974. (Merril West Publishing—Intuition Consultant)

Jonathan Wygant, Consciousness Unlimited, 3079 Calle Pinon, Santa Barbara, CA 93105.

Michael Wyman, Global Acknowledgment Foundation, 135 MacDougal Street, #2-B, New York, NY 10012. Phone: 212-995-0532. (Acknowledgment)

ORGANIZATIONS

The Adizes® Institute, 820 Moraga Drive, Los Angeles, CA 90049. Phone: 310-471-9677. Fax: 310-471-1227. Contact Dr. Patrick Griffin. An innovator in Organizational Transformation, this international management consultancy has been coaching corporate changes since 1975. Founded and directed by Dr. Ichak Adizes, the Institute with 8 international offices has implemented the Adizes program in nearly 500 organizations worldwide, including Fortune 500's, start-ups, nonprofits, and social organizations. The Adizes Graduate School awards state approved Masters and Doctorates in Organizational Transformation. Distributes books, videos, and audios by Dr. Adizes and offers speaking services by Dr. Adizes and Adizes Associates. International headquarters. Internet: adizes@adizes.com. Web pages: http://www.adizes.com/adizes.

Center for Work and the Human Spirit, a division of John Scherer & Associates, The Paulsen Center, Suite 1600, 421 W. Riverside, Spokane, WA 99201. Phone 800-727-9115. Fax: 509-623-2511. Conducts an unusual personal development program called the "Executive Development Intensive." Senior executives and their spouses attend for the purpose of gaining insights about themselves, insights which their corporations hope will improve their effectiveness as leaders. The work is based on the premise that the quality of work we do cannot be separated from the quality of "self" we manage to create in our lives.

The Conference Board, 845 Third Avenue, New York, NY 10022-6601. Phone: 212-339-0356. Fax: 212-980-7014. Gina Walter and Anna Powell—Human Resources, organizational effectiveness research and quality research.

Covey Leadership Center, 3507 N. University Ave. #100, Provo, UT 84604. Phone: 800-255-0777. (Seven Habits of Highly Effective People)

The Great Game of Business, 3055 East Division St., Springfield, MO 65802. Phone: 417-831-7706.

Institute for the Study of Consciousness, 2924 Bienvenue, Berkeley, CA 94705. Phone/Fax: 510-849-4784. Internet: rueyoung@aol.com

Institute of HeartMath, PO Box 1463, Boulder Creek, CA 95006. Phone: 408-338-8700. Website: http://www.webcom.hrtmath. A nonprofit research and education center, providing individuals and organizations with practical, proven tools and programs for reducing stress and increasing quality performance by learning to listen to and follow the heart.

MMS Institute, 145 Canon Drive, Santa Barbara, CA 93105. Phone: 800-321-6342. Fax: 805-563-1028. MMS is a human development and management consulting firm with offices in California, Europe and Africa. Conducts self-esteem seminars and workshops on personal and corporate development and transformation. Also coaches entrepreneurs and executives in reinventing corporations for measurable results.

National Association for Self-Esteem, PO Box 1532, Santa Cruz, CA 95061. Phone: 800-488-6273 or 408-426-9246. NASE, the largest and fastest growing self-esteem organization in the United States, is dedicated to integrating self-esteem into the fabric of American society, so that the development of personal worth, responsibility and integrity becomes paramount and commonplace in families, schools, the workplace and government. NASE is a membership-driven, nonprofit association dedicated to bringing people the latest information on self-esteem resources, research and upcoming conferences through their quarterly newsletter, *Self-Esteem Today*, and through the sponsorship of annual national, regional and local conferences. The many local chapters also hold monthly meetings. Annual dues are $35 per year. You can join or receive further information by writing to the address above.

National Labor Committee, 15 Union Square West, New York, NY 10003. Fax/phone: 212-255-7240.

O'Leary Brokaw & Associates, 43 Aberdeen Place, Clayton, MO 63105. Phone: 314-727-2350. (Moving Beyond Current Realities)

On Camera, Tom Alderman, Carey Grange, 12233 West Olympic Boulevard, Los Angeles, CA 90064. Phone: 310-820-8818.

Partnerships for Change (Jacqueline Miller, President), PO Box 471647, San Francisco, CA 94147. Phone: 415-863-7301. Fax: 415-863-0543. A beyond profit 501C3 organization dedicated to accelerating social, economic, environmental and personal transformation. The purpose is threefold: to increase awareness of the importance of self-esteem in guiding people toward responsible productive living; to generate greater community self-reliance; and to reduce violence in the media. Strategic to fulfilling their mission is the use of new media technologies to deliver their message and empower others. They focus on bringing heart work to organizations. They also act as a catalyst bringing together groups to facilitate and accelerate social change.

Renaissance Business Associates, 404 South 8th Street, Suite 224, Boise, ID 83702. Phone: 208-345-4234. Fax: 208-345-3350. A nonprofit organization for people dedicated to demonstrating the power and effectiveness of integrity in their lives and in business.

Self-Esteem Resources, Robert Reasoner, 234 Montgomery Lane, Port Ludlow, Washington 98365. Phone: 360-437-0300.

Terma—The Box, The Gift of Remembrance, PO Box 5495, Santa Fe, NM 87502. Phone: 505-474-4707; 800-793-9395.

Upsize Project, Andrew Michael, 222 View Street, Mountain View, CA 94041. Phone: 415-968-8798. Fax: 415-968-1126. E-mail: amichael@igc.mpc.org. A conversion project and solution to the depleting downsizing process—Upsize retains and creates sustainable jobs.

U.S. Chamber of Commerce, Jeff Joseph and Angela Koons, 1615 H Street, N.W., Washington, D.C. 20062-2000. CLIN—Community Learning Information Network Project.

World Business Academy, Emily E. Worthington, Director, 1511 K Street, N.W., Suite 1101, Washington D.C. 20005. Phone: 202-783-3213. Fax: 202-783-3216. E-mail: wba@together.org

ABOUT the AUTHORS and CONTRIBUTORS

WHO IS JACK CANFIELD?

Jack Canfield is one of America's leading experts in the development of human potential and personal and organizational effectiveness. He is both a dynamic and entertaining speaker and a highly sought-after corporate trainer with a wonderful ability to inform and inspire audiences toward increased levels of self-esteem and peak performance in the workplace.

He is the author and narrator of several best-selling audio and video cassette programs including *Self-Esteem in the Classroom, How to Build High Self-Esteem* and *Self-Esteem and Peak Performance.* He is a regularly consulted expert for radio and television broadcasts and print media and has published ten books—four on how to develop self-esteem and four international best-sellers—including *Chicken Soup for the Soul, A 2nd Helping of Chicken Soup for the Soul, A 3rd Serving of Chicken Soup for the Soul, The Aladdin Factor* and *Dare to Win.*

Jack has served as a Member of the Board of Trustees of the National Council for Self-Esteem, Chairman of the Board of the Foundation for Self-Esteem, member of the historic California State Task Force to Promote Self-Esteem and Personal and Social Responsibility.

Jack addresses over 100 groups each year. His clients include professional associations, school districts, government agencies, churches, sales organizations and corporations. His corporate clients have included the American Management Association, AT&T, Campbell Soup, Clairol, Domino's Pizza, G.E., ITT Hartford Insurance, Johnson & Johnson, NCR, New England Telephone/NYNEX, Re/Max, Scott Paper, Sunkist, Supercuts, TRW and Virgin Records. Jack is also on the faculties of two schools for entrepreneurs—Income Builders International and the Life Success Academy.

Jack conducts an annual eight day Training of Trainers Program in the areas of self-esteem and peak performance. It attracts educators, counselors, parenting trainers, corporate trainers, professional speakers, ministers and others interested in developing their speaking and seminar-leading skills in the areas of self-esteem and peak performance.

To contact Jack for further information about his books, tapes and trainings or to schedule him for a presentation, please write to:

The Canfield Training Group
PO Box 30880
Santa Barbara, CA 93130
Call toll free: 800-2-ESTEEM
Fax: 805-563-2945

WHO IS JACQUELINE MILLER?

Jacqueline Miller, an internationally recognized expert and sought-after consultant and speaker in the self-esteem arena, founded and currently serves as President of Partnerships for Change,™ a nonprofit organization dedicated to accelerating social, economic, environmental and personal transformation and community self-reliance. Current pivotal projects include media projects, Community Summits,© the Resource Exchange Bank,© and innovative economic revitalization programs. Partnerships for Change catalyzes funding and networking for individuals and organizations.

She received national recognition from President and Mrs. Bush for a conference that she sponsored and coordinated under the auspices of Partnerships for Change™ on the topic of "Self-Esteem in the Workplace." In 1992, she represented the State of California at the UN Earth Summit Conference in Rio de Janeiro, presenting on the issues of self-esteem and community empowerment. Ms. Miller coauthored a National Legislative Proposal with Assemblyperson John Vasconcellos, organized a Senate briefing in Washington, DC designed to increase awareness of the issues of personal responsibility, self-esteem and community empowerment and was appointed by the Governor of Maryland to serve on the Maryland Task Force on Self-Esteem to promote personal and social responsibility. In 1993 she was recognized at the Eco-urbs conference, a large political conference of all the mega-cities on the earth, in Sao Paulo, Brazil for her work in human relations and sustainability (ecological and urbanization issues as they apply to business and the individual). Serving as an executive for several U.S. corporations such as the Sara Lee Corporation, Shasta Beverages and Capri Sun, Inc., and as a Vice-President of Human Resources at PHH Corporation, she has deepened her understanding and appreciation of workplace issues.

Jacqueline Miller serves on the Boards of the Humanity Federation and Earth Song, she has made numerous television appearances, and has been active in the Junior League in Baltimore and San Francisco. A graduate of Loyola College in Baltimore, she currently resides in San Francisco.

To contact Jacqueline for further information please write to:

Partnerships for Change™
PO Box 471647
San Francisco, CA 94147
Phone: 415-863-7301, 415-922-1851
Fax: 415-863-0543
E-mail: pfc@thecity.sfsu.edu   or   hello@heartatwork.com

About the Contributors

Ichak Adizes, PhD. Adizes® Institute, Inc. International Headquarters: 820 Moraga Drive, Bel Air, Los Angeles, CA 90049. 310-471-9677; fax: 310-471-1227. He now resides in Santa Barbara.

Sam Albert. President, Sam Albert Associates. 27 Kingwood Road, Scarsdale, NY 10583. 914-723-8296; fax: 914-723-2886; e-mail: SamAlbert@SamAlbert.com

Dr. Gilbert Amelio. Chairman and CEO, Apple Computer, Inc. One Infinite Loop, Mail Stop 75-8A, Cupertino, CA 95014. 408-996-1010.

Mary Kay Ash. Contact: Randall Oxford, 3219 McKinney Avenue, Dallas, TX 75204. 214-754-6077.

James Autry. PO Box 12069, Des Moines, IA. 515-279-1245; fax: 515-279-4065.

L.S. Barksdale. The Barksdale Foundation. PO Box 187, Idyllwild, CA 92549. 909-659-4676.

Joe D. Batten. 4505 SW 26th Street, Des Moines, IA 50321. 515-285-8069.

Joe Black. Executive Quality Management, Inc. 110 W. Wallace Road, Campo Bello, SC 29322. 864-468-4325.

Kenneth Blanchard. 125 State Place, Escondido, CA 92029. 800-728-6000.

Stephen Boehler. President, Mercer Island Consulting. 8856 SE 74th Place, Mercer Island, WA 98040. 206-236-0447; fax: 206-232-5274.

Nathaniel Branden. PO Box 2609, Beverly Hills, CA 90213. 310-274-6361.

Helice Bridges. PO Box 2115, Del Mar, CA 92014. 619-634-1851.

Joel Brockner. Professor, Columbia University Graduate School of Business. 715 Uris Hall, New York, NY. 212-854-4435.

Richard Brodie. Integral Press. Elliot Bay Plaza, 2415 Western Avenue, #512, Seattle, WA. 206-443-9449; fax: 206-727-6130.

Art Buchwald. 2000 Pennsylvania Avenue, N.W., Washington, DC.

Christina Campbell. CEO, President, Christina Campbell and Company. 115 Hixon Road, Santa Barbara, CA 93108. 805-969-2670.

Chérie Carter-Scott, PhD. 145 Canon Drive, Santa Barbara, CA 93105. 805-563-0789.

Jim Cathcart. PO Box 9075, La Jolla, CA 92038. 619-558-8855.

Terry Cole-Whittaker. Spiritualist. PO Box 2763, Malibu, CA 90265. 310-836-3738.

Susan E. Davis. 156 Whitington Course, Saint Charles, IL 60174. 708-876-1101; fax: 708-876-0187.

Jim Donovan. 4815 Cobblestone Court, Doylestown, PA 18901. 215-794-3826.

Richard Elkus. Vice Chairman, Tencor. 3333 Octavia Street, Santa Clara, CA 95054. 408-970-9500.

Dr. Ted Engstrom. World Vision. PO Box 78481, Tacoma, WA 98481. 800-423-4200; fax: 206-815-3140.

Susan Cunningham Euker. 35 Glenbrook Drive, Phoenix, MD 21131. 410-887-1905.

Richard Foos. CEO, Rhino Records. 10635 Santa Monica Boulevard, Los Angeles, CA 90025. 310-441-6566.

Sidney Friedman. President/Chairman, Corporate Financial Services. The Bellevue, 4th Floor, 200 S. Broad Street, Philadelphia, PA 19102. 215-875-8700.

Barbara Glanz. 4047 Howard Avenue, Western Springs, IL 60558. 708-246-8594; fax: 708-246-5123.

Joel Goodman. The Humor Project, 110 Spring Street, Saratoga Springs, NY 12866. 518-587-8770.

John Grimes. San Francisco Cartoonist and Illustrator, 45 Sutro Heights, San Francisco, CA 94121. 415-221-5042; fax: 415-750-1213; e-mail: luddites@aol.com.

Ronald E. Guzik. 1264 Chappel Court #302, Glendale Heights, IL 60139. 708-682-5837.

Thich Nhat Hahn. Plum Village, France.

Willis W. Harman. President, Institute of Noetic Sciences. PO Box 909, Sausalito, CA 94966. 415-331-5650; fax: 415-331-5673.

Wilson L. Harrell. 7380 Pine Valley Road, Cumming, GA 30131. 770-887-9944.

Lou Holtz. Head Football Coach, The University of Notre Dame. Notre Dame, IN 46556.

John Imlay, Jr. 945 East Paces Ferry Road, Suite 2450, Atlanta, GA 30326. 404-239-2410.

Kathy L. Indermill. 1163 Judson Drive, Mountain View, CA 94040. 415-941-2878.

Dr. Tim Johnson. Chair, Obstetrics & Gynecology, University of Michigan. 1500 E. Medical Center Drive, Ann Arbor, MI 48109.

Michael Jones. Conari Press, 2550 Ninth Street, Suite 101, Berkeley, CA 94710. 510-649-7175; fax: 510-649-7190.

Trevor B. Kwok. RE/MAX Royal City Realty, 310 6th Street, New Westminster, B.C. V3L 3A6. 604-526-2888.

Robert Levering and Milton Moskowitz. Coauthors, *The 100 Best Companies to Work for in America.* Penguin, USA, 375 Hudson Street, New York, NY 10014.

L. Hunter Lovins. CEO, The Rocky Mountain Institute. 1739 Snowmass Creek Road, Snowmass, CO 81654. 970-927-3851.

Kate Ludeman, PhD. Consultant, Author, *The Worth Ethic* and *Earn What You're Worth,* and coauthor, *The Corporate Mystics.* 4210 Spice Wood

Springs Road, Suite 205, Austin, TX 78759. 512-794-9272; fax: 512-794-9483.

Harvey MacKay. MacKay Envelope Corporation. 2100 Elm Street, S.E., Minneapolis, MN 55414. 612-331-9311.

George E. McCown. Chairperson, McCown & De Leeuw & Co. 3000 Sandhill Road, Building 3, Suite 290, Menlo Park, CA 94025. 415-854-6000.

E. J. Michael. Author, *Queen of the Sun*. PO Box 2738, Prescott, AZ 86302. 520-778-3190.

Emmett E. Miller, M.D. President, Source Cassette Learning Systems, Inc. 770 Menlo Avenue, #200, Menlo Park, CA 94025-4736. 415-328-7171.

Bob Moawad. Edge Learning Institute. 2217 N. 30th, Suite 200, Tacoma, WA 98403. 206-272-3103.

Bob Moore. 19-B Senate Plaza, Columbia, SC 29201. 803-799-0493.

Bob Nelson. 12687 Gibraltar Drive, San Diego, CA 92128. 619-673-4608.

James O'Toole. Jossey-Bass Inc., Publishers. 350 Sansome Street, 5th floor, San Francisco, CA 94104. 415-433-1740; fax: 415-433-4611.

Petey Parker. 320 Decker Drive, Suite 100, Irving, TX 75062. 214-256-4120.

Rick Phillips. PO Box 29615, New Orleans, LA 70189. 800-525-7773.

Horst M. Rechelbacher. Aveda Corporation. 4000 Pheasant Ridge Drive, Blaine, MN 55449. 612-783-4000; fax: 612-783-4041.

Alan Rinzler. Coauthor, *The New Paradigm in Business*. Putnam Publishing Group, 200 Madison Avenue, New York, NY 10016.

Anita Roddick. Founder, CEO, The Body Shop International. Watersmead, Littlehampton, West Sussex, BN17 6LS, England. 011-441-90-373-1500.

Martin Rutte. Livelihood, Inc. 64 Camerada Loop, Santa Fe, NM 87505. 505-466-1510; fax: 505-466-1514.

Bud Seith. 161 Bahama Reef, Novato, CA 94949. 415-382-8402.

Will Schutz. 65 Sunset Way, Muir Beach, CA 94965. 415-389-1303.

Walter Scott. Consultant. 564 Santa Rita, Palo Alto, CA 94301.

Ricardo Semler. CEO, Semco, Sao Paulo, Brazil. Author, *Maverick*. Warner Books, 1271 Avenue of the Americas, New York, NY 10020.

Gloria Steinem. 1 Times Square, 9th floor, New York, NY 10030.

John Vasconcellos. State Capitol, Room 4117, Sacramento, CA 95814. 916-445-4253.

Lillian Vernon Katz. Founder, Lillian Vernon, Inc. 570 S. Fulton Avenue, Mount Vernon, NY 10550.

James Wanless, PhD. Consultant, strategist, creative marketing. PO Box 1227, Carmel, NY 93921. 1-800-676-1256.

Jacklyn Wilferd, PhD. 2319 Vera Avenue, Redwood City, CA 94061-1227. 415-369-3299.

Steve Wilson, MA, CSP. DPJ Enterprise, Inc., 344 S. Merkle Road, Bexley, OH 43209. 614-268-1094.

Michael J. Wyman. President, Global Acknowledgment Foundation. 135 MacDougal Street, #2-B, New York, NY 10012. 212-995-0532.

David Zimmerman. General Motors Design. 30100 Mound Road, Troy, MI 48090.

ENDNOTES and PERMISSIONS

CHAPTER 1

Developing Your Personal Signature

[1]This story is excerpted from Barbara Glanz's latest book, *CARE Packages for the Workplace—Dozens of Little Things You Can Do to Regenerate Spirit at Work* (New York: McGraw Hill, 1996). We highly recommend it as a companion volume to this one.

CHAPTER 2

Self-Esteem and Work

[1]Thanks to Ron Luyet who created this exercise.
[2]Ron Luyet made the original formulation of these statements.
[3]The complete statement of steps two, three and four is presented in the instrument called *ELEMENT E: Self Esteem™*, available from WSA, 800-462-5874.

CHAPTER 4

The Power of a Blue Ribbon

[1]To order ribbons or inquire about a blue ribbon training for your corporation, school or organization write Difference Makers/Helice Bridges Communications, P.O. Box 2115, Del Mar, CA 92014; or call 800-887-8422.

Permissions

Developing Your Personal Signature. Reprinted with permission from Barbara Glanz. Excerpted from *CARE Packages for the Workplace—Dozens of Little Things You Can Do to Regenerate Spirit at Work.* © 1996 McGraw Hill.

The Acorn Principle. Reprinted with permission from Jim Cathcart. © 1996 Jim Cathcart.

Our Deepest Fear. Reprinted with permission from Marianne Williamson. Excerpted from "A Return to Love" by Marianne Williamson. © 1992 Marianne Williamson.

Who Will Play Your Music? Reprinted with permission from Conari Press. Excerpted from *Creating an Imaginative Life.* © 1995 Michael Jones.

Integrity and Self-Esteem. Excerpted from *The Six Pillars of Self-Esteem.* © 1994 by Nathaniel Branden. Used by permission.

On Living a Lie. Reprinted with permission from Richard Brodie. © 1996 Richard Brodie.

What Is Integrity, Impeccability, Respect, Caring and Big Loving, and *Reverence in the Workplace.* Reprinted by permission of Jack Hawley.

Entrepreneurs and Self-Esteem. Reprinted with permission from Wilson L. Harrell. © 1996 Wilson L. Harrell.

Victory Formula. Reprinted by permission of Lou Holtz.

A Million Dollar Lesson. Reprinted with permission from Petey Parker. © 1994 Petey Parker.

Do What You Love—The Money Will Follow and *Let Complainers Solve the Problems.* Reprinted by permission of the Pryor Report.

Work Is Love Made Visible. Reprinted by permission of Alfred A. Knopf, Inc. Excerpted from *The Prophet* by Kahlil Gibran. © 1923 by Kahlil Gibran and renewed 1951 by Administrators CTA of Kahlil Gibran Estate and Mary G. Gibran.

Mine Are the Small Initials and *A Most Important Question.* Reprinted with permission from *Guideposts* Magazine. © by Guideposts, Carmel, NY 10512.

Learning a Lesson. Reprinted with permission from Susan Cunningham Euker. © 1991 Susan Cunningham Euker.

The Question. Reprinted with permission from Bob Moore. © 1996 Bob Moore.

Look Where You Want to Go. Reprinted with permission from Jim Donovan. Excerpted from *Handbook to a Happier Life.* © 1995 Jim Donovan.

Fired. Reprinted by permission from *Guideposts* Magazine. © by Guideposts, Carmel, NY 10512.